Passive Income Ideas, blogging for Profits, How to Start a Business in #2021:

Make money Online working with Time & Location Freedom.
Dropshipping, Affiliate Marketing, Amazon FBA Analyzed

By

Ronald Roberts

TABLE OF CONTENTS

Passive Income Ideas

10,000/ month Ultimate Guide

Dropshipping, Affiliate Marketing, Amazon FBA Analyzed + 47 Profitable Opportunities to Make Money Online Working with Time & Location Freedom

By

Ronald Roberts

Introduction

Passive income is money you make off an investment without having to do anything after the initial setup. Earn without doing much work or any active participation. Being a passive income earner is about taking advantage of the working systems already in place to make some good cash not once, twice, but constantly as long as these systems exist. This means you can make the cash as you sleep, but of course, after working on setting up the systems that support the passive income.

The idea that you are not actively involved in managing the investment is an important one because there are a lot of scams and schemes out there in passive income sheep-clothing.

It doesn't take more than five minutes online to see one of these 'great opportunities.' Much of the time, the only person making passive income is the guy selling his strategy to others.

While true passive income is the Holy Grail for investors, few investments offer income returns with no involvement by the investor.

Sorting through the countless promises and strategies to passive income investment means striking a balance between how much work you're willing to put into the strategy and the income you can expect. Instead of a strict technical definition, we'll be judging investment strategies on a sliding scale for truly passive income. The fact that a popular passive investment strategy isn't completely passive does not mean that it isn't a great opportunity.

Unless you have been living under a rock, you probably know that many folks all over the place are generating a massive amount of income while they sleep, travel, or vacation, and all from working very little (and sometimes not even at all) every day or week.

While it may seem that these people are living the good life, the truth is that before you can get to a point where the income comes in no matter what you choose to do—to work or not, vacation, sleep, or whatever else—you have to do a few things upfront for things to work like that. You cannot possibly find yourself earning passively having not set up the processes.

Setting up passive income streams is a massive undertaking that involves investing a lot of time at first during which you get zero earnings. Keep that in mind.

While a successful business may eventually deliver passive income as you hire out daily management, we will not include it as one of the strategies. People don't generally start businesses explicitly for the immediate cash flow but more for upside potential in value and future income. For this book, we'll focus more on strategies that can provide an immediate, or very near-term, stream of cash flow on your investment.

Why Should You Build Passive Income?

Let's discuss how you stand to gain by making passive income.

1: Time freedom

Time is the greatest asset we have, which is why anyone who knows its value values it more than any amount of money. You can spend money and earn it, without a doubt, but you can only use up time once. Once the time passes, it passes for good. It doesn't matter whether you are Bill Gates, Mark Zuckerberg or a homeless guy; you only have 24 hours in a day! It is not possible to relive any moment in time no matter how great that moment was.

This very fact is one of the many reasons why a passive income is so important: for the simple reason that it offers you time freedom. When you uncouple yourself from the necessity of earning an income just so you can meet your regular monthly obligations, you gain the freedom of time.

Having the time freedom means you are flexible. You are not worried about making ends meet at the end of the month—as long as your passive income is outpacing your monthly expenses—this in turn means you are free to use your time as you desire.

You can travel, make more money elsewhere actively, spend time with your family, engage in a hobby, or do whatever else you please: the choice is yours. A passive income gives you the freedom and power to choose what you want to do with your time.

2: Reduces anxiety, stress, and fear of what has to come

One of our biggest fears is being unable to pay our bills at some point or being unable to do the things we love. When we face even the smallest of financial strains, we fear that they may persist, recur, or become worse. We fear the financial obligations that might surface sometime in the future that we think we might not be able to meet. You know the 'what if' scenarios that encircle our minds, sometimes bringing fear, pressure and desperation to get something better that will make you feel more secure.

Perhaps you need to know that each time you live in fear of the future, it is difficult to be present. You cannot enjoy what you have presently when your mind is occupied by the endless doomsday scenarios.

A passive income helps you alleviate all the worries of the future. With a reliable passive income in place, you stop worrying about what would happen if you lost your job or another financial crash similar to the one experienced in 2007-2008. You feel more relaxed mentally, emotionally, and achieve some level of physical vitality. You also get the motivation and energy to achieve more because you achieve the all-important financial momentum, we all need in life.

3: Instead of focusing on what pays the bills, you can focus on all the things you love

Are you passionate about some things but always find yourself putting them off to later because you are busy earning money you can use to manage your lifestyle, pay off bills, debts—we are talking about the proverbial never-ending cycle of interest and payments?

On the other hand, perhaps you earn enough money but are never daring enough to take a time out (because your time equals money and therefore, when you take time off, you lose money). Passive income frees you from this problem.

With a reliable passive income in place, you have the time to do everything you love as you make money. The time you spend doing these activities does not affect the income you generate at the end of the month; even as you pursue the things you love, you can comfortably pay the bills and as a bonus, become happier since you will be engaging in things that impassion you.

4: It offers you freedom to be creative

When you work for someone (working at a regular job, perhaps one where you work 9-5), you have to follow rules; you cannot do whatever you want. There are working methods laid out and that you have to follow; you also have to do specific tasks with a particular focus on precision.

Most regular jobs across many industries do not embrace creativity. For instance, if you are an artist working on design projects, you may find yourself limited to the creativity relegated to what your clients are demanding from the company. Deciding to become your own boss through setting up passive income streams allows you to set your own rules, follow your passions, and take time to hone your skills in the area.

We do not need to go any further; you get the idea. The benefits of a passive income are simply endless! Actually, you will discover most of them yourself along the way.

Mindset of a Winner

Winners are separated from losers not by the amount of money they have, but the quality of mindset that they formed over the years. Unlike those who gave up on their dreams early, winners do not stop. They have an entirely different way of looking at failures and even their own achievements. It begins with how they look at the world around them. Winners do not lose, because losing isn't a part of their vocabulary.

In psychology, one's sense of 'self' defines everything else that happens to him. One's thoughts are powerful because it elicits emotions, can trigger him to do a specific action, and can affect his environment. Even his own physical health depends on the quality of his thoughts, for the brain is the center of his being.

This is not to say that winners have different brains than the rest of the world. In fact, all brains are the same in terms of structure, weight, and anatomy. Not taking congenital diseases into account, everyone is born with exactly with the same brain capacity, though it changes through time.

The changes in the brain aren't only a result of natural development based on nutrition. In fact, the brain is the most dynamic organ in the body in terms of function. The anatomy of it stays the same for everyone of course, but as a person grows older, he will be using his brain differently. Such changes may come from experience. As a person experiences something new, his brain will create new connections or maps by changing the way neurons send signals to each other. Thus, there will be no obvious physical change in terms of size, but there will be changes in activity. When scientists say that a person's brain is more 'developed', they only mean that there are more neural maps and brain activity. The size and structure stay the same.

Much of what is going on within these 'maps' cannot be observed objectively through behavior. In fact, about 70% of brain processes do not really translate into actions. When people dream, for example, there is an ongoing firing of neurons as though the person is awake. Because the body remains asleep, no one can tell what exactly was going on in the brain. Scientists have yet to find out if neural firing in the language area of someone sleeping means they're talking in their dreams.

This simply means that whatever goes on in people's minds, it is something related to their experience. In order to increase one's brain activity and development, he has to allow himself to experience many things. This is what winners do. Winners let themselves experience mistakes, failures and disappointments. Instead of looking at these negatively, they use it as food for their brains. They learn whatever they can and apply them in their lives.

Winners look at their experiences differently from the rest. While many people avoid negative emotions, winners acknowledge them. While most of them fear mistakes, winners look forward to it. It is through negative experiences that winners thrive, for without these, there is nothing to learn.

Here are some of the unique thought processes that winners have:

1. Winners think of their end goal at all times – Winners appear brave and confident because they know that the things, they do are necessary steps to their success. Instead of looking at their task as it is, they look at it as a valuable experience that prepares them in achieving their success. All the things that they do will have an effect on their future, so they treat it as a necessity. They know that to move on to the next step, they need to make their first move. They do it for the sake of achieving their goals.

2. Winners do not lose – Winners just do what they have to without worrying, because they know that they will not lose. Losing only happens to those who didn't even start. Because winners are always motivated to be successful, they see themselves as winners as soon as they start moving. For them, it is just a matter of time before their dreams are fully realized. All the obstacles they will face along the way are a part of winning.

3. Winners always gain something – As previously mentioned, experiences are precious to winners. It doesn't matter how much setbacks they encounter, or how many detours they have to take to get to the end of their journey. For as long as they experienced it, it's fine. It will be a part of their learning.

4. Winners always give themselves credit – Winners are very much in touch with themselves. They acknowledge their strengths and use them. They know their weaknesses and they do something about it. They accept everything that they have and strive to be better. When it comes to making mistakes, they hold themselves accountable and not point fingers at people. When it comes to making achievements, they pat themselves on the back and promise to do much better next time.

5. Winners do not stop at winning – When winners win, they find another battle to join. For them, winning is a lifetime affair. Just because they have met their goals doesn't mean they should stop moving. They treat themselves as people with the potential to change the world, which they can only do if they keep winning.

6. Winners encourage others to win – Winners do not believe in the rat race. For them, one's life is his own battle. There is no need to step on other people's dreams to win. Winning doesn't mean being on top of other people. For them, it is possible to win together, and the more people who win, the better. Because of this, they share what they know to other people.

7. Winning isn't about having material wealth – The ultimate goal of winners is to be able to live a healthy and happy life. They would like to be able to do what they love without depending too much on the things that they own. You will be surprised to know that those who are truly successful do not really use their money. They do not need it. Those who have achieved ultimate success get what they want using their abilities. They gain power and influence not because of their wealth, but because of what they were able to do.

8. Winners know that their biggest assets are themselves – Winners believe in themselves so much that no matter how many people discourage them, they will still keep going. They do not walk around bragging about their abilities, but they are also not shy to show it off if the situation calls for it. They know their strengths and they make sure that they maximize it.

Business #1: Dropshipping

Drop shipping is a fast and easy way to turn a buck. With products being developed and shipped all over the world, the drop shipper can connect the supplier with the consumer without ever leaving their home. You simply advertise the product to the potential customer, when the order comes in, collect the payment and notify the supplier where to ship the product.

With this type of business, you simply serve as the middleman. You do not have to warehouse a lot of goods nor do you ever need to handle the product at all. Your primary focus is on advertising and promoting the different products you sell.

With the right website, you can drop ship hundreds of different products this way and never have to worry about packaging, storage, or shipping hassles. The supplier never has to worry about marketing his products or finding his customer base. There is no limit to how much you could make with this type of business venture.

One of the great things about drop shipping is that you will never have to invest a great deal of money into inventory to get started. However, you will face a number of challenges and disadvantages. Make sure that you connect with legitimate suppliers so that you're not caught in the middle of a scam. And make sure that they are reliable and trustworthy. Even legitimate companies do not always have the best of reputations.

Dropshipping is a wonderful method to earn passive income, but not without a little effort on your part. Like with most successful passive income revenue streams, they take a good amount of work upfront. Some of them take a ton and then time-to-time maintenance to keep everything in tune. Drop shipping is no different. You will need to establish a website. It includes buying the domain name for the website, buying hosting so the site is able to go live, and finally either getting a web designer to design the website or designing the theme yourself through something like WordPress and Optimizepress. This website will provide products that you do not store in your home but buy directly from the warehouse.

You are going to buy your products from a third party, and have it directly shipped to the customer from that third party. You will never see or handle the product. The reason this has a low overhead and low cost to you is due to no inventory. You do not own inventory or have any stock to keep track of. The manufacturer or wholesaler is going to handle the merchandise directly.

With drop shipping, the best way for you to make money is to use a site like Shopify. You are able to connect with wholesalers and manufacturers on the website, as well as gain notice around the world with it.

Before explaining more about sites like Shopify, let's take a look at the benefits of drop shipping.

- Less capital is needed to start your passive income strategy. With drop shipping, you never buy the goods you sell, so you can launch an ecommerce store with very small investment. The drop shipping concept allows you to buy as you make sales, thus you will only need to purchase the product right away, if you have already been paid by the customer.

- You can get started very easily since you do not need to pay for or manage a warehouse, pack or ship your orders, track the inventory for accounting purposes, handle returns, or inbound shipments, or continue to manage and order products. All you will really need to pay for is a Shopify account, possibly domain name, and hosting.

- You can run your business from your home office, thus you have minimal overhead. In fact, your computer, Internet, phone, fax, and printer are about the only things you will need to spend money on. You will have a little electricity that goes toward your business, but it is minimal. This energy usage is particularly very little if you are converting time you used to search online to make passive income.

- You can choose a wide selection of products, as long as they fit within your niche. Let's say you are starting an essential oil business. You would want to sell essential oils, bottles to mix essential oils, soap making kits for those who want to use them for soap, and the list can go on. The point is you can choose to sell one product and its related products as a means of making more money. Anytime a supplier lists something on their site for sale, you can upload it to your site.

- You can eventually end up selling your drop shipping "store", aka your website, for thousands of dollars. A few friends of mine have put in the effort and created great drop shipping stores and have grown them over the course of a few years, then they sold them for between $40,000 to $60,000. There are others that have sold for much more than that.

There is one caveat to selling multiple vendor items. Your wholesaler or manufacturer may offer many products for several different niches. You may not want to post everything on your website that they offer. What would you think if you came across a site that sells pet food and saw a blockbuster DVD for sale? It would be confusing, correct? Now, if the savvy website owner was selling pet DVDs and pet food, it would make sense.

So, when you choose what products to sell, make certain it is within your niche and not something completely outside of it. If you are going to sell more products than what is in your first chosen niche, you need to start a new website for those products. You can link your two sites and have others link to you, but you definitely need to have two sites or make it very clear that you are more like a "big" box store offering multiple products. This second option takes multiple pages in your menu, with clear distinctions and a good tagline to get people to your site.

It is often more work than multiple sites that are niche based.

- Flexible location is also a part of drop shipping benefits. Without a need to have your business in a brick and mortar location, you can take your laptop anywhere you have an Internet connection and fulfill orders. When an email order comes in, you can select to fill the order from your drop shipper via the Internet, and within minutes, the drop shipper is going to receive the order and put it in their queue. You will need to communicate with the customer to let them know when the drop shipper is projecting an arrival date. You also need to keep in contact with your suppliers to ensure your orders are being filled on time.

- You can increase your sales, without increasing your time. Once you have established your website and are making sales, it will not matter if you become busier with sales. The drop shippers you deal with are going to pick up the additional orders, allowing you to expand your business without worry.

As with any business, even those that offer passive income, you have drawbacks.

- You can get started so easily because there are low margins in this business. By low margin, it means it is a highly competitive industry, where you have to sell products at very low prices to gain revenue. If your website is poorly constructed or without decent customer service, you are going to find your profit destroyed instantly.

- Shipping can be complex. You may offer several products on your website, but they are all from different suppliers. For instance, say you are selling a hard to find book. This book is available through wholesale publishers, used. You have to contact four suppliers to get four copies. The books will not arrive at the same time for the customer, and the shipping will be tallied for each supplier—not just once. If the book is $1.00 from two suppliers who charge media shipping at $3.99, and the other two books are $2.00 with media shipping at $3.99, then the customer is charged 21.96, not $4.00 for the books and $3.99 for the shipping. It can make a customer hesitate to purchase the items they need; especially, if the competition has one supplier, they can purchase all items from.

- Inventory can be an issue. When you stock items you own, you know exactly what you have to sell. With drop shipping, you are depending on the inventory being available or at least accurate on their website. Sometimes syncing your inventory records with wholesalers or manufacturers is not as accurate as you would like.

- Suppliers can also make errors. You get blamed for the errors because you were the face of the supplier, and you also have to accept responsibility. You have to apologize, attempt to correct the mistake or provide the customer with their money back. It damages your reputation versus the suppliers.

At this point, you are probably asking if it is worth it. It is, when you offer drop shipping as a service and not as a role. Manufacturers, wholesalers, and retailers can all act as drop shippers, just like you wish to do. This is why your role is not a part of the supply chain, but as a service to offer a better price than other companies. It takes having the proper arrangement with a legitimate manufacturer or wholesaler.

How the process works:
A customer is going to place an order online at your website.

You are going to confirm that you received the order.

You will then check with the supplier or suppliers you work with. You will find the best price for the item, including the best shipping option.

If the goods are available, you will send a second email to the customer, letting them know the expected ship date.

When the item is confirmed as shipped by the supplier, you will charge the customer's credit card or PayPal or another account.

The customer will wait for their package, track the package via the wholesaler, and only contact you if their product shows up late, broken, damaged, or otherwise incorrect. The wholesaler or manufacturer is totally anonymous to the end customer. Your logo and return address are on the label. The drop shipping wholesaler only works in stocking and shipping the products. You, the merchant, are responsible for the website, marketing, customer service, and all other areas of the "merchant" business.

Ratings
Profitability - Always remember that in dropshipping, you don't own the products and you don't ship them as well. In addition, the money you make is nearly all profits. However, you still have to deal with customer support issues when they arise. **8/10**

Perspective in the future - Scaling a dropshipping business is a matter of either adding more products to your inventory or creating another online store. **9/10**

Difficulty - I would describe dropshipping as very simple because you can pretty much automate the whole thing. As long as your online store is set up, there's not much else that you do. The only challenge here is learning how to effectively drive traffic to your website/online store. **8/10**

Budget for starting - $500

Business #2 Affiliate Marketing

If you are already part of an online community that is based around a hobby or interest, then you can likely leverage that community into an affiliate marketing-based passive income stream. Affiliate marketing is a type of dedicated advertising where you work with companies or other types of merchants for the purpose of helping them sell their products in return for a cut of the profits of every item sold. This passive income stream req

uires a bit of work to set up effectively, but it can generate a constant stream of profit when done correctly.

How Affiliate Marketing Works

Affiliate marketing works in different ways based on how the company you are working with is set up. Some affiliate marketing programs have a tier structure, which is how the myth of a pyramid scheme got started. The first person to offer affiliate marketing is usually the company; they reap the most from the sales. They hire and offer a deal to a person like you, who signs up for a specific commission amount based on sales. When you make a sale, you earn a piece of the pie from the sale of the goods. Your piece of that sale is larger than affiliate marketer B and C. B signed up after you and under your company code. They help you market the products with their own website. C also has a website. Both B and C will make the same commission. If they get someone to sign up with their code, then they split a piece of the sales, earn a higher amount than their sign-up marketers, and still earn less than you do for the sales.

Since the idea is about the more advertising there is online through e-mail marketing, pop-up ads, contextual advertising, and web banners, the more products a company can sell, companies work hard to find hundreds of affiliate marketers. You really can earn a commission off of an affiliate product through so many ways. Having an email list to promote product offers, having a YouTube channel where you can link affiliate products that you use and recommend under each video, having a social media following - it goes on and on.

It creates stiff competition. It is also the reason that you want to find a deal that offers a high commission based on the industry calculation for pay. If you can get paid for cost per mile or cost per click versus cost per sales, then you will be paid more just for sending someone to your site or the company's website.

Some great websites where you can find plenty of physical and online products to earn affiliate commissions off of are Amazon and Clickbank. Actually, Amazon has a policy where if you promote an affiliate product for them and someone clicks on that product and does not buy it but ends up buying anything else off Amazon within a certain time frame, you will earn an affiliate commission off those products.

Find a niche: The first thing you need to do is to consider the type of customers you are going to be marketing to. As previously mentioned, if you have a hobby that people are dedicated too then this is a good place to start. You'll be spending a good deal of time with products related to the niche and having an interest in them besides money making will make the process easier in the long run. If you don't have an idea already in mind, then you should choose a hobby for people with a good amount of discretionary income and a steady stream of new products always coming to the market.

Do some research: With a niche in mind, the next thing you want to do is to take some time and visit existing websites where these types of individuals spend their time. Consider the types of things that are important to them and the type of products they are likely to buy the most frequently. It is important to take note of their thought processes, the things that are important to them and the slang they use. Sounding like you are one of them is key to making them trust your opinion when you tell them to buy one product over another.

Create a website: In order for this passive income stream to work, you are going to need a blog where you can collect your thoughts and your affiliate marketing articles. When creating your site, keep in mind the types of things you saw on the sites you researched and strive to create a space that members of your niche are going to feel comfortable in. Additionally, create content that is more than just advertisements to ensure that niche members get in the habit of visiting your site on the regular.

Affiliate programs: While there is plenty of different companies that offer affiliate programs, the easiest to get started with is Amazon. Once you sign up to be an Amazon affiliate, you can choose to sell practically any product you want, and they will send you a unique link to that product. Then, whenever a purchase is made through that link, you will receive a commission for the sale. Many new affiliate marketers go straight for the big-ticket items, as the commission on these will naturally be higher than cheaper products.

This is a mistake, however, as it takes much more convincing to get someone to spend several hundred dollars on an item compared to something that is in the fifty-dollar range. When looking for items to sell, quantity is almost always going to trump quality. Another good route to take is to find items that are already discounted on Amazon and let your readers know that if they click on the link you provided, they would get a discount on the item in question. Remember, you aim at closing the deal as quickly as possible because even if your review sways a customer in a given direction, if they have to think about the purchase before making it then it is less likely they are going to use your link to do so, which means you won't get credit for your hard work.

Making the sale: When it comes to convincing visitors to your site to purchase things, it is important to do your due diligence with the item in question which means purchasing it for yourself first. As an affiliate marketer, your word is your business, which means that if you promote low quality items, then your total conversions are likely to drop and will be unlikely to rise again. If you buy a product and it isn't worth the money, be sure to write about that as well, having negative product reviews as well as positive ones will make the positive reviews you do write more believable.

When using the product, be sure to take plenty of pictures of yourself doing so. Seeing the product in use will make it easier for readers to picture themselves using the product. Each review should include a breakdown of the product describing its pros and cons, but still leaving out a bit of relevant information to ensure that the reader is more likely to click the link you provide (several times throughout the review) to find the information that you left out. Once they are on the purchase page, they will be more likely to go ahead and pull the trigger.

Another good option is to talk about the product's strengths but then discuss how it is too complicated for all but the most knowledgeable users, as this will make some users even more likely to purchase it. You will also want to try and create a story around each product, discuss what you were doing while using it and generally give readers as many different ways to connect with the product as possible.

Additionally, it is important to ensure that you market yourself as well as the products you are trying to sell as the more your regular readers feel that you (or a persona you create for this purpose) are an expert in a given field, the greater the weight your reviews will have when they are making up their minds whether or not to purchase a product. The more you go out of the way to make readers relate to you on a personal level, the more they will listen to you when you say that a given product is superior to its competition.

Ratings

Profitability - Affiliate marketing remains as one of the best ways on how to generate passive income. If you have a website that's full of valuable evergreen content, it can keep on earning you money even if you don't work on it for weeks or even months.

Perspective in the future - It's really easy to scale an affiliate marketing business considering how cheap domain registration and hosting are these days. You can create a dozen affiliate websites that will cost you as low as $100 a month, monetize them with high ticket and relevant affiliate products, drive traffic to them, and earn passively. That is truly a bargain.

Difficulty - Affiliate marketing requires a good amount of work. You also have to be smart with your product selection, commission/pay structure, etc. It may be easy to build a YouTube channel, or a website monetized with affiliate products, but it takes time to build an audience around it.

Budget for starting - $120

Business #3: Amazon FBA

Almost everyone has heard of Amazon, but only a few people know what Amazon FBA is. But if you have any plans of selling specific merchandise, this might be the absolute easiest way to get your products into the hands of the consumer without having to worry about shipping, handling or marketing. It is the best consideration for businesses experiencing difficulty warehousing a large quantity of any product.

FBA simply means fulfilled by Amazon, and since they house your products on site, once you have delivered it to Amazon, there is nothing left for you to do but collect the money. Ensure that it is the right arrangement for you and for your customer base. Using Amazon to connect you to your customer is one of the easiest marketing strategies you can have. With their already large customer base, you will likely reach far more potential customers than you might ever do on your own.

You simply set up your own Amazon account, scan your list of products into the system, print out the barcodes, a packing slip, and then choose a pick-up location based on where you live, and in just a few days, your products are safely stored in the Amazon warehouse. At that point, just wait for the orders to be placed and the money to roll in.

The benefits of this arrangement are obvious. You not only get easy access to the millions of consumers that log into Amazon every day, but you also save time and money in shipping items to different places around the world. Amazon covers the storage of your merchandise and the shipping costs related to it. If you choose a relatively popular item, you stand to earn quite a bit of money on simply reselling the merchandise you were already planning on selling anyway.

How to Find a Product

The key to finding a great product that will sell well is to look at what is *already* selling well. Yes, you can spend money on software that will do the work for you, but guess what? Amazon already does!

If you go to Google and type in "Amazon Top 100 Sellers," it shows you the top selling products on Amazon. You can filter by any department you want — Arts and Crafts, Electronics, Sports & Outdoors, Pet Supplies, etc.

Now you instantly know that everything on that page is already selling like crazy. There's a full list of 100 potential products that you know are best sellers.

When analyzing a market for a product, Will (my entrepreneur friend, an expert in Amazon FBA) looks at the review to revenue ratio. If there are $100,000 in total sales on the first page of the search results, and 1,000 reviews, that's $100 per review, which is a great ratio. But if there are 10,000 reviews on the first page and only $100,000 in sales, $10 per review isn't as strong a ratio. This is a very easy, quick way to gauge where the product is in its life cycle, and whether the market is already saturated.

Will uses JungleScout.com for his analysis. Jungle Scout is a must have for all Amazon sellers, as it breaks down the competition for every search. All you have to do is type in your search, and then hit the Jungle Scout button. You'll get an entire page of data from the search results. From revenue to daily sales cost, it has every data point you will ever need to identify a strong market.

The main key to finding great products to sell is to stay niche. There is no point in competing against 1,000 other sellers of the same product. When you're doing your research, think like a buyer. If a person is searching "Power Tools," they don't know if they actually want to buy tools or not — they are just looking around. But if they search "12V Battery Powered Cordless Drill with Accessories," chances are they NEED that drill for a project and are looking to buy.

Market for "needs," not "wants." If someone is actively searching for knee scooters, the odds are that they need the scooter due to an injury. It's not a want; it's a necessity.

In the ecommerce space, it's about being creative and finding different ways to market your niches and finding niches that haven't been developed yet. Even better, look for a niche of a niche. Avoid electronics, things with a lot of moving parts, and extremely competitive products. For example, Will mentioned there are spin mops on Amazon — that's a pretty niche marketplace in itself. But instead, go for the niche of a niche and sell the industrial spin mops, which sell for a much higher price than the regular ones.

Get lost on Amazon. Go deep into the "Items suggested for you" and don't be afraid to get obscure.

Keep an Eye Out

Finding the products to sell is one of the easiest parts of the process, according to the experts. But many individuals trying to get started say it's the hardest. They don't want to pick something with too much competition. They don't want to pick a loser. What happens to these people? They never start anything!

How does a multi-million-dollar seller find products to sell? Will explained that when he first got started selling on Amazon, he was a huge UFC fan. One night, he was watching a fight when he noticed one of the fighters wearing shorts that said "Hayabusa" on them. He decided to head to his favorite site, Amazon, to check out some of Hayabusa's products.

When he searched for Hayabusa, he noticed that all of their listings were very poor quality and, being the expert, he knew he could sell more products for them. He decided to call Hayabusa directly and offer to sell their products for them. He found out that they sold to mostly smaller-sized UFC gyms across the country, and most of the sellers don't have enough cash to keep their product in inventory because they offered five different colors of gloves in five different sizes. It would cost too much in inventory for the sellers to stock everything.

Will recognized that Hayabusa needed someone with a strong cash flow to be able to stock enough inventory, and he realized he could be their main seller. He asked if the company would let him be the only authorized reseller on Amazon if he could keep all of their gear in stock. Initially, he was selling the gear in his other Amazon accounts alongside generic products. Hayabusa said they wanted a standalone Amazon account that was only selling their product.

Will created a standalone Amazon account called Fighting Factory. Every month, he would buy $30,000 of inventory from Hayabusa and then sell it for $40,000 - $45,000, and it was all on repeat through FBA. Will does none of the R&D and none of the marketing — all he has to do is reorder until the product sells out. Amazon handles all the shipping and all the returns on the customer service side of things. That's $10,000 in profit every month, without doing any of the real work!

I know what you're saying: "Yeah, but he's a pro. I could never contact real companies, why would they want me to sell?" Think about it. You're a free sales rep. Why wouldn't they let you do that? In the case of Will and Hayabusa, the company is getting one of the best Amazon consultants in the world for free. They don't pay him a dime because he buys the product from them. It's a win-win all around.

Here's a recap: Will went from a UFC fan watching TV, saw a product and contacted the company, convinced them he could sell it better, set it and forget it, and now he earns $10K/month with Amazon FBA.

Retailers
The next time you are walking around Target or Walmart, take a look at the products on the shelves, particularly everything at eye level or on the ends of the aisles with nice displays. The retailers obviously want you to see those specific products. Why?

Those are the most profitable products. Those are the high margin products that the store wants you to buy so that they can make more money. Those same products can also be high margin for you, so take a look around and get some ideas to kickstart your sales.

Infomercials
We've all seen the infomercials for cool new products. The companies that make those products wouldn't pay all that money for infomercials if the products weren't making them money. There is a demand for those products among people watching television, which means there is also demand on Amazon for those types of products as well.

Ratings
Profitability - Managing an Amazon FBA business can take a lot of your time and resources. Some of your time will be spent communicating with your suppliers, optimizing your listings, running promotions/giveaways, optimizing your Amazon sponsored ads, etc. However, profitability can be improved by outsourcing some of these tasks to virtual assistants who will take care of them for you.

Perspective in the future - It's easy to scale your Amazon FBA business. Once you are accepted into the program and you have successfully launched your first product and familiarized yourself with the process, scaling is as simple as adding more products to your inventory or expanding your product offerings (i.e. offering your customers complementary products as part of a bundle).

Difficulty - Starting a business with Amazon FBA can be very complicated because there are a lot of hoops you have to go through. You have to apply to the program. You need to make sure that the products pass certain standards (e.g. packaging and safety requirements), etc. And you have to be communicating with your manufacturer/supplier, inspectors, etc. to make sure products are manufactured to specification. Language barrier and time zone difference could present challenges.

Budget for starting - $3,000.

Business #4: Blogging for Profit

One of the biggest passive income myths is that of making money online. Follow the promises of some blogs, mainly those offering blogging services or "how-to" manuals, and you need only register your website name and wait for checks to deposit into your bank account. While blogging can offer some passive income potential, it is much more a traditional job than a passive income investment.

Developing online assets is similar. You take an undeveloped spot on the Internet and build it into a valuable asset, usually with almost no cash flow until you do. As someone that owns two blogs and has contributed to others for more than five years, I know the work that goes into developing an online asset and the income you can expect.

How to Set Up a Blog

Millions of blogs are out there. Remember the discussion on finding a niche? You need your blog to serve a need that will gain attention. You have to find the 1% topic that everyone else is overlooking. It is tougher now than when people started blogging more than two years ago.

But, don't worry, you can find a topic. You just have to think outside of the box. You may already have something from your personal life that provides you a unique experience. For example, going through the loss of a loved one that suffered dementia has given me a unique perspective. Discussing topics that scientific sites and the ALZ organization doesn't touch is easy.

It is what you do once you find a topic in a niche that can make blogging a little difficult.

1. You need to meet a need.

2. Discover who your target audience is.

3. Ensure your readers can depend on you.

4. Diversify.

5. Be disciplined.

6. Find and support advertisers.

7. Have an IT back up.

The topic you decide on should help you narrow down your target. Going with the dementia topic, there are more than two types of dementia. There is a pseudo-dementia that comes from underactive or overactive thyroid, FTD, Alzheimer's, vascular dementia, mixed dementia, and the list goes on. Each of these dementias will have a different target audience because a family member who is acting as a caregiver needs to know about their family member's type of dementia. It is the same as a person who owns a Dutch Shepherd. They want information on their dog breed, not mixed dog breeds or small dog breeds like wiener dogs.

The hard part comes in when you need to help your readers believe in you. First, get rid of the idea that you can create the perfect blog without mistakes. Everyone makes a mistake now and then. It is difficult to catch every grammatical mistake, even with the help of editors and editing software. Just look at the NY Bestsellers list, choose a book, and if you look hard enough, you will spot a grammatical mistake. The truth is—the people who are going to notice these are English professionals and those who tend towards analyzing everything to a tee. Most of your audience is a hard-working group who wants to read about a topic, is not looking closely for errors, and will trust in your information if it is reliable.

This doesn't mean you should only spend 5 minutes on a blog and upload it. You still want to strive for perfection, but don't worry if you miss something and find it later or have someone point it out.

When discussing reliability, it is about providing information that is correct. For example, if you are creating an entertainment website about local places, you don't want to be wrong or unreliable. If you tell someone to eat at a restaurant, then you better be honest about that restaurant. You need to provide the proper pricing for food, such as appetizers being between $6 and $12, meals being $12 to $20, etc.

If I were to write a review about a local restaurant I like to go to, I would tell the readers I know the owners. I would tell them what I like and do not like about the food choices. I would also be honest about any issues I've had. For example, I would warn them about one of the servers who is never friendly, but still has a job at that restaurant. I'd tell the reader not to be put off by that one server because everyone else, including the owners, is great at customer service. They also know there is an issue with that server. You have to look past the server to enjoy the amazing onion rings, pizza, salad wedges, and awesome hamburgers. The ambiance is also wonderful because it is on a river, with plenty of nature to observe.

You can see the point I am trying to make. I'm sharing the benefits, letting people know, I know the owners, and being honest about one bad server. If I didn't mention the server or failed to mention that I know the people who own the place, I'd be doing a disservice to the reader. It is also a way to establish trust in what I talk about. A reader is more apt to trust me the next time if I was honest about my review versus leaving the important details out.

Let's say you are using your blog to help sell the eBooks you are an affiliate marketer for. You need to be honest about your reviews of these books. You also need to let people know that you are making money when they purchase a book. It would be like saying, "hey buy this $300 textbook that I hated," if you were not honest.

You are going to be associated with your brand. Do you want hundreds of hate websites to pop up about you or worse be accosted on the street by someone who recognizes you and your blog? Of course not. You want to earn money; thus, you need to be reliable.

Diversification is necessary because you cannot just make money from advertisers. Many people who own a blog also use affiliate marketing. They allow ads to be posted on their website, but then sell products through affiliate marketing sites. Their blog is actually a marketing tool for those sales.

The key to making money and keeping your readership is to be disciplined in when you post. You need to religiously post at the same time each week, every few days, or each day. If you have something to say or review, you might provide a blog post each day. However, most people have two to three posts a week.

You need new content for SEO purposes, but also to help remind readers that you are still online and have valuable information for them.

Also make sure you have an IT option should your home Internet or computer break down or stop working for a short time. You never want to be late with your post. If necessary, write a post and set it to upload automatically at a certain time of day, on a certain day. This is possible.

Finding Advertisers
It is fairly easy to find advertisers, but do you want everyone you find? No. You want to be relied on. To be reliable, you need to have ads your target audience is interested in and have advertisers you trust. You can be approached by numerous people asking to post ads on your site, but you are not going to choose everyone that asks. You are also going to search for advertisers, but again, you will only choose advertisements you

can trust. If you trust them, then you know your readers can. It will limit the money you make, but on the other hand, you want to make passive income without having to redo your advertising arrangements because your reputation has been blown.

Cash flow on blogs is low compared to other passive income investments. While your return on the money invested in your blog may be high, as long as you don't spend much, the cash return on your time spent will be next to nothing for at least a year.

Overall, blogging is a poor source of passive income though it can be a great profession and a good source of active income. The benefits from blogging include pride of ownership and editorial control over your own work, as well as other non-monetary benefits. You can blog from anywhere in the world, giving you the freedom to travel or live where you like.

Ratings

Profitability - The earnings you make won't be 100% passive. You still have to perform tasks like reading and replying to comments, brainstorming for new ideas, and communicating with advertisers and partners.

Perspective in the future - Blogging is highly scalable in the sense that you can duplicate your success in a specific niche by applying the same tactics in another niche. In addition, the same blog that serves 100 people can also serve 100,000 people without any significant increase in your fixed costs.

Difficulty - Starting a blog is rather easy. In fact, you can create one in just a few minutes.

Budget for starting – from $100.

Business #5: Create your Affiliation Network

A successful Network Marketer learned a very valuable lesson the hard way. After selling a single product to a customer, she made a decision that this customer would never be interested in more products, hosting an in-house presentation, let alone becoming part of her team to sell products herself. She took it upon herself to count someone out. Never had a conversation or asked any questions. She simply passed judgment, moved on and never extended an invite to get involved.

Then one day she was speaking with the direct manager in her up line about an eager new recruit that came to her after trying one of the products. This particular recruit was on-fire and passionate about growing a team. And who was this recruit? The very person she pre-judged and never invited to get involved or host an in-home presentation.

1) Make your genuine focus on people NOT product or money.
2) Ask support from your up line. Get them involved and ask for their help.
3) Don't be a salesperson. Successful Network Marketers take on the role of teacher. Your job is to educate prospects on the benefits of how what you have will help them meet and exceed their personal goals.
4) Avoid giving prospects just enough information to let them make an **uninformed** decision. Set a meeting with the prospects for a full presentation to enable them to make informed decisions. Go for the AIN. (An Informed No). Get an answer. Warm maybes are your enemy.
5) Use email and mass social media invites as a last resort. These types of invites are very impersonal and rarely successful. Try to use traditional invites through mail, phone or in person as much as possible.
6) Continue to add prospects back to your FOLLOW UP list until they have experienced your full presentation.

7) Avoid saying things like, "I just recently started..." or "I just recently joined..." or, "I want to take you to an opportunity meeting."
8) Get serious about your recruiting strategy. Recruit above your expectations.
9) Brainstorm names of people you know on a blank piece of paper. Write down any name that pops into your head. Do NOT judge and count anyone out.
10) Build partnerships with business owners that are a natural match for your products. For example, skin and nutrition products are a great match for a partnership with salon owners. Make an appointment to present to a salon owner and get them interested in your product. Imagine the reach of prospects tapping into the salon owner's client base.
11) Create a loyalty reward from interested prospects who bring a friend.
12) Figure out the stats. One successful Network Marketer has discovered they must touch a minimum of ten prospects per week, have two parties per month to meet his recruiting and sales goals.

Ratings

Profitability – In the short term, it is not a profitable venture. Once you attract a high traffic flow, you will be able to earn passively.

Perspective in the future – Once you gain ground, the network is projected to expand with time.

Difficulty – You will have to take time to learn about the different tools that are essential in establishing your network. Such tools include landing pages, product feeds, product discovery tools, and link generators.

Budget for starting - $200.

Business #6: Kindle-Publishing

Outsourcing is one of the ways many of the books are getting published through Kindle. There are writers who are not confident enough to publish under their own name, do not have the savings to publish and market their books, or simply want to focus on the writing versus the marketing of books.

Writers are hired to ghostwrite various topics. They may have a special niche that they deal with or a vast knowledge that allows the writer to discuss more than one topic. Savvy writers choose concepts they consider themselves experts in, as a way to offer validity of the products they are hired to create.

A publishing company may contact a pool of writers directly. They will create a writer's persona and have the writer create the product based on an outline or a title heading. The writer will get a flat rate with no potential to earn royalties from the book sales.

The publishing company or person is the one that receives the royalties. Sometimes there is a middle person who gets work from the publisher, passes it on to their pool of writers, and makes passive income from simply getting the completed book back to the publishing company.

Kindle allows anyone to publish a book. Quality is not always the best because Kindle doesn't check, with as much scrutiny, as other eBook publishing sites. There are certain things that Kindle looks for, such as sensitive topics like inappropriate photos, foul language, broken grammar, etc. Other than that, nearly anything can be published.

All you have to do is set up an account with Amazon, in their KDP department. It is free to set up a publishing account. When you set up the account, you gain access to free tutorials on how to publish, the template you need to use, and the various options for making money from the published book. You also gain access to emails that help you see what is hot or trending right now. Furthermore, Amazon will help you get book covers from a pool of template images. When the book is published, you can choose to make it exclusive to

Kindle, meaning you will not publish the book elsewhere. This helps you gain a higher royalty amount. You can also opt to sell it in multiple locations to garner more customers and make less on the royalties at these various publishing locations.

How to Make It Work for You:

As you can imagine, there are certain ways for you to make more money from Kindle publishing than others.

- You can write the book.

- Upload it.

- Market it.

Your other option is to pay a flat rate to a writer, so they get the time-consuming work of researching the topic, writing the book, and editing it. Then, you reap the rewards of uploading it and marketing it.

The money is truly in where and how you market the book.

Marketing with Kindle Publishing

One of the great things about Kindle is that they do market your book for you. However, you have hundreds of books being written each month, on similar topics, so even Kindle cannot market each book with the same success.

You want to take advantage of what they will do to market the book, but also have your own methods.

- Use email lists

- Set up affiliate marketing sites

- Create a blog

- Use social media

The email list option that will be discussed later will help you garner people that are more interested in the books you are selling. Of course, they have to buy or read your book first.

The key here is to offer your book for a limited time at a "free to read" price. This is where you put it in the Kindle Unlimited option for free. Someone sees the topic because they are interested in it, reads it, and then opts-in to read more books when you publish a new one.

When you have readers through Kindle Unlimited or offer the book for free for a short time, you want these individuals to leave a review. You should ask in the email or at the end of the book for a review. You don't have to be obvious about it but ask the person to let others know how much the reader appreciated the content.

Obviously, you want more positive reviews than negative reviews. If there are issues with your book, a rewrite to correct them should be made, so that you are selling a quality product.

Using affiliate marketing sites, you can create multiple online websites selling the books or at least products related to the books' topics. For example, if you grow pineapples, set up a website to sell pineapples. Post that you have books on how to grow, care, and repot pineapples available on Kindle. An interested customer will click through to your Amazon site and purchase the book. You have just made a sale to them for a pineapple plant and a book. Now you have two sources making you passive income.

You will always need a blog. When a new book comes out, you will use a press release or a book review by a customer to post on the blog. Readers flock to the blog, follow the link, and buy the book. The link they follow is, of course, an ad for that book.

Social media outlets are also ways to let people know that you have a book available to read. You can use your friends, family (with permission, of course), as well as anyone who stops by your social media websites.

Ratings

Profitability - Most of the hard work in Kindle publishing is over once you have finished your book. After submitting and publishing your book, the majority of the proceeds are passive in nature.

Perspective in the future - To scale your publishing business, you can either write more books or create bundles using your existing books. The more books you have the more royalties you can earn from sales.

Difficulty - As long as your manuscript is up to par with Amazon's standards, there are very little barriers along the way. You can have your book published by Amazon in a few days.

Budget for starting – As low as $100.

Business #7: Retail Arbitrage on eBay

If you are interested in selling physical items online and don't want the hassle of opening your own online store, then retail arbitrage might be for you. Originally an exclusive to those who traded in the foreign exchange currency market, arbitrage is simply the idea of purchasing a commodity at one price and then selling it elsewhere for a higher price. The rise of online marketplaces means that anyone can participate in retail arbitrage, as long as they are able to purchase items at a price that means they can be resold elsewhere for a profit.

Starting out: The biggest asset when it comes to retail arbitrage is a good nose for a great bargain. Your two biggest assets in this quest are going to be the Amazon Price check app and the eBay seller's application as these two sites are typically going to be the best place to go to sell your items for a profit. Both of these applications will help you determine the baseline price an item is selling for so you can decide if the price you are considering purchasing it at is worth the trouble.

In addition to these free applications, consider the Profit Bandit application. While it has a $10 upfront cost, it provides you with a wide variety of information that the free apps lack. Specifically, it will tell you how the current price of an item stacks up to the price of that item overall and also if the product is being sold by Amazon directly or if it violates their code of conduct and why. It will inform you the amount of profit you stand to make off of an item based on the amount you are paying, the amount you will sell it for and any extraneous costs that might be incurred.

Finding the best items: When it comes to finding the right items to sell, many people automatically think of big-ticket items, under the rationale that, if they can be found on sale, then the profit would be substantial. While these types of items will occasionally pan out, you will almost always find a more reliable return on basic items that everyone needs as they will sell faster and more readily is found for a discounted price. While this isn't the most exciting advice, products like batteries, diapers and ink cartridges are always going to be able to ensure that your retail arbitrage business turns a profit.

While they won't necessarily sell right away, a great type of product to consider selling is seasonal items such as Halloween or Christmas decorations. These items can typically be picked up for pennies on the dollar in the days immediately following the holiday and if you are willing to wait almost a year to sell them, will always return a reliable profit, especially if you wait to a week or so before the holiday to post them for sale. The downside with this being you only have a limited window in order to ensure that the item sells or else you have to hold onto it for another entire year.

Another good choice is to keep your ear to the ground when it comes to new trends and then purchase a large amount of the new hot item in bulk before the price catches up to its new level of popularity. For example, these days' kids are all about fidget spinners that have led the price of many versions of this product to increase dramatically. If you had hopped onto the fidget spinner bandwagon early on, then you could now sell them for a significant profit.

Finally, items from the dollar store that feature popular licensed characters such as Disney princesses or Marvel superheroes are always going to be able to turn a profit. While these products might not sell for much more than their purchase price at the moment, if you wait until a specific product is hard to find, typically four to six months, then you can easily sell it for five times what you paid for it to parents who are desperate for new content for their child who has already consumed everything else with their favorite character's face on the box.

Additional concerns: Outside of just looking for the best deals, give special attention to how a given item is likely to ship before buying in bulk. Keeping this factor in mind will make it easier to prevent a rash of returns on products that are exceedingly fragile or are otherwise difficult or exceedingly costly to ship. Furthermore, you will want to avoid items that are going to be complicated to ship as, if things go well, you will be shipping them out on an exceedingly frequent basis.

With these types of items, a good rule of thumb is to only move forward with sales that will net you at least 50 percent profit on the sold item. The only exception to this rule is if you have a specific idea in mind for the product when you purchase it and don't mind making less from it overall.

eBay to Amazon arbitrage: If you are looking to get into arbitrage without having to purchase any physical product, then you can actually play eBay and Amazon against one another. Specifically, what you do is spend time searching both eBay and Amazon for specific items and then, once you find a product that is selling for more on eBay, simply post a new auction and then, once it ends, purchase the product on Amazon and send it to the winner of the auction as a gift. While Amazon currently frowns upon this, it is not, strictly speaking, breaking any laws.

When it comes to completing this type of arbitrage sale successfully, it is important to ensure that the items you choose aren't on sale on Amazon for an exceedingly limited time as once an auction has been won it is difficult to get out of sending an item, even if you aren't going to make any money for it. Additionally, it is important to always only post a single auction at a time. Not only will this prevent you from losing money if the price changes on Amazon, but it will also make the buyer more likely to pull the trigger because of the apparent level of scarcity that having only one option provides.

Ratings

Profitability - You are directly selling products the way traditional stores do. So the income you earn is mostly direct income.

Perspective in the future - You can easily scale the business by adding more products in your eBay store.

Difficulty - The business model is really simple. Buy products from retail stores then list them for sale at a profit on eBay.

Budget for starting - $1,000.

Business #8: Paperback-Publishing

Kindle allows you to publish both eBooks and paperbacks. What's great about the platform is that you have control over your rights for the book and you get to set your own list prices. Furthermore, you can make changes to your books any time you want. As far as earnings are concerned, you can receive up to 70% in royalty from your book sales. For example, if you priced your eBook at $2.99 per download, your royalties will be $2.093 per eBook sold (excluding download fees). That may not look like much, but it quickly adds up once your sales start to pick up. The 70% royalty applies to numerous countries with huge Amazon markets.

I sell more paperbacks than Kindle editions of my books. That is common for non-fiction writers, less so for fiction writers. However, creating a paperback from your existing Kindle manuscript is easy, so why not? Until recently, Createspace was Amazon's print-on-demand service, but they've now moved it all under the one "KDP" roof. Having both kindle and paperback publishing in the same KDP account makes things even easier. Let's get started.

If you are creating Kindle books, it's relatively easy to convert those books into physical paperback versions, without having to pay anything upfront. It works like this:

1. Create your book in the "paperback" format.
2. Submit it for publication.
3. When approved, promote your book.
4. Let Amazon do the rest.

If you make a paperback sale, Amazon prints a copy of your book then packages and sends it to the customer. At this point, Amazon takes its cut and adds your royalty to your monthly income report.

As you can see, this is pretty much hands-off on your part. All you need to do is promote your book, but Amazon will also do that for you. You don't have to worry about taking orders, shipping, refunds, etc. All you do is collect your royalty payments every month.

You've already created your Kindle book from your Word document and we'll now use the same Word document to create the paperback version. Most of the work has already been done. All we really need to do is decide on page size, create a cover, and then do some final checks of the document.

Business #9: Audiobook Publishing

An audiobook is a representation of a written book through voice recording. It may include background music and some sound effects. Such recordings are rewarding in terms of sales and income.

You need to create an effective marketing strategy for the audiobook that may include such plans like social media campaigns and notable online retailers. Consider such sites like Amazon and ACX/Audible. The best way is building your own online strategy, get various distribution outlets and work with firms with reasonable costs and splits.

You may also decide to do a book promo through the print media and the cable stations available in the region. Unlike normal books, audiobooks do not take much room in the house. They are easily stored on a device by occupying megabytes space on the device's hard drive.

Business #10: Domain Flipping

Domain flipping has existed for long as a way of making money on the Internet. Since the dot com era, lots of savvy Internet entrepreneurs have cashed in on the business of domain flipping. Understanding how domain flipping works is quite easy. It is the understanding of how the market works that gets you the real money.

Buying a domain at a low price doesn't mean you will sell it for a higher price. You might fail at it if things are not laid out well. The important thing to consider when going into this business is the market. How do you market your domain?

Before we proceed, allow me to show you just how profitable it is to flip domains. There have been major milestones surpassed in domain flipping. Some domains have sold for over $30,000,000. The website Marijuana.com sold for $8,888,888 in 2011 on heels of the mainstream cannabis adoption. But that's not all. There are regular domain auctions on www.flippa.com, an online website and domain auction platform.

Getting Started

Over 300,000 domains are being registered daily and this comes to about 109,500,000 registered domains a year. Looking at these numbers tells you that there is a huge market for domain flipping.

This is the catch: Most of the domains registered yearly don't get to live past their first year. Oftentimes, once they expire, they are abandoned.

This is the business: These expired domains can be bought by you for pennies on the dollar and then sold for hundreds if not thousands of dollars. Because new businesses are always looking for popular domains, you can cash in on this and make some good money for yourself. Your responsibility is to find good domains, make them yours for cheap and then sell to eager buyers.

Finding the Right Domain

Finding the right domain to purchase for flipping is essential to your success in this business. I will provide the best five factors to consider and the tools to help you make a successful decision. It is important that you know how to judge the quality of a domain and its value.

These are some of the factors to consider when getting your domains:

Consider DOT COM (.com) Domains Only: You should invest only in .COM domains. This is an ideal domain for businesses. Most customers assume the domain to be a .com when told the web address. This is also the domain extension with the highest resale value. Over 50% of all domains sold are .com extensions. You can even leverage your name by purchasing other link extensions and link them to your .com extension.

<u>Pick an Easy Name:</u> The name should be easy to remember and pronounce. Most people have a better affinity with 2 – 3 syllable domains, although this is not the norm and all I am saying is avoid unnecessarily long names, like names with hyphens or numbers. Keep it short and simple.

<u>Look out for Branding:</u> You will have to be a little creative here. Names that sound like brands sell faster and attract more value. For instance; consider a name like cookieJar.com, this name sounds brandable. This is not difficult to do, just think about it a little and it will come to you. Businesses are looking to pay thousands for names that sync with their brand. Sometimes, it is the domain name that gives them an idea of what to call their business.

<u>Keywords Only:</u> This involves finding names that match specific niches. Someone setting up a medical business would want something along the lines of medicine. Domain names that are keywords, or are keyword related, sell faster and have good value.

<u>The Right Value of the Domain:</u> This is the most critical point in finding the right domain. If you make a mistake here, you could lose a lot of money. The value of a domain lies in the number of its backlinks, its relevance and quality. The more backlinks a domain has, the more powerful and valuable it becomes. The position of the backlinks is also important as backlinks within the content matters more. There are several tools online that will determine this, including the Moz site explorer.

When purchasing domains, make sure that the domains are of good quality, and although the earning potential may be huge, you can still get a loss sometimes if you don't apply the right strategies.

Business #11: Shopify

Profitable opportunities abound for online storefronts. There are several sites like Shopify or WooCommerce that make it easy to set up your own storefront to sell all sorts of products. You will need to obtain an SSL certificate and set up a way for your customers to accept payments, but once that is done, you are good to go.

There is no need of limiting yourself to the products; you could also set up a storefront where you can provide consulting services directly from your site. All you need is a good website, a merchant account, and a target audience to market to.

Once it is set up, you can easily earn a sizable income from a regular stream of customers making it worth the initial hassles you will meet in getting started.

Shopify is a platform you should seriously consider using for your e-commerce store. There's a reason why this platform is one of the biggest players in online commerce today. Hundreds of thousands of entrepreneurs and merchants use the platform to market and sell their products. Shopify is great for two things. It's great for starting an e-commerce store. And it's great for building a dropshipping business. The company offers several plans for those interested in using their services. These plans and their corresponding rates (as of March 2019) are as follows:

- Basic Shopify: $29 per month

- Standard Shopify: $79 per month

- Advanced Shopify: $299 per month

- Shopify Lite: $9 per month

- Shopify Plus: Flexible rate starts at $2000 per month

You can always test the Shopify free trial version before making your final decision. This trial version allows you access to Shopify's most basic features and functions for free for a period of fourteen (14) days. There are no strings attached. You can cancel and terminate your account any time you want. To proceed with the service, you will be given time to choose from the various plans (i.e. Basic Shopify, Standard Shopify, Shopify Lite, Advanced Shopify, and Shopify Plus).

Using Shopify to build an online business is quite easy and hassle-free. This is one of the most important selling points of the platform. It allows you to create a professional-looking e-commerce store even if you have very limited knowledge about web development, coding, and programming in general. The platform has a website builder wherein all you have to do is choose the template and customize it using prefabricated options, features, and functions. There are dozens of templates that you can use for free. Another great thing about these templates is that they have been designed specifically for certain niches and markets. For example, there are templates that have been designed for online stores selling shirts and other apparel.

If you don't have your own products to sell, no problem. You can always choose the dropshipping route. What you do is create your Shopify store and list products that you will be ordering from a manufacturer or supplier. You will not be keeping any product inventory. In fact, you won't even be the one shipping the products to your customers. If a customer orders a product from your Shopify store, your store orders the product from your supplier who ships the item to the customer.

Although the product came from your supplier, it looks like it came from you. This process can be 100% automated which means you earn money round the clock. It's nearly 100% passive income. You don't make the products and you are not the one shipping them. The cost of running the business is really cheap. Your major expenses will only be composed of your monthly dues from Shopify and any amount you spend on advertising and other marketing campaigns.

Business #12: Day Trading

There are two divisions when it comes to professional day traders. The first one is those who work alone. The second is those who work for a larger company. Most traders who do this kind of trading for a living will work for a large company. This is helpful because these individuals will have access to a lot of tools that an individual trader only dreams about. These can include some expensive analytical software, a lot of leverage and capital to start, and a direct line to the trading desk. These types of traders are looking for profits that are easy and ones that can be made looking at news events and arbitrage opportunities.

This doesn't mean that an individual trader isn't able to do day trading on their own. They may not have a trading desk of their own but they may have some strong ties to a brokerage and some other resources. If you are an individual trader, you won't be able to compete with some of the larger companies, but there is still a niche market that you can join.

If you wish to use day trading as a method to make a living, then there are a few things that are required to make this happen. These include:

- Some sort of access to a trading desk.

This tool is often reserved for those traders who work for a larger company or those who will manage a lot of money. The dealing desk provides these traders with the ability to do trades instantaneously which is very important to the success of day trading. If you don't work for a large financial organization, you may need to discuss with your broker what options are available for you here.

- Several news sources.

The news is going to provide you with the information you need to pick the best trades in day trading. You need to be one of the first to know when something big is about to happen. Then, you can jump into the market in the beginning and get a good price. Once everyone else catches on the news, you can sell your security and make a profit. Having at least three or four news sources that you look through each day can help you figure out the right trades to make.

- Analytical software.

When it comes to day trading, analytical software is going to be so critical. It may be a bit expensive when you get started but it is a necessity for most day traders. For those who are working on swing trades or technical indicators, you will rely more on this software than the news. Some of the features that you will want to find in your software include:

- Pattern recognition that is automatic.

This means that when you work with the trading program, you want it to identify technical indicators such as channels and flags. You may even want some complex indicators such as the Elliott Wave patterns.

- Neural and genetic applications.

These are programs that will utilize genetic and neural networks to help make your trading systems better. They are good at making more accurate predictions when you are trying to figure out where the price is going to move in the future.

- Broker integration.

Some software applications are going to make it possible to interface directly with the brokerage. This makes it easier for an individual trader to do an automatic execution of trades. Not only does this help you to get into and out of the markets at the right time, but it can also take some of the emotions out of the game.

- Backtesting.

Backtesting can be useful because it allows a trader to practice a bit. You will take your strategy and test out how it would have worked if you used it in the past. This is not always completely accurate, especially if the market turns a different way. But in some cases, it can give you an idea of how your current strategy will work in the market by basing the information on historical data.

When these tools are combined, they can provide a trader with a big edge over others in the marketplace. And when it comes to working with day trading, they are really important. Without them, many traders without the right experience can lose money in the market.

Business #13: Forex Trading

Forex trading is also known as foreign currency exchange trading, and it is the trade of international currencies. The prices of currencies fluctuate over time and as a Forex trader, it is your responsibility to look out for trends that foretell the direction in which a particular currency will fluctuate.

Currencies are like any other commodities in the world, their value is also affected by market forces, and thus the currency either rises in value (Bullish) or loses some of its value (Bearish).

The global online Forex market is the largest financial trading market in the world. There is conflicting data as to exactly how large the market is, but there is one common denominator and that is that the market has a daily trading volume in the trillions of dollars. The market is a 24-hour, 7 day a week market that attracts traders from all over. It is quite easy to trade Forex which is exactly why people do this. Aside from the ease of setting up an account, the Forex market offers significant leverage, low startup cost, opportunities to practice strategies before taking the plunge, and a range of investment options. There is no need to worry about driving traffic here nor do you consider the impact of SEO/SEM, but you must be ready invest a lot of time in education (which is absolutely free by the way) and the practice of new techniques.

<u>Rule of Thumb:</u> Forex is not for everyone, so it is important that you determine if you have the right temperament and mindset required to successfully trade Forex.

Summary

Forex, simply put, is the exchange of currencies. The currency in use in the US is the dollar ($), the currency in use in Germany is the Euro (€). You would have to exchange your dollars for euros when you get to Germany because with your dollars, you can't make purchases. One important thing to consider when exchanging your dollars for euros is that the rates are subject to fluctuations. You could get a higher rate today than what was exchanged for on the previous day.

If that is understood, let's then consider this same practice of exchange is moved onto the online world and ordinary people engage in the exchange with a motive of profiting from the fluctuations. This is online Forex trading. You invest in a particular currency pair exchange (USD/EUR, USD/GBP or GBP/EUR etc.) with the motive to profit from the rise in the value of one currency over its pair.

The beauty of this kind of trade is the ease at which it occurs. You can trade from your living room, kitchen counter, patio, office or from anywhere else. All that is required is an Internet enabled mobile device or computer, an account with a broker, and your first investment.

Business #14: Dividend Investing

When you're seeking to invest in companies, you need to seriously consider dividend stocks. However, what exactly are dividend stocks, and how do they really assist you in profiting effectively? To begin with, dividend stocks send out regular payouts to investors, called dividends. This means monthly, quarterly, yearly you will get a check informing you how good the company is performing, and may also take those funds and even reinvest it back into the company or perhaps cash out your stocks altogether and go invest with another person or business who might use your hard earned money a lot more sensibly. Dividend stocks, if chosen sensibly, can give you real protection for the future and bolster your portfolio.

A dividend is a payment by a corporation to its shareholders. Often, but not always, it is paid in cash; it is a form of compensation for the funds invested by shareholders.

I learned about dividend investing while I was still in a **growth investing** mindset, and I believe that most beginning investors are in the same position.

Investing for growth means buying stocks in the hope that their share price will go up after you buy them. The old saying, "buy low and sell high," is an apt description. Investing for growth means you don't make any profit from your stocks until you actually sell them – and only if you can sell them at a higher price per share than you paid for them.

Dividend investing is sometimes called "investing for income" because dividend stocks pay you income on a regular basis (usually quarterly), regardless of their share price. Not all stocks pay out dividends, but at first glance, dividend stocks look just like any other stock. They're publicly traded on the major indexes, and you buy your shares through your brokerage account. Sometimes their price per share goes up, and sometimes it goes down. As a dividend investor, you will want to "buy low," just as a growth investor would, but once you own the stock, any growth in share price is added to the fact that it's likely to pay dividends for as long as you own the stock.

Dividends that you earn from the shares make for a regular income. The share prices go up but you also get a regular income from the dividends. The companies share the profits with the shareholders on a regular basis. At the end of every financial year, these profits are divided. Some companies may also give them more than once a year. The dividend income is not guaranteed and if the company suffers losses, it might decide not to pay anything. Some companies invest the profits back into their work-flow.

Something you have to remember when you are dealing with dividend stock investments is the fact that you will need to make certain you take your time; this is planning for the future so you will have to be comfy giving your money in different stocks even when they're not really doing that great at a certain time or simply having a horrible quarter.

Business #15: Mining Cryptocurrencies

By now, most people have heard about the crypto craze. Stories abound about people literally making fortunes overnight. It is true that there is money to be made in this type of venture, but before you jump in with both feet, it pays to do your research. This is a very new market, and things are very unpredictable, so enter this income stream at your own risk.

Everyone has heard of Bitcoin, but there are more than 1600 cryptocurrencies you can invest in. You must exercise extreme caution when investing in new coins because, in addition to the volatile market, many coins may not be able to compete in such a flooded market. For that reason, it is important for you to do more than the usual research when it comes to choosing the right coins to invest in.

Business #16: Options Trading

An option is defined as a contract granting the buyer the right to buy or sell an underlying asset at a specified price on or before a specified date. It is a binding contract with very strictly defined terms. Here's a very easy example: Let's say you find a super sexy Chevy Corvette z06 that you just have to buy. Unfortunately, the cash is not available right now, but you will in two months. You talk to the owner and agree on a deal that gives you the option to buy that car in two months for a price of $50,000. Since you don't have the cash upfront, the owner makes you pay $2,000 for this option.

A few different scenarios can take place in those two months:

Scenario 1: Let's say it's discovered that the car actually has a factory upgrade that it wasn't supposed to have. Now it's the only z06 in the world with this upgrade, so it's a one of a kind car and is now worth $200,000! Since the owner sold you the option, he is contractually bound to sell you the car for the agreed upon $50,000. You just made a profit of $148,000 ($200,000 current value - $50,000 purchase price - $2,000 option = $148,000). Not bad.

Scenario 2: It's discovered that car is actually a lemon with a salvage title. It's only worth $5,000. Although you originally fell in love with the car, it's not all you once thought it was. Even though you bought the option, you as the buyer are under no obligation to go through with the sale. You only forfeit the $2,000 price of the option.

These scenarios exemplify the two most important aspects of options. When you buy an option, you have the right to buy the asset, but not the obligation. You may decide to allow the expiration date pass, at which point the option has no value. It also demonstrates that an option is merely a contract that deals in an underlying asset (in this case, the Corvette). This is why options are often referred to as derivatives — they derive their value from something else.

Types of Options
When it comes to stocks, there are two types of options available: calls and puts.

Call Option: A call option gives you the right to buy shares. You make money as a stock rises in price. You are hoping the stock will increase in price substantially before the option expires.

Put Option: A put option gives one the right to sell stocks. You make money as a stock drops in price. You are hoping that the price of the stock falls before your option expires.

That's the great thing about options — they allow you to make money as something goes up in value, or even as something goes down in value.

Let's take a look at an example. Let's say we have a company called Tucker's Agency. On June 1, the stock price of Tucker's Agency is $50 and the premium (cost of the option contract) is $2 with an expiration date of August 15th and a strike price of $55. Because each option contract represents 100 shares, the total price of your contract would be $2 X 100 = $200.

The strike price is the price a stock must go above (for calls) or below (for puts) before a position can be exercised for a profit. In this the contract, the strike price is $55, so the stock must rise above $55 before a call option is worth anything. And since your contract is $2 per share, the actual break-even price $57.

Four weeks later, the stock price is at $60. The options contract has increased and is now worth $6. $6 X 100 = $600. Subtract what you initially paid for the contract and your profit is $400 (($6 - $2) X 100 = $400). You have just doubled your money, but only if you decided to actually sell when the price of the stock was $60. If you do not exercise your option and the stock then dropped to $45 by the expiration date, you would lose your initial investment of $200.

Business #17: Freelancing

Freelancing is taking over the world because many people are doing this work more than actually working a 9-5 job. There are so many people losing their jobs nowadays because of the outsourcing of companies. It has gotten so bad that even people with degrees find it hard to obtain a job. The Internet offers you a chance to make some money with people worldwide who want and need your talent.

Freelance work means that you're always available to work for a specific job. And the beautiful thing about freelance work is that there are normally no time restraints holding you back. Therefore, you can complete it anytime you want. That job could be temporary, or it could be long term, depending on the availability of work for clients.

Freelancing jobs could include graphic design, data entry, website designer, website coding, website creation, IT (Informational Technology), marketing, virtual assistant, online accountant, translator, online tax preparer, programmer, and more. Some websites that offer work for freelancers are: Freelancer, Upwork, Getacoder, Guru, Fiverr and others.

Business #18: Online Consultancy

Are you an expert in something? Maybe you are a good social media marketer. Maybe you are a pro in Web Design. If you are skilled at something, you should consider offering your knowledge as an online consultant. Anyone from around the world can become your client. You can create an income source from your skill or experience by simply offering advice to people.

Online consultancy is a very competitive niche so you should be smart which fields or industries you enter. Getting clients for your consultancy business is all about proving to your potential customers that you are who they're looking for. You have to show them that you got the goods. Aside from providing samples or testaments to your previous work, you also have to constantly work on your personal branding. You have to get your name out there. The best way to do that is to keep on providing exceptional services to your clients.

It is advisable to create your website, own a blog and command a high social media presence. Get to platforms that you will use to promote your services.

Business #19: Personal Branding on Social Media

It is essential to have a unique personal brand. You may not earn money on the short term but it is a scalable business with time. Ensure that your account is up to date with complete and accurate information. You will be able to attract the traffic you target to showcase your skills.

Business #20: Social Media Influencer

In this age of social media, there are a few roles that have been erected and these roles serve as rallying points in this online space. One of the roles that has become popular in recent years is the social media influencer.

Defining a social media influencer is as straightforward as it sounds. We can refer to a social media influencer as a person who has a very large following on the various social media platforms and exerts a measure of control over his or her followers. By virtue of who they are, they can influence the buying decision and the thoughts of a lot of their followers. Celebrities, sports stars, actors, politicians and leaders all fit this bill.

You fall under the latter group. You see, I am guessing that you are not a celebrity, a sports star, an actor or a politician. We want to grow our following as normal people and if we become social media "celebrities" in the process, that is just a bonus.

Influencers are those people consumers look to before they decide to make a purchase. As more and more technology is developed, people are less likely to pay attention to promotional ads before making a decision on a product or service. They usually will refer to those who have previously used the product and seek out their advice.

Social media sites have become a rallying point for a lot of people, especially from the younger age group. These individuals span different niches including gaming, fashion, sports, comedy and information technology. These people are not celebrities in the real world, but in the online realm, they are kings and queens.

Who is a Social Media Influencer?

Social media influencers are passionate people. It was their passion that made them popular. They stand for an idea and express their passion. Some are great teachers, others are inspirational speakers, and some are fashion experts. They have passion as a common feature.

In business, a social media influencer is someone who uses his or her influence to promote a particular brand, service or interest to his or her followers and can convert them to customers for the respective brand or company.

How Do Social Media Influencers Earn?

There are several techniques you can set yourself up as an influencer. Most do YouTube videos reviewing certain products while others may insert their views through Facebook or Instagram. A popular influencer could easily generate a six-figure income with just a few videos. Even a lesser-known influencer can generate a pretty stable income with the right audience.

Social media influencers are one of the biggest earners in the world today. A majority of their income comes from branding. Earnings for social media influencers vary a lot. There are no fixed amounts but their following, to a large extent, determines how much they can earn. Also, the client's budget and marketing objectives also make a difference.

Brand Rep/Ambassador: Social media influencers can monetize themselves by taking advantage of their popularity to become brand ambassadors or representatives for major brands.

Sell Digital Products: They can use their influence and sell digital products such as eBooks, how-to courses, or videos.

Make Sponsored Posts: In this case, you can use your profile as a potent advertisement tool. Make sponsored posts for brands and companies for a one-time fee.

Physical Products: You can sell physical products. Even when you don't manufacture anything, you can sell other brands' products through your profile.

Affiliate Marketing: One way you can take advantage of your followers is by becoming an affiliate marketer. Affiliate marketers have the medium to reach millions of people and earn well for themselves.

How to be Successful as a Social Media Influencer

There are certain practices that will put you ahead in being a successful social media influencer. But first, your personality must be built on trust. Any untrue aspect about yourself should be disclosed upfront, if not it will come out when you start becoming popular.

Build a Following: The easiest way most social media influencers have come to prominence is through their content. They all have great content that suits their niche. Creative content is the major elixir. Even if you invest in driving traffic and advertising, if you do not have good content, you will lose the following after a short while. It is great content that encourages a user to follow and invite others to do the same.

An investment in growing your following is not a bad idea especially since you are just starting out. Organically growing followers these days is very difficult. So, you have to act wisely to invest in boosting your following. There are agencies and freelancers who would do this for you for a small fee.

Business #21: Create and Selling Online courses

Selling online courses is another option for passive income streams. There are two ways you can do this: write an online course and market it, or market online courses written by other people. There are advantages to selling online courses. You believe in the education of others and wish to help them gain new materials that will help them gain what they require. However, the disadvantage is that you can go terribly wrong when creating content or selling online courses from other sources. You can provide improper information if you are not careful.

- You never want to sell an online course, or you write, if you are not an expert on the topic.

- When selling online courses that others write, you need to check their expertise. What is their degree? Have you seen their diploma? Have you read any of their work?

You never want to sell anything you cannot validate. This is why you need to choose online courses to sell that you actually have knowledge about.

How to Sell Online Courses

- Choose valuable content.

- Identify the audience you hope to sell to.

- Visit forums where your target audience will hang out. If necessary, rewrite your course based on what you learn from these forums. Sometimes people complain that they are not learning what they feel is important or they don't understand a concept and wish for more explanation in a simpler manner.

- Market your material based on the target audience you hope to sell to.

- Choose a niche.

- Offer a hook to get your audience's attention, such as time saving tips and tricks for Office Programs.

- Have more than one course that fits the learning needs. You want a series of courses on offer, where the person finishes one course and wants to take the more advanced course. Your plan is to sell a series of courses to one customer versus one course to multiple courses. Return customers will help you gain their friends.

- Choose a platform to sell on. It needs to be one that will confirm appropriate standards for your online courses. To provide validity for your course, you need the SCORM standards. Udemy is just one location that has a free open-source learning management system that provides standards that allow people to trust in your courses.

- You are going to need a dedicated website for online learning courses you sell. You want to have a catalog and shopping cart that ensures buyers can quickly and effectively purchase your courses.

- Tie your website to a blog where you can share relevant content, as well as make money from the advertisements on that blog site.

- Social media, including Facebook, LinkedIn, Instagram, and Twitter accounts are necessary. You can publish articles, discuss what you sell, and help get your audience engaged and to your online course website.

- Use online search engine indexes to get your courses noticed. Try offering affiliate marketing as a way to get your courses noticed.

- Once you sell a course, stay in contact with your learners. Figure out what they liked, would like improved, and what else they need. A great review can help you sell more courses. It also shows that you care about what they are learning and you want to ensure they are getting what is required.

Selling online courses once you have established your reputation is about keeping up with the content, making sure it is updated when new information is discovered, and marketing it. It is the marketing part of selling online courses that will take the most time, unless you are writing your own courses.

You can make money whenever someone buys your product or a series of your products. You can make money on the advertising and affiliate marketing set up you create.

Business #22: Coaching Online

You can earn passive income by teaching online courses. There are a number of sites that will allow you to create a video class featuring your unique set of skills or talent in any area of your personal expertise.

If you enjoy creating content and teaching people what you know, then this could turn out to be very profitable for you. Whether you are an expert guitarist, or you have the secret to baking the perfect cake, you can generate your own following and teach people what you know.

Udemy is one of the best places to get started with teaching your courses, but there are other sites as well. Whether you want to teach technical courses that focus on something complicated or you want to explain some skill that is hard for people to acquire, you can end up with a global classroom with thousands of people willing to learn what you have to offer.

Through them, you can share all of your knowledge and talents to a whole world of students and generate a nice little income at the same time. The beauty of it is that once the video is made, it will continue to generate income for as long as you keep it up there.

Business #23: Podcasting

Don't like to talk in front of a live audience in person? Are you a chatterbox? Do you like sharing your opinions to a fault? Well, podcasts are for you. Talk, talk and more talking is what you need to do start a podcast business. Podcasting is similar to talk radio to a degree. You don't have celebrity guests, but you do have friends and family that you could invite on to share contrasting opinions. You could even live stream, but all in due time. If it resembles your kind of party then I would suggest you start today!

Tons of free web hosting sites are out there so there isn't any excuse to start today. It's going to take some legwork to get your podcast site out. Visit forums and share your web address, and there are tons of affiliate programs that you can post on your podcast site to generate that passive income in addition to the membership area. My wife ran a podcast for 4 years and we shared some truly fun times, respectfully debating and taking input from our streamed feed. But having newborn twins kind of put a wrench in her podcast, for now. She plans on returning to the Internet airways in the future. She really loved her podcast.

Business #24: Online Auctions

Online auctions operate exactly like what you'd expect. You list a product in an auction site, set an auction period, set the minimum bid, and then click launch. Customers will bid on your product listing until the auction period ends. Whoever bids the highest after the auction period expired will get your product. This can be a lucrative online business if you are able to target a niche and build an army of loyal customers.

Online auctions require a little bit of work because you need to regularly check which of your auctions have expired and which auctions are still running. Products that didn't get any bids have to be manually relisted. So yes, running an auction business can be time-consuming. But it's worth it if you have products that are easy to sell.

Business #25: Royalty from Photographs

If you are already familiar with what is required to take a great photo, and you have a way to take photos that is more advanced than your Smartphone, then taking photos and selling them to stock photo websites can be an easy way to generate a steady stream of passive income.

Getting started: There are several major sites that you can apply to if you are interested in pursuing this type of passive income stream including iStockPhoto.com and ShutterStock.com. Each of these sites allows aspiring photographers to post content to their site in exchange for a percentage of the profits when a third party pays to license a picture. These sites generally take between 50 and 85 percent of the profits from each photo with more experienced photographers getting a larger percent of the profits. What this means is that selling stock photos is a numbers game with a number of sales being key to success in the long run.

Understand what sells: The first step towards making money through this type of passive income stream is determining what type of photos customers are looking for and understanding how to reproduce the quality that you find. Assuming you are already familiar with the basics of quality photography, that means spending some time looking through various categories of photos you are interested in. You will want to find a category that is active enough to make it worth your while to contribute to it, while not being so stuffed with content that it is going to be difficult to get yourself noticed. You will also want to take note of the photos that seemed to be picked the most so that you can get an idea of what types of pictures those who frequent those sites are looking for.

Take some pictures: After you have a clear idea of the types of pictures you are to take, the next step is to get out there and start taking pictures. It was mentioned before, but it bears repeating, if you want to find success in this passive income stream then you are going to want to use something nicer than your Smartphone camera. While those pictures have the potential to be relatively good quality, especially considering where that technology was just a few years ago, if you try and submit Smartphone pictures to these sites, there is a very high chance that you will be rejected.

Once you have a number of shots that you feel are of the quality required to get your foot in the door, before you submit them, go over them with a fine-toothed comb. To do so, blow them up to the largest size possible and keep an eye out for small imperfections that might not otherwise be visible. You never know what size photo customers are going to be looking for and you don't want to lose out on a sale just because something isn't right at the largest size. Besides that, always stick to an exposure rate that is set to 100 percent and to also use a tripod, as blurry pictures are almost never going to be accepted unless the blurriness is obviously done for effect.

Submit the photos: The submission process for the major sites is relatively straightforward, you simply choose a few of your best shots and then send them along to be analyzed by a team of professionals who work for the site in question. Once accepted, you then create a profile. Once you have been given access to post new pictures at your own discretion, ensure that each photo you upload features descriptive text that makes it clear what the photo is of as well as a variety of descriptors that will make it more likely to show up in as many different relevant searches as possible.

Include common keywords as well as those that are outside of the box as your idea will sometimes rub potential customers the right way and they will go for it when they otherwise would have picked something more mainstream. This doesn't mean you list your photo in every category possible, however, as doing so is only going to cause people to start ignoring your work, even if it comes up in a category that is actually relevant.

If your work doesn't get accepted to the major sites, you may find success with some of the smaller stock photo sites out there that have much less strict application requirements. As almost anyone can be accepted to these sites, if your work is better than average, but just not quite good enough for the major players then you may even find that these sites work in your favor. What's more, they typically pay a larger cut even to new photographers to make up for the fact that they see a fewer number of customers on average. Remember, stock photos are a numbers game so the more places your photos can be seen by the masses the better.

Promote your photos: When posting your photos to the sites you have been accepted to, it is important to not ignore the free photos section. While posting free photos might seem like a bad way to make money, in reality the opposite is true. If customers aren't ready to pay for a photo quite yet, getting your name in the free section is a good way to get them thinking about your work so that when they are ready to purchase, your name is already in their mind. Consider this as an advertising cost and you will likely see more productive hits in the long run.

Business #26: Real Estate REITS

This is an easy way to get into real estate without actually purchasing real property to rent. You won't need to have a large amount of cash to invest in because you are merely purchasing "shares" in the real property.

There are several REITs you can invest in including residential, retail, industrial, office, hotel/resort, and storage.

REITs are companies owning commercial real estate like retail spaces, office buildings, hotels, and apartments. Investing in REITs accords you the benefit of investing in real estate without necessarily purchasing individual properties. REITs usually pay high dividends, which then makes them a viable retirement investment.

REITs actually hold above $2 trillion worth of commercial real estate globally. And the good thing is; typically, REITs do not have to pay corporate income taxes so long as their investors receive at least 90% of their income. With this huge advantage, you can understand why returns from REITs are usually higher.

Because of this, we have large companies such as Sears and McDonalds who have considered selling their real estate into REITs and then renting it back in order to gain from tax benefits.

As an investor who does not want or need the regular income, you can invest these dividends automatically to grow your investment even further.

NOTE: REITs can be complex or varied. Some will trade on an exchange such as stock while others do not trade publicly. One of the biggest factors in the risk size you take on is the type of REIT you buy because the non-traded REITs are not easy to sell off and can be difficult to value.

As a new investor, stick to publicly traded REITs you can buy with the help of an online broker. This therefore means that you will need to have your own brokerage account; if you do not have one, you can open one in at least 15 minutes.

Currently, there are 3 kinds of REIT shares available in the market:

Equity REIT – The REIT Company invests and owns their own real estate.

REIT Mortgage –as opposed to Equity REIT, this type loans money in the form of mortgage to prospective buyers of real estate.

Hybrid REIT–the REIT Company buys their own properties as well as offers mortgage.

REITS may be publicly traded or privately traded. They can also be highly specific to an area, a city, a state, or even the type of real estate invested into. For example, some REITs invest only in retail mall space while others are concerned with residential properties. It's possible to settle for a REIT company that focuses on a specific industry but for the sake of diversification, it's usually best to opt for one that takes all real estate types into account.

Benefits and Risks

The beauty of REIT is the fact that you don't have to spend an exorbitant amount of money to get started with real estate investing. Much like stocks, it's also fairly easy to buy, trade, and sell – unlike direct ownership which takes negotiation on your part. This makes them *liquid* assets in the sense that they can be easily sold off if you happen to need cash fast. Their growth, however, is not in line with stocks and bonds, which means that there's room for diversification. For example, should your shares in Apple start to fall, the real estate market will not fall with it.

Of course, risks are present as with any investment. The liquidity of REIT shares depends largely on whether they're traded publicly or not. A publicly traded REIT is often easier to unload for cash. Private REITs can also be tough to pin down when it comes to value per share. Hence, if you're just getting started – it's usually best to settle for a publicly traded REIT for the sake of transparency.

How to Buy and Sell REIT

Fortunately, the Internet makes it easy for you to buy and sell REIT. There are currently several websites dedicated towards real estate trading and for complete beginners, you can start with E-Trade or Scottrade.

Different companies have different requirements for their REIT shares. The whole process, however, is much like opening a bank account or purchasing bonds and stocks in the market. The selling process is pretty much the same because when it comes right down to it, you *are* selling shares in a company that invests in real estate. For the sake of reference, Scottrade requires you to fill in the Brokerage Application Form which can be easily submitted online.

How to Choose a REIT?

Much like buying company stocks, you'll have to perform some background checks before making your purchase. Here's a typical guideline for choosing and buying REIT:

Property Types – What properties are they investing in? Currently, the biggest and most stable earners are those in the multi-family residential market. Hotels and single-person apartments are usually the riskier options, and everything in between often provides average returns in the market.

Company Growth – Company growth is something you can easily determine with the information typically provided by the company themselves. An excellent indicator is the FFO or Funds From Operation. This takes into consideration income and subtracts expenses so that you get a clear look at how much the company currently has. Of course, you might want to take a look at other indicators in the Account Statement but for the most part, this should get you going.

Value per Share – Of course, don't forget the value per share of the REIT. Ideally, this should be increasing over time, although not necessarily at a quick pace. If you're gunning for passive income, then chances are you simply want to collect on the dividends but if you're holding on for long-term investment, you'd want to see growth in the shares themselves.

Visit a Property – If it's possible, you can try visiting one of the properties owned by the REIT Company and see how well they handle their holdings. You'd want to find a property that's properly maintained with long-lasting tenants; otherwise it, might bode badly for the future of the business.

REIT and Taxes

The great thing about REIT is that it's not subject to double taxation unlike other companies. Although you still have to pay your taxes on them, the company itself doesn't have to. What difference does this make? A large one, if you analyze it mathematically.

Let's say that there's Company A and B. Company A is a REIT company while B is your typical corporation. They both have a yield of $10 per share before paying tax. Company B will have to pay the required amount of tax – say 20% - lowering the yield to $8. This is how much you will be paid and in turn, your $8 will ALSO be subject to tax, this time filed by you.

REIT doesn't do the first level of taxation in that the whole $10 will be given to you. Any tax payment will be done by you based on the $10 yield.

If you want to decrease the taxable income in your REIT investments, you can try directing them to your retirement funds. In this situation, you'll catch a tax break and still be able to save up money for future purposes.

Business #27: Flipping Houses

Flipping houses is about taking a property that needs repairs or modern updates, making those changes, and selling the property for more money. Flipping houses rely heavily on understanding the current real estate market and buyers. If you buy a house, you need to have someone who will buy it from you once changes are made.

The wrong location can jeopardize your sale. When real estate agents say, it is "location, location, location," it is because it is true. Families, expectant mothers, and couples planning for the future are looking at school districts, safety of the neighborhood, and family-friendly entertainment in the area.

Single people are usually looking for an entertainment scene that is affordable and close to their place of employment.

Flipping houses is all about knowing the customer base you want to target. It is also about finding housing deals that will turn a profit. If you buy a house for $200,000 and the neighborhood comparison prices are all $210,000, then even if you put $50,000 into renovations, you are unlikely to gain a higher price.

Older homes can have structural issues like foundation, electrical, or plumbing problems. These problems can be expensive, without increasing the home's value enough to cover them. Sometimes adding a new bathroom may seem like a value increase, but the reality is it costs more than the little added value.

Requirements:

- A strong network.

- Money in the bank or the ability to leverage.

- Construction knowledge, expertise preferable.

- An eye for value.

You may have seen the shows about fix and flips? There are plenty of them on HGTV, where someone or two partners thought they could do a lot of the work themselves, to save time and money. Only to end up spending more than they budgeted and not selling the property for enough to cover their costs. Do not be this person or partnership.

If you are going to flip houses without any construction knowledge, you will need the money to hire a contractor and other subcontractors. Only fix and flip with your own talents, if you have actually worked in the industry.

You will also need to pay the full price for the house or have the ability to get a mortgage. Understand that while you are working on the house, you are paying the mortgage until the house sells.

It takes talent to assess homes and determine which houses will turn a profit based on current market sales, neighborhood, demand, and price. It is not always possible to find something worth fixing and reselling.

Business #28: Business silent partner

A business silent partner is an individual who is not actively involved in the operations or management of a business apart from capital contribution. The silent partner is entitled to a percentage of the income.

Business #29: Cashback Rewards on Credit Card

Using a cashback rewards credit card is a nice way to get back a percentage of your purchases. If you do a lot of your shopping online or if you use your credit card often, you should consider making use of one that offers cashback rewards. A cashback is basically a rebate of a percentage of the purchases you make on the card. There are three main types of cashback reward cards. These are category bonus cashback cards, tiered rewards cashback cards, and simple cashback cards.

Business #30: Membership sites

A membership site contains content that can only be accessed by registered members. You pay a membership fee to gain access to the content. These sites are filled with valuable content, which you can only access if you register as a member and pay the relevant fees.

How do you earn passive income from a membership site? Aside from the membership fee which you can collect monthly or yearly, you can further monetize the content of the site through various methods like affiliate marketing and advertising. You can also directly sell digital products to your members. Content in membership sites can include PDF files, eBooks, video tutorials, software downloads, webinars, exclusive forums, consultancy services, exclusive chat rooms, etc.

Business #31: Cashback Sites

A cashback website is basically a reward website that compensates its members by giving them a cut of the money it earned from goods and services that their members purchased through the site's affiliate links. Buying goods and services through a cashback site is called cashback shopping. Technically speaking, you are mostly saving money instead of making money when you use a cashback site. However, some cashback sites offer other services where you can earn some income. Such services may include online surveys and crowdsourcing tasks.

Business #32: Online Real Estate Auctions

You have been to several auctions, and real estate auction is not different. This is an innovatively structured and effective process of buying and selling of property. It is a professional and market niche accepted way of real estate marketing that involves the public in the selling process. The effectiveness of real estate auction accelerates property marketing becoming the choice of many. It is an open cry but yet competitive process that also caters for the non-distressed as well.

Simply put, an online real estate auction sale is a process where you sell property online by allowing buyers to bid, analyzing the bids and selling to the highest bidder. Due to its ascending nature, it is the ideal auction for your real estate. This is the open auction.

It is upon you to decide to go with the public or private auction. In private auction, you have a special setting where the identities of the bidders are not disclosed. Those who visit your auction site will not have access to what bids their competitors have placed. This way when people do a search, your private auction will not disclose the identities of others interested parties.

Business #33: Rent properties-rooms-spaces Online

Why:
You can get a steady monthly income if you have tenants renting your place without you having to do anything other than making sure the tenants are giving their monthly rental fee on time and maintaining and managing the property.

Now, if you want it to be a totally passive income, you can hire professional property managers. However, that would take a portion of your income since they usually charge around 10% of the rental fee. So, if you can manage the property, don't hire any property managers. It wouldn't take a lot of your time anyway.

If you got the property through a bank loan, the monthly income you get from the rental fee can be used to pay your mortgage, so you don't have to worry about your monthly loan payments. Then, once the loan has been paid off, the rental fee is all yours therefore, increasing your monthly cash flow.

Where:
Consider the location of your property. Is the property strategically located? For instance, properties near universities, colleges, malls, companies or corporations are more likely to have more tenants than those that are in far flung areas.

How:
Calculate how much income you'd like to get from the rental property and consider the cost of the property, taxes and other expenses. For example, if target earning is $500 a month and you have to pay $2,000 for mortgage plus $500 for taxes and other expenses, then, the monthly rental charge should be $3,000.

Reality:
Getting income from a rental property is an effective way to earn. You should consider a few things like (1) the cost and/or expenses of the property; (2) how much ROI (return of investment) you want to get; and (3) what the financial risks are in having a property rented.

Rental properties can be zoned residential or commercial. Residential rental properties include single family homes, duplexes, condos (townhomes), multi-family homes and apartment buildings. Commercial rental property can be a part of a strip mall, a group of offices, an office building, a single office, indoor mall, or a single building. The zoning for commercial property means it cannot be used as a residence or a portion of the building is for a business, while another portion is zoned residential. For example, buildings with businesses on the ground floor and towers of apartments above are commercial property, with residential apartments above.

Commercial property requires a larger buy-in, different insurance, and offers a larger return on investment than residential property.

Requirements:

- You need to understand rental property law, including landlord and tenant laws.

- Anyone with the right network can become a landlord. There are no special qualifications.

- There is an option to be highly involved, speaking with tenants on a monthly basis, hiring a management company, or being minimally involved. Minimum involvement is checking in when the rent is late, changing air filters, conducting maintenance, and maintaining the outside of the building.

Rental properties are often a more comfortable position to be in, when a mortgage or investment partner is required. You can leverage the property, make money from the appreciation of the property, but also have the tenant covering the mortgage on the property. If you have a mortgage that is $500 per month and a renter pays $750 per month, you not only pay the mortgage, but also gain a profit. The $250 may be used for maintaining the home, emergencies, paying the insurance you need for the building, or other expenses. Appreciation in a home only pays off when you sell the home, so you want to make sure you are covered for emergency, maintenance, and insurance expenses.

Choosing a Rental Property

When choosing what rental properties to buy, there are a number of important criteria that you have to keep in mind. We have already mentioned the neighborhood, the property is located in, as well as easy access to schools and other amenities. Here are some other criteria that you should keep in mind:

- **Average rents in the area:** This is an important consideration since it will affect your profitability. Is the average rent enough to cover your expenses and ensure that you have enough left for a profit? If not, can you charge more without deterring tenants from renting in your property?

- **Employment opportunities:** Areas where it is easy to find work will naturally attract more tenants. In addition, having a major business in the area will probably raise property values, and may be a signal for you to consider unloading your investment.

- **Crime:** This is a major concern for tenants so if the area is considered unsafe, you should definitely avoid it. Apart from looking at police presence in the area, you can also look out for indicators such as petty vandalism that may indicate the property is undesirable.

- **Amenities:** What are the amenities in the area? Is there easy access to parks, malls, groceries, movie theaters, and other leisure activities? In addition, you should look at how easily you can get to the area using public transportation. Are there public transport hubs near the property?

- **New developments:** If there is a lot of new construction going on in the area, it is probably a growth area with lots of potential for you to charge high rents. Also consider if the developments will hurt property values in the neighborhood, i.e., if they will cause the loss of amenities that will make it a less attractive place to live.

- **Property taxes:** Paying property taxes will naturally impact on your profits so you want to know what the local rates are. However, this may not be a consideration if you intend to hold on to the property for the long-term.

- **Vacancies and listings**: If there are a lot of listings in a neighborhood, it may signal that the area is undergoing a seasonal fluctuation and that conditions will eventually correct themselves, or that the neighborhood has become undesirable. You should also look at the vacancy rates since low rates mean that you can charge higher rents to tenants.

Business #34: Create a software

Software can be an extremely lucrative source of passive income.

Just like anyone else, I'm assuming you have your fair share of problems. Write them down and brainstorm ways to solve them. You can't track which of your students has paid for their lessons? Create software that can track it for you!

Brandon was a music teacher and couldn't keep track of which of his students had paid and which hadn't, so he decided to create a very simple application to help track the payments. Eventually this got a little more sophisticated and began generating $1,000 per month. Today, Brandon's software includes a full suite of offerings, as well as a DIY website element.

When he first reported on it to Tim in late 2011, it was already bringing in $25,000 a month (90% of which was passive income!).

Don't know how to program software? I know I don't. Outsource it! Just like almost everything else in this book, it's extremely easy to find programmers online in different places. Any programmer worth their weight will be able to create basic software, and basic is all you need to start.

Business #35: Create an App

Unless you hibernated to an island for several years and out of touch with society, you know there is now an app for nearly everything. In fact, there's even an app to keep all of your current apps organized. No, this is not a joke. So, if you haven't gotten on board the app bandwagon, it may be time to rethink that decision.

Designing applications for the many different mobile devices has become big business these days. No matter where you are, who you are, or what you are, there is a good chance that you're using some type of application to get the things you want to be done. If you're in search of a highly lucrative opportunity and you have the skills to develop these apps, you are in a very enviable position.

Before getting surprised "This is a great idea, but I have no idea how to make an app" it's okay! You don't have to have any type of programming abilities to make an app. In fact, most people who opt for this path have no clue as to the first step of programming. There are plenty of other people who have more than enough knowledge to help you with this part of it, it's how they make their living. Seems weird right? If they have all of this knowledge, why not just make them for the apps for themselves instead? We can't begin to understand the whys and what for's, just suffice to say these people exist and that's a good thing for you. Why? Because even if you did happen to know the ins and outs of programming, it is smarter to outsource this to someone else to free up your time to multiply your efforts elsewhere to generate passive income.

So what kind of app is best? Truth be told, pretty much any kind of app can be successful. Sure, we are all familiar with the wildly successful iTunes apps – they are the most well-known, the most downloaded and obviously produce the most profit. For your app to be successful, you have to have a bit of a roadmap to follow. For example:

Do you want your app to promote a business? In other words, if you want your app to promote and showcase your favorite adult watering hole and you have a bang-up, spiffy design and idea, your first step would be to hire someone to develop it for you. This doesn't have to be expensive – in fact, some apps can be designed for around $125; however, keep in mind that the more bells and whistles you have in your design, the more programming effort will have to go in and of course, the price goes up. Be careful with apps being used to mainly promote business. Apps that are mostly used as marketing material will have a harder time being published.

The important thing to understand before getting started is what people need. This means that you should expect to do a bit of market research so that you know exactly what type of application will have the most appeal to the public.

Once your application is designed, you can easily offer it in the Apple Store, Google Play, or another online store for sale. Remember that Android and iPhone are two different operating systems, so you may want to consider only choosing one in the beginning to help keep your costs at a minimum. General consensus when trying to make this decision is this: if you want to make money with your app, stick with iPhone. If you are trying to simply promote a business then without a doubt, Android is the way to go. Research is the hardest process. If you have the skills to create an application that can meet the needs of the public and simplify their time on their devices, you are good to go.

To do this, you will need at least some programming skills or the money to pay someone to do the programming for you. This may happen to be easy money once it's all done and could generate income for many years if done well.

Free or Not? Every app category is different when it comes to deciding how to price it. Games and other apps used for entertainment purposes are typically free.

As with any path to passive income, creating apps will take some time whether you build it yourself or hire it out. When your first app goes live, you will no doubt develop a serious addiction to your computer. Stick with it, especially in the beginning and watch that hard work pay off.

Business #36: Network marketing

Network Marketing is a unique business opportunity as it provides the means for both residual income as well as passive income. While we won't be discussing residual income in this publication, I will definitely show you how passive income can be generated through this industry. Unlike affiliate marketing that you can do on your own with little effort, network marketing will require a bit more time, particularly in the early stages.

On the surface, network marketing often gives the appearance of repeat customers that are overwhelmingly happy with the products they are purchasing and that's what keeps them around. Don't misunderstand that statement – the customers ARE that happy, but when you dig below the surface you will discover that while the products a networking marketing company offers may be second to none, they aren't the only reason people tend to stick around.

Many people decide to enter the world of network marketing not for the products, but rather the hopes of earning some extra money for starters and eventually enjoying financial freedom. In the case of network marketing though, you not only have the ability to help yourself financially, but others as well.

The entire process is actually quite simple. You choose a company whose products, mission, and program appeal to you and you become a home-based distributor. In some cases, you may need to purchase a starter kit or a few samples, but not necessarily every time. Once you are set up and working your own program, you then begin to share your success with others – with the ultimate end goal being to bring them into the company where they have the same opportunity to enjoy the same success. Long story short, when a network marketer helps others become wealthy and successful, they themselves enjoy the same benefits.

So why does it work? Network Marketing is based on three simple but important ideals:

People will always need or want extra income.

People will always be unhappy with their current employment situation.

People will always to want to get and maintain control of their time.

Getting started is the hardest part, but once you build the machine to make others successful, there is no limit to the amount of passive income you can generate.

Business #37: Start a YouTube Channel

You've probably already heard about how many people are making home videos, uploading them to YouTube and collecting lots of money in the process. With the right know-how, you can generate income for yourself as well. However, there are some things you must already have in place in order to make this type of plan work.

You cannot rely solely on your smartphone camera. You need to have quality equipment to get the best results. This means you'll need a camera dedicated to recording, a good microphone, and the right lighting situation. This might require an initial outlay of cash to get started, but once you do, you can generate quite a bit of income.

It is also advisable to have a website that people can connect to. Your own website can generate a great deal of money for YouTubers. Those who enjoy your videos can connect directly to your site for more information. This site, in turn, can link to your Facebook or Twitter page.

You can create a video on just about anything you might think of. If you feel you are good at any topic that might appeal to others, you'll find that creating a video can be a great tool. Many people would prefer to see a 10-minute video on something they want to know rather than reading an article or book on the same subject.

Your goal in creating a video should be on giving your audience something they wouldn't otherwise learn or understand from other sites. To make this avenue a success, there are several things you must keep in mind when making your videos.

1. Target a specific audience.

2. Don't make it too long, get to the point quickly.

3. Be enthusiastic—avoid the tendency to talk slow and give your audience some energy.

4. Be unique—the more successful videos offer something that no one else has.

As long as you plan your video content carefully and think about your audience, you have a good chance of a successful venture. It is astonishing to know how much money can be made from a successful YouTube video. While YouTube does not pay you directly for any video content you upload to their site, when your video gains traction, you will create a following, which can generate income in and of itself. In addition, you will attract the attention of advertisers who will be more than happy to piggyback on your success and pay you for the privilege.

The important thing to remember is that you have to be unique. No one will pay you for something that everyone else is doing. The more you can stand out from the crowd, the more money there is in your future. As long as you make your views informative and entertaining, you will eventually attract a following that can generate lots of money for your future.

Also, look for something with viral appeal. In other words, you want something that will compel people to share the information with others. This will help to spread your name around the YouTube community generating additional income for you as it goes.

It is important to understand that in order to generate a steady stream of income, you will need to put up videos on a regular basis. Whether this is weekly or monthly, the more consistent you are with delivery, the more reliable you'll be, attracting more and more people to your site on a regular basis. Whether you choose to release a video once a week or once a month, make absolutely sure that you stick to your schedule and do not waver. The more loyal you are to your viewers, the more money you will make.

Many people who have a YouTube channel already know that the videos they have on their channel can be monetized. Actually, this is usually the main purpose of starting the channel in the first place. Typically, the monetization scenario involves obtaining an audience for the video and then allowing Google to attach adverts to the video.

At first, at least 10,000 video views were necessary for any video to have eligibility for monetization. When a video achieves 10,000 views, every subsequent viewing would then earn some subsidy for the advertising exposure. Today, monetization does not need viewership minimums.

We have YouTube AdSense that requires no minimum viewership for profit sharing. The payout rule just stipulates that you have to earn at least $100 in that given month; otherwise, the balance will roll over into the subsequent month to have additional growth of funds.

In case you have not heard about it, Google AdSense is a program designed to place ads in videos on various YouTube channels. As an advertiser, you publish your ads through Google AdWords. The ads can display as videos, images, or text on the various websites and then pay per click.

If you possess a unique passion, hobby, or something in which you know more than the average Joe or Jane, you have a niche right there! That may include teaching people how to speak well in a particular language, singing, teaching things to do with beauty and fashion, and so on. If you love animals, you can teach people about pets, how to love them and take care of them. If your pets are funny (or unusual in a funny way), you can also create revenue-generating videos out of that; In other words, possibilities are endless!

To get started, just create a channel if you do not already have one.

Displaying ads is not the only way to make money on YouTube. In fact, it is the least profitable way to make any money on YouTube. What other ways can you make money then? Well, here are some of these ways:

Other ways to earn with YouTube

Promoting other people's products with AdSense is not the only way you can generate income on YouTube. We have other ways that include the following:

1. Using YouTube to drive traffic to your money-making blog, ecommerce website, your online course, etc.
2. Come up with a web TV series where you create your own shows with stories about anything you can imagine. It could be a drama series, a comedy series, or even a talk show. Just make sure you publish regularly and that every episode is interesting so that you keep your audience entertained constantly.
3. Crowdfunding: Crowdfunding is a model where your audience contributes money directly to you/your channel. Such funds can actually help you jumpstart a new project on YouTube to make even more money such as buying new equipment (cameras and important tools for instance).
4. Creating products and then promoting them on YouTube.
5. Using YouTube to drive traffic to affiliate products to earn a commission.

Business #38: Watch Videos and TV and get paid

If you spend a lot of your time watching videos online, why not try to make money from it? There are actually several companies out there that will pay you just to watch videos and TV. Most of the time you will have to register with an app or sign up with a website where you get access to videos and television programs which you can watch and be compensated for your time in watching them.

Business #39: Social Lending

Social lending, or Peer to Peer (P2P) lending is, simply put, a way for any individual to request a loan from sources other than banks. These lending sources are just regular individuals like you and me who put themselves on the line to assume a portion or all of a loan. The process is simple enough, but you do have to do your homework a bit before agreeing to assume a loan or even a part of it.

This is possibly one of the more involved, but not necessarily more difficult, methods of creating a passive income. This is also perhaps the most costly to start yet can produce a very healthy income if handled correctly. But again, as stated above, you have to do your homework before you get started. Being interested in this type of lending is one thing, but actually taking the steps to invest your own hard-earned money is quite another. Becoming involved in social lending is going to force you to use a lot of personal information in unfamiliar places in addition to your initial investment. For some, this can be a huge turnoff and send others running for the hills with their hair on fire.

If you are willing to accept the risks that are involved, then by all means keep reading. There are two major players in the Social Lending forum – Lending Club and Prosper. For one to be qualified as a peer to peer lender, you will need to register with either of these sites to be approved. Once approved, you are then able to invest in loans that are pending with either of the above-mentioned forums.

Here's where the process gets tricky and even risky – it's nearly impossible to determine which of the hundreds or thousands of loans are good ones and which ones are not. With every loan, obviously, there is the chance that the borrower will default. Granted, this is a very small chance as both Lending Club and Prosper do an extensive credit check on all of their potential borrowers, but a chance exists, nonetheless.

With social lending, the best advice that the P2P gurus can offer anyone getting started down this avenue, is to go slow. Do your homework. Learn the process as much as you can before investing even the smallest amount of your own money.

The two power players in social lending have both setup easy-to-use systems that even the most computer-illiterate can follow along, meaning once you get started working and generating an income with social lending, it can be done in as little as a few minutes each week. You can log into your account to see what type of funds you have available for lending, browse the loans that are available to you, filter out the ones that are best for your current situation. Once you find a loan that looks like a good fit all the way around, you invest a small amount into it. This is called a "note." Both lending platforms strongly encourage their lenders – especially new ones – to not invest more than $25 in each loan. This allows you to absorb a smaller risk per loan, but also frees up your funds to invest in several loans should you choose to do so.

Once you have invested, it's important to remember that the repayment on the loan doesn't happen overnight. There is nothing very quick about this operation. Each loan will have to wait until it is fully funded and then there is a 30-day period for the borrower to make his or her first payment. Once all of the planets are in line, you begin to receive monthly payments for the term of 3-5 years.

OK, so your account is set up, you've invested in your first loans and the repayments start rolling in – now what? Here is where the road forks and you have two choices to make with your new funds: reinvest or withdraw. Letting the funds sit in an account and not working for you does not help you earn interest on that money. Make a habit to check your accounts at least once a month in the beginning – more frequently as you move forward – and keep your money working for you.

On a side note, you should know that some states do not allow peer to peer lending. Before you begin and set up an account with either lending platform, you'll need to do some research and make sure these activities are permitted in your state.

Business #40: Launch a Crowdfunding website

Why:
Crowdfunding is similar to peer to peer lending. In crowdfunding, a large group of people will give small amounts of money to help fund a project or venture. It's like collecting a capital from different individuals.

Crowdfunding is a source of passive income because of the benefits it provides. For example, in rewards-based crowdfunding, you will contribute to a business financially in exchange for a reward which is normally the company's products and services.

Now, if you're into equity-based crowdfunding, you will have more leverage. By being a financial contributor to the business, you will be part-owners of the company. Since you're part-owner, you are entitled to receive a portion or share of the company's profits plus the return on your investment (capital contribution). Though it asks for a monetary investment upfront, you still don't have to do anything. Isn't that passive enough?

Where:
There are different crowdfunding sites that you can visit to look for projects or businesses you may be interested to participate in. Gofundme.com is the number 1 crowdfunding site based on the traffic data from Alexa and Compete.

Kickstarter.com, indiegogo.com and teespring.com are some examples. There are a whole lot more.

How:
You can start on crowdfunding either by proactively looking for projects or businesses that need capital or

by waiting for a friend, colleague or family member to inform you about crowdfunding opportunities.

The thing is, you need to thoroughly review the project before you decide to be one of its contributors - especially if it's equity-based crowdfunding. You would want to have that guarantee that the business can give you the passive income you're looking for.

Business #41: Buying an Online Business

Why start a business from scratch when you can just buy one that's already been established? This is the concept behind the idea of scouring the Internet for businesses that are up for sale. These are usually online businesses whose owners simply don't have the time in operating and managing them. These can be in the form of authority websites, forums, affiliate sites, membership websites, subscription-based websites, Amazon FBA businesses, and so on and so forth. To find these businesses for sale, you need to search for listings in online marketplaces like Flippa.

Business #42: Online Stores

If you have spent any time thinking about making money online, chances are you've given some thought to niche websites to do so. Creating a niche online store or website can be one of the more trying methods for generating passive income but one of the easiest in the long run.

Even starting out, building a niche site that can generate about $500 a month isn't so tough to do and as with any of the other methods I've talked about so far, there's a pretty simple and solid roadmap to get you where you need to go. Because we don't have time to dedicate to a lengthy description in this particular eBook, I'm going to touch on the finer points of building a niche presence online to help you get started.

First, you're going to have to have an idea of what type of niche you want to be involved with so the first step is to sit down and make a list of as many niches that you can. Start with your favorite hobbies, interests, things you know a little bit about, etc., and go from there.

Once you have a good list, you then begin narrowing it down by creating another list in direct reference to the niches you have chosen:

The amount of products/services related

Are there plenty of affiliate options?

Is anyone already making money off these?

Is the niche something you can comfortably write at least 100 articles about?

Now it's time to set up your online presence. Make a decision on the domain name for your website and set up the hosting. If you're familiar with WordPress, then you know this is the way to go. It's the most user-friendly builder there is and will allow you to create your site fairly quickly. Don't forget your social media presence too. Facebook is a given but depending on the type of niche you choose, you'll also want to consider Twitter, Instagram and Google+ just to name a few.

Once your web presence is set up and functioning properly – don't forget to run a few tests to make sure you have all the pistons firing – it's time to create your content. Here are some pointers to help get you on your feet is:

Pick the five most popular items in your niche and write an article about each of them

Next, do some type of how-to tutorials – at least three

Finally, write three list posts related to your niche

Got all that done? Good! Now do it again... And then sign up for the affiliate sites that are within your niche and get them listed on your new site. Let your friends, family, co-workers, acquaintances, favorite bartender and mailman know about your new site and of course don't forget your social media presence. If you aren't using social media to promote yourself and your business, you are quite literally leaving money on the table.

Yes, as with other passive income generation methods, there is some work involved with building an online niche store, but it doesn't have to all be drudgery. Have some fun with it – after all, loving your "job" and having fun with it means never having to "work" a day in your life.

Business #43: Exchange Traded Funds (ETFs)

Exchange Traded Funds (ETFs) are like traditional mutual funds with an extra facility to the holders to buy and sell them like stocks on the stock exchanges. In other words, it is a type of security and has characteristics similar to the close-ended mutual funds, which are listed on the stock exchanges. ETF's are bought and sold on the stock exchange throughout the trading day just like a stock and see price changes continuously.

ETFs track an index, a sector, or a commodity like an index fund. ETFs own assets such as stocks, bonds, commodities, etc. The stockholders, who indirectly own the fund assets, get a portion of the profits, interest or dividends. Some financial institutions buy and redeem ETF stocks and large blocks known as creation units.

ETFs started in 1989 with the Index Participation Stocks, which was an S&P 500 proxy and traded on American Stock Exchange. Standard & Poor's Depositary Receipts (SPDRs) was introduced in 1993, and the fund soon became the largest ETF in the world. Barclays Global Investors launched the iStocks in 2000, which became the largest ETF by 2005. Over the years, ETFs proliferated with various niche ETFs catering to the specific needs related to different sectors, commodities, regions, etc. By 2014, the number of ETFs crossed 1,500 with assets above $2 trillion.

ETFs provide diversification, tax efficiency, and low expense ratio. At the same time, they also provide features of ordinary stock, like limit orders, options, short selling, etc.

Advantages of Exchange Traded Funds (ETFs):

Lesser Costs: ETFs have lesser costs as compared to most of the investment products, as they spend less on marketing, sales, and administrative expenses. Reason being that most of the ETFs are not actively managed, and secondly, they don't spend much on buying and selling of stocks for accommodating the purchases and redemptions.

Buying and Selling Ease: You can buy or sell ETFs easily on a stock exchange during the trading day. You can buy ETF stocks on margin. You can use stop orders and limit orders specifying the price points.

Tax Efficiency: ETFs are tax efficient as they have a low turnover of portfolio securities, and don't need to sell securities to meet redemptions.

Diversification: ETFs have a diversified portfolio and provide you diversification across a full index, industry, sector, etc.

Transparency: ETFs have transparent portfolios. Moreover, their prices are set at frequent intervals during a trading day.

Types of Exchange Traded Funds (ETFs):

Index ETFs:
Most of the ETFs are index funds and replicate the performance of a particular index. The index can be based on stocks, commodities, bonds, etc. The index ETFs invest proportionately in accordance with the underlying securities in an index.

Stock ETFs:
Many ETFs track stocks and some index like S&P 500. Stock ETFs have different styles like large-cap, mid-cap, etc. ETFs may be a sector fund e.g. IT or banking. It can be global or country specific. Thus, you can have a lot of options, while investing in an ETF.

Bond ETFs:
Many ETFs invest in bonds like government treasury bonds, blue chip company bonds, etc. These are very good investment options during a recession, as the stocks don't perform well in such times.

Commodity ETFs:
There are ETFs that invest in commodities e.g. precious metals like gold, other metals like copper, agricultural produce, etc. Many commodity ETFs are index funds that track some non-security index. These are riskier as compared to other ETFs, as the commodity prices are affected by many factors and also due to speculative activities.

Currency ETFs:
Some ETFs invest in currencies of different countries such as USD, GBP, EUR, etc. They track a single currency or a basket of major currencies. These are very volatile due to the extreme volatility of the underlying i.e., currencies.

Summary
You can pick ETFs based on your investment objectives and individual needs. You should buy an ETF, which gives you the desired risk-reward ratio; an ETF with a good track record, low expenses, low tracking error, etc.

Exchange Traded Funds (ETFs) are a very good option for investing. You can buy and sell ETFs like stocks, and also go short. You can get the diversification of the mutual funds with the versatility of a stock. ETF investment is like buying an entire portfolio of stocks as if you are buying a single stock.

Business #44: Franchising

Franchising is a business arrangement between the owner of a brand, business concept, or an arrangement (franchisor) and you, the franchisee, who gets the rights to operate a business associate with the franchisor based on the franchise agreement.

The franchisor will let you use the trade name, business methods and in return, you accept particular restrictions on the way you conduct your business. You then pay the franchisor royalties/franchise fees.

Simply put, this kind of investing involves a licensing relationship where a company licenses to you its products and operating system. This means you get the right to advertise, distribute goods and services using the name of the business and systems for a certain time. You are bound to earn immediately because the company is already established.

Some of the various franchises include:

1. Restaurants

2. Home cleaning

3. Medical clinics

4. Car repair

5. Child learning centers

6. Floral shops

Investing in a franchise entails numerous upfront costs. When the company grants you the right to conduct operations using their products and trademarks, you give them upfront and ongoing fees.

How franchising is passive

As you know already, opening and operating a franchise requires a lot of work and input in terms of time and money. However, when you establish it and your income keeps growing, the amount of work actually reduces as you hire people to help run various areas of the business. Ultimately, you can have a great management team run the business for you—getting to this point is actually the key.

Business #45: Webinars

While creating digital content that other people are legitimately interested in purchasing can take more time and cost more money upfront than selling physical products, eventually you will reach a point where the profit is rolling in without having to do nearly as much work. When you factor in the fact that you don't have to deal with shipping or storage costs, it may even be the more profitable option. While creating the content itself doesn't necessarily need to be terribly time consuming, you will need to spend a good deal of time marketing yourself if you hope to be successful in the long run.

Finding the right topic: In order to create a successful webinar, the first thing you will want to do is to determine what hobbies, talents and skills you are intimately familiar enough with to ensure that other people would be willing to hear you talk about them. It is important to be fluent enough in a given topic that you can provide insight greater than what can currently be found on YouTube regarding the topic for free. You should understand the topic inside and out; you need to be able to clearly and concisely teach it to others as well.

If nothing immediately comes to mind, the first thing you will want to do is to make a list of all your best skills. Almost everyone has something that they are adept at enough in order to generate at least one webinar; these skills can just be hard to see because you do them well without thinking about it. These topics can be anything from general self-help and how-to topics to more specific things that many people often think of as innate skills such as time management or organizational skills. If you are so good at something that you don't think of it right away, then this is likely a good candidate for a webinar.

Express your content clearly: With a viable topic in mind, the next thing you need to do is determine the best way to express your topic in a way that makes it easy for other people to follow along. Depending on the topic you choose, this could be something as simple as recording yourself talking about the topic while doing it or it could be more complicated and including some type of PowerPoint presentation. While the exact way you go about explaining your content doesn't matter, it is important that the visual and audio quality is professional, after all you want to come off as an expert in the field, not someone who is trying to make extra money off of a YouTube video recorded on their phone.

Build a website: Once you create your content, it is important that you find a place to put it online that adds to the entire experience. This means you are going to do more than simply throw up a link to the video and a link to PayPal, you are also going to need to create free content that makes visitors interested in seeing what's behind the paywall. This means creating plenty of blogs, and even some free videos that show you are knowledgeable on the topic to the point that visitors are willing to trust you enough to pay for your expert level webinar.

If you have never created a website before, there are plenty of options when it comes to creating something that is functional, if not necessarily flashy. While completely free options are available, invest at least enough in your platform so that you can have your own domain as this will help to build your professional brand. Having an official sounding name will go a long way toward legitimizing your content, which will make it more likely that visitors will be willing to pay for it.

Market your content: Once you have a website that is full of content, both paid and free, the next thing to do is get the word out about your webinar. The first thing is to spread the word via social media and encourage all of your friends and family to do the same; you never know when something might go viral and word of mouth is enough to boost the sales of a webinar significantly if it gets in front of the right people.

With that out of the way, the next thing you will do is visit websites that the people in your chosen niche are likely to congregate around. Once you find these sites, spend time in their forums, answering questions that people pose about the topics. Every time you do so, credit your site as the place you found the information. With enough posts all carrying your website, you can be sure that word will start to spread, and you will start to see additional hits on your primary site as a result.

Finally, it is important that you include the right type of Search Engine Optimization for your site. This means including the right key phrases as well as a well-thought-out description to help you show up when people search for the topic you are discussing. The right SEO is extremely important which means that if you don't know what you are doing it is worth paying someone else to do it for you, whatever the cost, you are likely to make it back tenfold from the extra hits you will receive.

Create an email list: As part of your checkout process, it is important to offer users the ability to sign up for your email list so they can be told when new webinars are available. There is no better audience than one that has already purchased your content, which means whenever you create something new, you send out an email letting these folks know that it is available.

Business #46: Building an Email List

Email lists are another way to make money. The key to email lists is not to sell them for profit, but to use your email list to sell products, services, or information you have. Years ago, it was okay to sell email lists to interested parties. Now, it is aggravating, leads to scams, spam, and while not illegal, frowned upon. Why mess with potential income streams just to generate email lists and sell them, when you can make more from keeping your customers happy.

If you are going to generate email lists for sale, then you need to be transparent about it and let your customers know why you are selling the lists. For example, you might garner a list of suppliers and email lists to help affiliate marketers or dropshippers find companies offering the services these individuals need.

Given the trouble building and selling lists can make, the focus from here on out will be about how to build the list using opt-in options, landing pages, email autoresponder, and then how you can profit from the list.

Email lists can be very important tools for businesses to use in conjunction with other passive income methods. The idea is for you to build a list of customers, build on that list from customer's friends, social media sites, and other locations.

Here is how you can build an email list:

- Create remarkable email content that will get someone's attention. Oftentimes this is referred to as writing "sales copy". The content needs to be something you would truly share with your friends, without being considered spamming them. People like your friends and family can make purchases from your site or at least help you gain leads from other people. The idea is that the people who subscribe to your emails are going to forward them via email or something like Facebook, to friends, colleagues, family, and other people they know, so you get more income from the emails.

- You want to keep your current subscribers updated and sharing information, so you have to include things like social sharing buttons and email to a friend button.

- You always need your email list to be optional. So, while you want to share it with your own friends, make sure you send it on to these friends and family with a request, such as "can you look through this and see if it would get your attention." Let your friends know you need help in building your opt-in email list. More often than not they will help if it is a worthy cause. Don't forget those closest to you can help. But, don't rely just on them. You still need to target your main consumer with an opt-in option.

- Promote online contests, so people have to sign up for the contest and give you an email address. Make sure you are not spamming the email account. Let the person see a welcome email, with new deals, and explain the details of the contest. Ask them to opt-in again if they wish to receive more than just communication about the contest coming up.

- Have more than one email subscription option. You want to have targeted content for the audience you hope to turn into customers. This means you need to include things your customers have already bought or would be most interested in, from the pages they already viewed when they sign up for your email.

- You do not want to over-send emails, so only send campaigns out when you truly have something to share. For example, if you do a newsletter each month, send it out with a call to action. In the middle of the month, send out coupons or a contest offer.

- Every once in a while, send out an email with an opt-in response. Sometimes people forget you exist until you have great offers for them. By sending an email with a request to help you update your email, as well as a coupon to use you will get them to make a purchase.

- A great way to build a huge email list is through putting a little sidebar on your blog website where people can click "subscribe" and they will be prompted to enter their email address to gain exclusive content from you or some type of giveaway.

For email lists, you have a couple of options for how to send the emails. You want to generate an email in an autoresponder that lets the person know you received their opt-in request, gives them a deal, and gets them back to your site. You also want to use email opt-in on various landing pages to help clients sign up. Do not make this a pop-up. Instead, make it obvious at the bottom or top of the page. Something like, "sign up to get a 20% coupon off your first purchase." Aweber is a great autoresponder that you can use to get emails out to your target audience.

The reason you should use an email program is to not only auto-respond to your customers, but also to generate emails on a specific day that will be sent out at a time of your choosing.

When you have an email sent out on a Sunday, but you made the email on the previous Monday, you don't have to work on Sunday just to earn money. The point is you want a passive income stream that takes little time, so the more you set up to send out at a different time, the better. You could even draft 10 emails all in one day and have them sent out throughout the next two months.

Business #47: Sell Lesson Plans

If teaching is not your cup of tea but you have a lot of knowledge, you might want to sell your lesson plans. This is an ideal setup because you only have to create a plan once and then you can sell the same plans over and over again. If your plans are good, you won't have any trouble getting busy teachers to pay money for them. It saves them both time and effort, and it can be a great benefit to the students as well.

Business #48: Web Design/Graphic Art

If you are a Graphic Artist/Designer, your options for creating a passive income with your skills are plentiful. Creating templates that other designers can use for their own, for example, is just one way. Before you shake your head and think "No way, I'm not giving away the store" think of it this way: designing and selling products for other designers not only earns you a tidy income, it also helps establish who you are in the graphic design community by increasing your credibility.

A beautiful thought to using your web designing or graphic artist abilities is that you can combine your talent with nearly every one of the previous incomes generating methods I've already described in this eBook.

One way is through affiliate marketing. You'll remember this is one of the easier methods used to produce passive income. As a designer or artist, affiliate marketing is wide open for you. On Amazon alone, you can review and sell any number of products from books to laptops, all relating to your expertise. With Amazon offering a commission rate of 4-10% based on your volume (there is an earning cap on things like laptops remember), you are looking at a healthy chunk of change each month.

Like the idea of helping others learn the tools of your trade. Why not try creating an online course on any of the Adobe programs you may be using. Online courses are convenient and how-to courses for say Adobe Photoshop or even Adobe Illustrator are in high demand. You can create these courses easily enough through sites like Udemy or Skillshare and again, with a high payout rate of 30-50% on these types of courses, the passive income is going to build.

Would you rather offer more of a showcase of your own work? No problem – create fonts and sell them. Again – not a difficult way to make a decent passive income. Once your work is ready to be shared with the world, you can do so through sites like Myfonts.com for example.

Are you getting into the idea of promoting your own work? Great! You can put the starving artist in you to work designing and selling promotional products like t-shirts, can koozies, posters – basically anything that can have a company logo or design – you can create. And here's the kicker: once you make one customer happy with their promotional products, the word will spread like wildfire and soon you will not only get repeat business from your existing customers but also new business from the referrals they send your way.

The point of considering website design and graphic art in the passive income point of view is to sustain your income while waiting for other client work to come through. This can take some time if you are just starting out and haven't paid your dues, so why not grab the bull by the horns and help yourself financially?

Business #49: Review Music

This is a great idea for anyone who really loves music. By joining sites like Slicethepie.com, you can review new and unsigned musical artists online and get paid for your opinion.

The money you make will be slow in the beginning, but once you've built up a good reputation, you will have more people looking to you for your views on new music. Once you sign up, it is easy to get started. It is not difficult; all you do is listen to music and give your opinion, a great job for a true music lover in their own right.

Even though they are totally international, all money will be paid in US dollars. Anyone can sign up and create a review regardless of age, gender, or any other factor.

Business #50: Testing Apps

There are many companies that will pay you for installing their apps on your mobile devices. You get paid for every month you use them. Check out sites like Nielsen Mobile Panel, and the MobileXpression. It only takes a few minutes to download the applications, answer a few questions and you're all set to start making money. Each of these sites will earn you about $50/year, and some will also reward you with prizes each week.

Conclusion

Passive income is a real thing. It is not a myth and not something you should consider as a pyramid scheme. You have learned a great deal about many of the best passive income streams you can choose to do, as well as how you can combine the different options to increase your overall income.

Now, you need to choose what you think is going to be the best option for your situation. What do you have the time for? What skills do you have that will fit the passive income schemes available?

Once you know what you are dedicated and determined to do, you can start to slowly earn $1,000 per month in extra income. Yes, it will take time. Some people strike the right marketing trick right away and keep up the momentum for years. Others have a slow, but steady start eventually making $10,000 per month after a year of building their online clientele.

You don't have to be one or the other. You simply need to take the information provided and see what you can do. Your life is different from every person who is trying to make passive income. You have different, unique experiences that might provide you with a new revenue avenue.

It is my experience as a writer, blogger, entrepreneur, and someone who has had hands on experience with making money online, it has given me an edge in certain topics over others. Find what you know and are an expert in to make your money. You can do this.

Just remember it takes time, effort, and in time you will make money with little effort because all you will need is to write a new blog, send out a new email campaign or generate new leads via social media.

If you enjoyed this book and feel inclined to leave a review, please do so! Honest Feedback is always welcomed!

BLOGGING FOR PROFIT:

10,000/month ultimate guide – Make a Passive Income Fortune using Effective SEO Techniques & Affiliate Marketing Secrets leveraging your contents on YouTube & Social Media

By

Ronald Roberts

Introduction: Why Blogging?

Blogging has gained traction for people seeking passive income in the past decade. This is because the internet is readily available in almost all parts of the world. The speeds are also very good to sustain heavy usage by many customers. Many internet providers are doing a good job in innovating which encourages a lot of users. A blog is a website in which the author passes information in written form. The messages are passed using blog posts where the author can pick almost anything to talk about. With more and more people getting most of their information from the internet, there is someone looking for whatever you want to talk about.

With so much information online, your content is bound to get buried in the noise. The only thing that will separate you from the rest is if you infuse some of your personality and opinions. Everything that we shall discuss in this book has been done and will continue being done, therefore, you have to make sure your personal perspective comes out in the way you write or conduct this business called blogging.

The main aim of blogging is to create an intimate communication between yourself and your reader. There is a comment section in every blog where the reader can leave their questions, thoughts, and feedback on the topic in the blog post. The readers that will follow your blog are people interested in what you have to say, and you must do your best to be authentic and trustworthy so that they can support your business. You have to ensure that you create a loyal fanbase who will support any business venture you may want to start.

Many people have argued that it may be too late to start blogging in 2019 because there are way too many people blogging nowadays, but I beg to differ. There will always be a gap in what you can offer in any field even if it is saturated. There is always something you can contribute, either new or additional. Another myth is that you need to be a master or expert in the topic you want to write about. You don't need any prior knowledge or to be a master of writing at all. You just need to be able to conduct research on your niche or topic and be able to give true, accurate, and useful information. Once you do that, boom you are an expert in the area that people will respect and seek out.

All the tools you need are available online and there are many courses, books, video, and many other resources that are out there for beginners. They explain step-by-step ways on how you can move from amateur to expert in almost any field or niche. Does it sound too easy? Don't be skeptical, just realistic. Blogging requires patience and dedication. There is no overnight success in making money blogging, especially if you don't do it consistently.

The main thing you will need to have in this business is a passion for both learning and the topic you choose to focus on. These two things will keep you motivated even if you don't make money the first couple of months or more. The reason passion is very important is because readers will see through your act very fast and you shall miss out on some loyal readers. Basically, as a PASSIONATE blogger, you are set to reach out to other passionate fans or curious novices of your niche. Strive to hit the loyal fan ratio of 500 hundred people that will give you just 20 dollars per month, and trust me, there are many ways of doing that! Read on to discover them.

Chapter 1: Blogging for Profit

Sam's Story

Sam loved food, in fact so much so, that she was over 300lbs by the time she was 35. She knew something had to change, so she started on the Keto Diet. She was hooked as the weight melted off her and all her blood and medical tests came back normal (unlike the prediabetic state prior to her weight loss). She had to tell people, so she started a blog. It started as a daily record of her weight loss journey, noting what she ate and how she felt. Within 3 months, she had 2k followers that were logging in several times a week. Some wanted to do more, so she partnered with AdSense to monetize her site in hopes she could work out of her day job and help people full time.

It went fairly well, but she was only generating about 300 dollars per month with her 2k followers. So, she started adding special posts for those that wished to support her on the social media site Patreon. The posts were emailed to them for as little as 1 dollar per month. She also started a Facebook group for her followers to meet and talk about their own struggles and a YouTube Channel to turn her Blogs into VLOGS. Within 3 months, she had an additional 3k followers between all the sites. She finally wrote a Keto Cookbook (using the recipes she posted on her blog and others she created), as well as a Keto 101 e-book. She offered them for paid download on all her sites and on Kindle. Within 6 months her income had jumped to 10k a month and she was able to devote full-time efforts to her following. Soon she will hire a freelancer to help her manage her sites and will start appearing at Keto and Weight Loss conferences/organizations for paid speaking gigs and sales of the hard copy versions of her books and t-shirts she created.

Want to be like Sam, read on.

Why Start in 2019?

Don't listen to the naysayers that whine about if you are not already established as a niche expert, then don't even bother, because your field is all saturated. Shake that off and remember that trends change and evolve and so do the needs of the knowledge seeking public. Therefore, I guarantee that you can bring a fresh perspective to any niche and package it in a way that is more appealing than what is already out there. So, keeping that in mind lets go over why blogging is a worthwhile pursuit in 2019.

1. **You get to make money from any part of the world.**

There are literally no limitations as to where or when you can blog. As long as you have internet and a portable computer, or even a smartphone or tablet, you are set to start. As long as you have created a great blog that has a loyal following, you can even make money as you sleep. Some bloggers become digital nomads because they have understood that blogging gives them the freedom to travel and still make money. Some of them even live on full time blogging because they earn enough money to sustain their lifestyles. There are literally no limits to the money you can earn, if you act smartly.

2. **Tell your story online**

Blogging isn't just about making money for everyone. Some people find it therapeutic to put their life experiences, real or fictional stories, and other personal information on the internet. Some stories are meant to inspire, educate, and stimulate the mind and need to be shared where everyone can see. There is also a need for escapism for many people, so they turn to the blogs and vlogs (which we will talk about later) of people living different types of lives to experience the adventure they don't see in their own lives. There is a wide audience that is meant to enjoy these stories and appreciate the candor.

3. **Put yourself, your brand or business out there**

The importance of setting up a website and social media in today's business world cannot be understated.

This is because people want to see what you are all about before they commit to buying from you. Google, Bing, and Yahoo searches are some of the ways in which people discover new people, products, and the services that they may have been searching for. In addition, searches on Facebook (with 1.8 billion users), Instagram/Twitter (with millions of trending hashtags), and YouTube (the 2nd largest search engine in the world) are another necessity for modern branding. All of these methods can be used to sell your main product and blog. A blog just makes it easier to sell yourself to potential readers and clients, because it allows your followers to get to know you more than just having a website. They see you as a real person, not just a business owner.

4. Build an online community

You may never meet some of the people who share the same interests as you from other parts of the world, but this is easy with blogs. People are able to share and discuss on the topics they are interested in and support each other thanks to a community created by a certain blog. Blogging allows you to learn from other people as well as share the knowledge you already have. If you share your contact information, you may make some lifelong friends thanks to blogging.

How to Turn a Blog into Profit?
Choosing the Right Niche

It is important to remember that even if you are passionate about a certain topic, it may not be as profitable as other topics. This is unfortunate but true. You can blog about anything you want as long as you are just doing it for fun. However, if you want to make money, you have to choose the right niche that people are interested in. The same applies for what you are an expert in. Blogging for profit is dependent on the audience rather than what you are good at. You will be very fortunate if the area you are an expert in and are passionate about is what people are looking for online. Working hard at a niche that isn't profitable won't make any difference at all.

Some of the most profitable niches include:

1. **Health and fitness** – People have recently joined the health and fitness bandwagon and are looking for natural ways to stay healthy and fit. You can choose topics like healthy meals with basic foods or something more extreme like Keto/Carnivore/Low Carb Lifestyle, Intermittent Fasting, or Plant Based. Also, some other topics might be simple exercises one can do at home to complicated gym routines, and natural supplements or vitamins for better health etc.

2. **Personal finance** – topics like how to make passive income, side hustles that make you money, how to budget your income, how to make money from home or paying off debt.

3. **Parenting** -young parents are clamoring for help in raising children, so any experienced parent or caretaker has a wealth of information to offer.

4. **Holistic or Natural Medicine**-there is a market for those who wish to take a more natural approach to healing. Topics like reflexology, Chiropractic, Eastern Healing for the physical body or spiritual concepts like the Law of Attraction offer a wealth of possible readers.

5. **Home Schooling**-the home-schooling trend is fast accelerating and advice or curriculums for better methods are always a hot commodity.

To pick the right niche which you can focus all your efforts in, you have to consider several factors:

o   People have to show an interest in the niche, whether rational or irrational e.g. Bullet journaling.

- You have a solution to people's problem.

- People should be willing to spend their money on products or services related to the niche.

Creating Content for your Blog

If you are interested in blogging for profit, I am sure you have already come across the phrase, "Content is King". The reason why this statement is quoted in every blogging for profit book, blog, or course is because, content is the only thing that will separate you from your competition. Whatever niche you pick, there is probably someone who already beat you to it. That's not to discourage you because readers are always looking for engaging, mind stimulating, and useful information out there. The only tool you have to do this is the content on your blog. There are three things that you might want to keep in mind before creating any content for your blog:

- What you are brainstorming and thinking about may not necessarily be what people are looking for.

- Use frameworks that are already working when creating content.

- There is nothing new that your post has to offer the reader, instead you have to put a new and interesting slant on it.

I don't mean to discourage you but to help you get rid of the "know-it-all" mentality so that you can succeed. You are starting from scratch when you choose to start blogging and it should reflect as such in the way you come up with content for your blog. You have to give more importance to the needs of readers rather than your own. I repeat, this doesn't apply if you are blogging for fun or personal use, but to for profit blogging only. Write down your personal thoughts and ideas and after you have researched, you can find areas that need those ideas.

Remember these three important levels when you are trying to create content for your blog:

- Find the most popular topics in your chosen niche and stick to them.

· Research and learn the frameworks that other successful bloggers have already established and use them when creating content. This saves you from making silly mistakes that could lead to the slow growth of your blog.

- The content you deliver should provide useful information that readers are interested in. It doesn't have to be unique (but that helps), just valuable.

Now how do you go about the technical or physical production of your blog, there are several options online for blogging sites or extensions for already established websites. In chapter two I will suggest the easiest and most straightforward site for producing blogs.

Chapter 2: Setting up a Blog-The Basics

WordPress-why it is the best?

WordPress is the best option for any blogger when they want their presence felt online, as it is the most used and has the widest reach via search engines and word of mouth. This is a CMS or Content Management System that will run your website smoothly and efficiently. It comes with different features, templates, and tools that ease the process of customization. With so many potential choices in WordPress, you will thrive online and be able to adjust to new trends very easily. The CMS is free (if you do a direct download of the software and use it to set up your own site or integrate it into an existing site, the online version and use of the WordPress site to host your blog is $2.75 a month), yet strong and flexible to accommodate your eCommerce needs. Read on to see why WordPress is your number one option as a blogger:

WordPress is Easy to Use

WordPress is easy to use, even for beginners. The first time you have to use any software, you might feel intimidated. But this CMS makes creating your first website easy despite not having any experience with such platforms, as it is a click and do type of set up.

There is no coding involved, and even the admin dashboard comes in straightforward language. Navigation is smooth whether you are looking for the best themes, installing plugins, customizing settings, or writing content.

For the seasoned internet gurus, the simplicity of WordPress should not turn you off, as it will enable you to do more, quicker than doing your own coding. This is a powerful CMS that will enable you to customize your website the way you want.

Ready to Use Themes and Plugins

The outlook of a blog is determined by the theme you choose to use. The theme is not customizable in every aspect, but it does help you get a unique look. The elements you add help your blog stand out among others with the same theme. However, it shouldn't be overdone because excessive customization can affect how the theme is presented by different web browsers and screen resolutions.

Excellent for a Static Site

WordPress is updated periodically and therefore makes the best platform for a static website. This CMS will help your blog rank high with the search engines. If you have been marketing your blog using a static HTML website, moving to WordPress will bring many changes.

This is due to the platform's plugins that make your website easy to rank high. Besides, this CMS' dashboard does not require a tech guru to make any necessary changes. Furthermore, it allows easy integration of your site with different social media platforms. Nothing increases your chances of appearing on the first page of a search page more than a social media connection.

Easy to Use with Your Mobile Phone

Mobile users outnumber other types of devices by a huge margin. Those who go online via a smartphone every day are more than those who use desktops, tablets, or laptops. So, if your website is not mobile friendly, you will be losing big business opportunities. WordPress takes the guesswork out of this process by offering a wide array of themes and templates that are mobile compatible. It makes adopting a blog that offers a mobile friendly web design very easy and a built-in function of the software. This simply means your design will adjust automatically to display content clearly regardless of the mobile device's size, via WordPress.

Compatibility with All Popular Web Browsers

WordPress is compatible with all the major web browsers, with no known issues or errors. People use different web browsers, depending on their devices and location, so your blog should be strategically placed where everyone can access it. Choose a theme that will appear as intended and avoid any that might look too small, too big, or will rearrange all of the elements when viewed with some browsers.

WordPress has a compatibility that you can use to see how your blog looks in its mobile and web version when viewed using various web browsers. The top web browsers include Mozilla Firefox, Internet Explorer, Opera, Safari and Chrome.

Unique, But Intuitive Look
The intuitiveness of WordPress is related to its customizability. It allows you to choose to customize themes to get a unique look by using a plethora of colors, design, and layout. As a blogger, you know the brand you want and communicate it to your readers via the look of your site.

The easy to navigate WordPress site will ensure your visitors will not struggle to find the icons to click. The links and all navigation buttons are laid out clearly without any distracting ads. Just because WordPress allows you to create something distinctive, your site does not become complicated or complex for users, as the built-in functions keep the site smooth and fully visible.

Buying the Domain
Finding a domain name is a primary step when creating a website. Where you buy and register the domain name will not affect your WordPress in any way. You just choose the site with which you would like to register your site (a list is below), based on the important things like if their price is within your budget, if you like their interface or if they have extra services that want to access quickly. You can buy your domain from any of the following companies, without worrying about the compatibility of your blog.

HostGator
HostGator is one of the popular domain registrars. They also offer hosting after you have purchased your area. The hosting packages vary from as low as $3 per month. They have high-quality services, which include 99.99% uptime. By buying your domain from them and seeking their hosting services, your blog will start its journey online on a good note.

NameCheap
Namecheap is easy to use and incredibly intuitive. They are excellent in domain management services, which is usually very helpful. The domains are reasonably priced, plus you get a free DNS service combine with WHOIS protection. If you want tight security, this domain registrar offers SSL encryption.

Hover
Hover is an accredited online registrar, launched in 2009. It is an offshoot one of the biggest ICANN accredited registrars online known as Tucows Inc. Hover is straightforward making domain registration easy via a seamless process. They also have superb support, and their pricing depends on the top level of the domain you choose to use.

GoDaddy
GoDaddy is a famous domain registrar that also offers web hosting services. They are a big company and the largest name registrar worldwide. Apart from selling domains, they also have other services to support websites online depending on what you need. Their annual cost for a domain is $14.99, but sometimes they have incredible offers where you can buy a domain for as low as $0.90

Gandi
Gandi is a great place to buy your domain. It has been in the business for two decades and they have no

hidden fees. Their packages are straightforward, and you will not be asked to make extra payments. To register a domain with them will cost you $15.50 and transfer charges are $8.00.

Dreamhost
Dreamhost was established in 1997 and today, it offers both domain registration and web hosting services. They have features such as free privacy services for your domain and ability to control the settings of your domain.

Name.com
Name.com has been in domain registration business for years. Besides selling domains, they also offer web hosting, email services, and a website builder. Using their unique feature to search domains, you can see all the domain extensions available for your domain. They have different services on a single platform, and their prices are reasonable. Both .net and .com extensions will cost you $12.99 and a .org is $10.99

1and1
1and1 manages millions of domains. It has been in the field for a long time and works perfectly for online users looking for pocket-friendly services. For all first-time users looking for domains to buy, 1and1 offers each at $0.9. However, renewal goes to $14.99. They do not have additional registration and ICANN fees, and so the price is constant.

Network Solutions
Network Solutions offers domains and web hosting services according to your needs. A domain name will not cost you more than $9.99. They have customer support, which is available any time of the day and will help you navigate their platform if you need some assistance.

Hostinger
Hostinger is a well-established domain registrar and web hosting company. Their pricing attracts many online users with .coms available at $11 annually. The less known domain extension cost $0.99. Anyone looking for affordable domain registration, Hostinger has a solution.

Flippa
Flippa is a marketplace dealing with websites and domains. They usually have many domains on sale and great discounts where you can buy a domain name for less than a dollar. If you are getting started online as a blogger, Flippa is excellent. It has a solid backlink profile that will increase your ability to rank high with search engines.

Domain.com
Domain.com targets small businesses with various affordable web hosting options. They also have useful tools for blogs and small businesses. Their loyal customers get huge discounts. There are coupons to allow other users to enjoy discounts when buying domains from Domain.com.

Bluehost
Bluehost is a big name in the web hosting industry. You can register your domain name with them and also use the hosting services. With all services on a single platform, Bluehost helps you get started with your blog immediately. Their stellar support service ensures your questions and requests are attended to immediately regardless of the time.

Wix.com
Wix is a simple straightforward site, where you can buy your domain and host it there if you choose. The rates are very reasonable, and they have a plethora of options like click and build sites or full integration

with a prebuilt site using WordPress.

Web.com
Web.com is very similar to Wix and offers domains a low prices and full web hosting and integration if needed.

Installing WordPress
WordPress is easy to install, and the whole process does not take more than five minutes to accomplish. There are some web hosts with tools that enable automatic installation of WordPress so the process there would be a bit different, but the five basic things that you must do regardless of the methods you will use to install your WordPress are:

Getting Web Server Access
Before installing WordPress, get web hosting services from a reliable company. This is what enables your blog to go online and reach your readers. So, select any company from the list above that sell domains and also offer web hosting services.

Get a Reliable Text Editor
Text editors are many, and a good example is the Notepad (which is free and preinstalled on most PCs). They allow you to access and edit text files without the need to format. It will ease the procedure of editing once you're in the WordPress files. Using word processors with their formatting such as Microsoft Word will cause damage to the codes and files. But in case you wish to use something other than Notepad, here is a list of both free and purchased text editors, just Google them for information:

1. Notepad++
2. Coda
3. TextWrangler
4. Sublime Text
5. Textmate
6. Atom
7. BBEdit
8. UltraEdit
9. Vim
10. Brackets
11. Coffee Cup HTML Editor
12. Espresso

Get an FTP Client
This is the method to use when downloading, uploading and managing WordPress files on the server. Basically, it is a method to upload, download, and manage files on a (usually private) server, but it is not needed if you choose to use a hosting provider since they will take of it.

Select the Web Browser to Use
This is simple and any web browser is good enough to download and install your WordPress.

Download WordPress-The Latest Version. Visit the WordPress site to make sure you only download their latest version.

Options to Use for WordPress Installation
1. Automatic Installation

Bloggers are lucky because some web hosting providers provide automatic installation of WordPress. Bluehost and Dreamhost are some of these hosts and are the best options if you are just starting out. You do not need to be an experienced web developer; if you get stuck, you can contact their support service.

2. Installing WordPress on a Computer

Installing WordPress on your computer is possible. It is not common with bloggers because most of them want to reach many people. Installing WordPress in your computer means that it will be available to you and other people cannot access it.

3. cPanel Installation

The cPanel installation is one of the best options for bloggers. You must have some basic web technical skills to install a tailor-made WordPress site. The hosting company gives access to cPanel. After signing up, you can use the credentials to access the cPanel dashboard and locate the section called "auto-installers."

Once you click on the auto-install button, go to the WordPress icon and click. You are redirected to another page where you will see "Install Now," click on it. Follow instructions; the first one is to enter your domain name. This page looks similar regardless of the auto-installer or cPanel you choose to use.

"http" is the default under "Protocol" and the best to stick with. However, if you have SS certificate installed, you should use "https." Besides, you will be given an option to enter "directory." Most people opt to leave it blank so that WordPress installs in their primary domain. When left blank, the URL appears like this: www.mysite.com. If you choose to enter, it will read this: www.mysite.cm/blog. It means WordPress will be installed in a small part of your website.

You also have the option to include your business name where it reads the business name and give a small description of what you do under where it reads the purpose of your website. You will find these options under the icon labeled "Site Settings". However, you can always change these details later if you want to.

Finally, go to the admin page and fill the necessary information. You need an email, admin username, and a password. Provide answers for all questions asked and click install.

To reach the backend of your site, you use www.mysite.com/wp-admin. This is the point where you edit admin details when needed.

Installing Manually with FTP
With so many web hosting companies offering WordPress Automatic installation and the auto-installers available in the cPanel, there is no need to install this software manually with FTP. However, it is possible to install your WordPress if that is what you want.

Step 1

Before you get started, you must have an FTP program like the FileZilla or SmartFTP. Start by completing the first five tasks before installation begins.

Step 2

Unzip the file from WordPress and upload to the public directory. It will appear like this: public_html.

Step 3

Move t to CPanel to the "MySQL Databases. It is easy to spot it; all cPanels have the same look. Create a database and next is the "user" creation for the MYSQL account. Enter the username and a password and click on "Create User.

Step 4

After creating the user, include their details and indicate the database where you want to add them. Move on to the next page and check the privileges you want to give them.

Step 5

At this point, the FTP transfer is complete. Go to your domain and complete the installation process. If you're prompted to select the language to use when you check your domain, installation is successful.

Step 6

You are almost done; this step requires to enter your Database Name, Your Username, Password, Database Host, and the Table Prefix. Click on "Run the Install. Then you have to provide your WordPress admin with information such as the username, site title, email, and password. All these are the ones that you created when installing your WordPress.

Finally, you are done, so simply click "Install WordPress." At this point, you can log in into your site using your username and password, and your site is ready for use

How to Link your Domain with WordPress
Once your blog is on WordPress.com, you can get your domain to help you brand the site. The free website's address is the blog's name.WordPress.com, which will not have a significant impact on your brand exposure.

However, to add your domain in WordPress is not free; you have to pay $14.97 yearly for a new domain and $9.97 annually to map a domain that you already own.

Here is How to Link the Domain
Login in your site and on the dashboard, click Upgrades and choose Domains.

Enter the subdomain or domain in the text box and click on the button labeled add domain to blog.

WordPress has to confirm the availability of the domain before registration. If it is, you get a registration form to fill after that hit the Register Domain button.

For a domain that is already in use, you get the following results:

If the domain is yours, you have the option to map it. So, go to the domain registrar account where you can change your server name like this:

NS1.WordPress.COM

NS2WordPress.COM

The DNS settings of the domain may look different. This is determined by the registrar you chose to use. But, you get something like this:

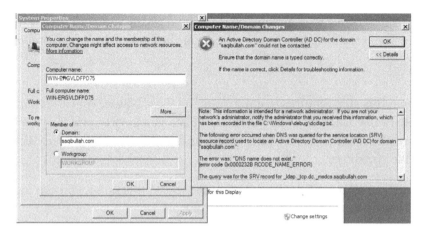

For a subdomain like blog.mysite.com, you need CNAME record. But, for this domain linking, you have to contact your registrar's customer support. Make sure you replace the subdomain, blog name and domain in the CNAME record.

Click *Try Again*, once you have the correct settings. However, you have to wait for some time for the DNS settings to update. When it's done, your screen should show you this:

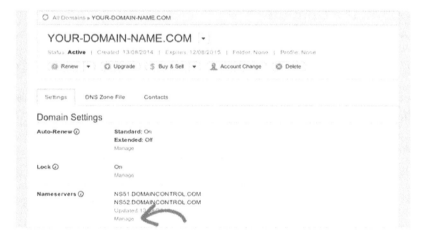

Hit the *Map Domain* button and the domain will be added to your WordPress blog.

At this point, you should pay for registration or mapping. Choose method of payment and follow the steps.

After payment, try your new domain and it will definitely open your blog.

Installing the Right Theme
Installing the right theme should be a hard task. You may want to check out a few before you settle for the best. Every time you activate a new theme, it changes the outlook of your site immediately.

There are four ways to install a theme in your WordPress site:

- Using access via admin area of WordPress

- Download the theme to your computer

- Accessing FTP

- Use of phpMyadmin

The easiest way of installing a free WordPress theme is through the dashboard. They have a directory full of free themes and you simply select what suits your niche. The "Feature Filter" helps you find what you require. It looks like this:

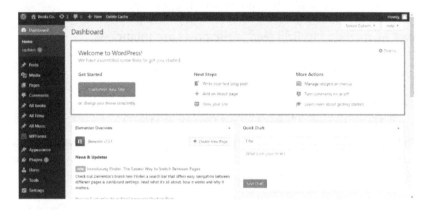

Once you find what is most suitable for your blog, click install, and you are good to go. It takes about five minutes for the new theme to be installed. You follow the same steps to install a paid theme from ThemeForest.

Another option to install the right theme is via dashboard. It can be either free or paid theme. Start by downloading the theme from the directory. Like this:

The downloading is easy. Then move to Appearance>Themes and click on the Add New icon like this:

Click on the *Upload Theme* icon and move to the **Choose File** icon and then browse through the themes and click *Install*.

If the uploading is complete, you will option to activate, live preview and return to theme page. You should click activate and theme installation is complete.

Page VS Post
Beginners in WordPress confuse pages and posts. This free platform has two content types by default pages and posts. What is the difference between pages and posts?

- o Pages are not timed, and posts are timed

- o Pages are not social while posts are.

- o Pages are usually hierarchical while posts are categorized

- o Pages cannot be included in RSS feed while posts are included.

- o Pages have their custom feature while posts do not

Tags, Ranking, and SEO
What are Tags and How to use Them in the Correct Way?
Tags help you group your posts with similar details. When a visitor clicks on the tag, WordPress opens the tag page and indexes all posts with the same specific tag. Tags help to keep your content organized and have a huge impact on SEO. Tags are basically how to make your contents visible.

The Importance of Search Engine Optimization on Page (SEO on Page)
How does Google work?

Google is an authority over all other search engines available. Over time, users get more value from Google search engine as it has invested in the best automated programs to ensure users get the information they need almost instantly. Delivering relevant results at any given time has been a plus.

That said, a smart blogger would want to know how Google works in order to position oneself. The primary goal here is the consumer. Google is available so that consumers get answers to all their queries and concerns. Google is out there to fetch the best results and deliver to a client. As a blogger, you are very secondary to Google. Google will prioritize you if you will in turn give the most value to Google consumers. Therefore, it is important to know that your content must be of top-notch quality and sufficiently meets consumers' needs on the web. If you are the most satisfying provider, it goes without saying; Google will rank you so highly that you will be on the first and top page of Google's search engine results page (SERP).

Google works with mathematical algorithms to filter through their database and deliver the most relevant of results to end users. They have not publicly stated what the algorithms are, and it is squarely in order so they remain anonymous since for one, they are in business and letting out why their search results are almost perfect would only be sharing company tactics and strategies with competitors. Secondly, publicizing the algorithms will not guarantee safety to users as rogue bloggers will have a chance to cheat the system. Over time, only smart and hardworking bloggers have learned how it works up the ladder. Those working right have seen their efforts bear fruit.

How Google Ranks Sites in 2019: Top Ranking Factors
The above is an all-time favorite question to any blogger who means business. It is important for one to have the understanding of Google's pagerank in mind in order to get the best out of the effort put to release quality content. Search Engine Optimization SEO is the lifeline.

Besides the fact that the top-ranking factors are anonymous to bloggers from Google, the following proven tactics have identified some factors to be true and proven to work. You cannot just fail consider them. It will be the difference between your success and failure.

Having in mind that 97% of Google users only look at the first page of the results and never bother to click on the next page, this is how to win a spot on the first page and possibly the top three organic results:

Content Quality
"Content is king" is not a cliché in blogging, rather, it is the motto. After all is said and done, the foundation of writing and having a viable presence online is quality content. Every other factor builds on this. You are already a success if you have mastered the art of juicy content. It all starts here and that is what will primarily drive people to your blog. We can't emphasize the importance of quality content enough; it is great that content quality leads to the other winning factor of quality backlinks.

Quality Backlinks
You must be an authority in your niche for another website to consider having you on their page. It means you have to have been of great value to them and they cannot do without a link to your resource. The many links to your page by other pages is a credible voting system for Google top ranking factors. The more backlinks you have, the more credible Google finds you.

While we are at it, do not forget the word quality. Having every Tom, Dick, and Harry backlinking you is not a smart move. Therefore, seek authority websites to link back to you, as the former might be more detrimental to your blog. Be wise and carefully check out those who want to collaborate with you.

Though we will discuss more about social media and blogging later on in future chapters, it is important to highlight at this point that your content going viral on social media and the inbound traffic to your page, is something that catches Google's eye. They are in the end always ranking your site on the quality backlinks when people choose to share your content.

Secured Sites (A shift from HTTP to HTTPS)
Google is out to protect her users from hackers and other people with ill-motives. They want to ensure that when a client is browsing through your website that all their information is kept safe from intruders. Having security in your blog will mean you mean well for your clients and it makes it a common goal for you and Google. Secure your sites if they indeed matter to you. Google will surely reward this effort.

Page speed
We live in fast times. Consumers want their results either now or now. Your page should take up utmost 2 seconds to load up. Anything other than that will see people moving fast to sites which seem to consider the value of time in this day and age. There is so much to do with so little time, so whether someone is online for work or for social reasons, you will be surprised how both do not have a second to waste.

Work on your page speed. Google in an effort to satisfy their clients, will give priority to sites with great page speed.

Webpage Content Length
After a long time of working to optimize web pages, we have learned that lengthy content wins the top ranks. We would want to assume the more you offer, the higher the chances of a client getting all they need on one stop. This is not in any way a call to have you stretching your content from East to Waste losing your focus and gist. In most scenarios, brief is sufficient. Jump in with both feet and through all lengths, short and long, in your site, watch and learn what works for you and your niche.

Mobile friendly Websites
Many websites only considered desktop user experience from the word go and as was pointed out in our

WordPress section, that is a big mistake. Mobile Devices are the easiest and most accessible tool at any given time. If you even realize half your audience is on the desktop while the other half is on their phone, it is only smart to be on both service points. The fact that almost everyone has a smartphone, means that once in a while they will be doing their searches on phone. Anytime a client visits a site on mobile and it is not friendly, almost all leave for a better experience. Why would Google risk it to prioritize you?

Domain age

Whether or not the age of a domain is anything to judge its credibility on is debatable. However, the age of a site can be judged by Google or any search engine on its viability. There are too many new bloggers who do not last, so being patient and focusing on why you started in the first place is critical. Being around for a while and offering consistent and quality content from the beginning will set you up as a better authority figure.

Google Updates and How to survive them

Google updates are responsible for the most severe fears that bloggers tend to have. Why? Because you might be ranking high or appear on the first page consistently for several years and then your ranking falls due to some changes in algorithm. If and when there are Google updates, this is how to survive them.

The above points we covered on Top ranking factors still hold true, so continue to use best practices in utilizing them. In other words, be proactive and continue to update them periodically (remember trends change, so stay on the top of the wave). For example, keywords are big to garner top rankings but how and when to use them is paramount to know. Today voice search is a big deal and it is obvious that Google is big on it too. Factoring the voice search engine on your site is non-negotiable now and in the near future. It could be a top reason as to why your rank is falling after an update.

Do not be hasty. You cannot diagnose the changes with Google updates at face value. It will call for time and a great deal of auditing and reflection on your site. It is also beneficial to contract experts to do the audit for you. Once updates are out, many sources run to explain the why and the how, but few are legit. It will take seasoned digital marketers and the Google team itself to get to the truth. Be careful not to follow masses blindly and instead let all your effort count and be timely while at it.

The competition for an audience and great conversions online is great. Google updates are bound to happen to cut out the fake and manipulative participants, as well to move people from comfort zones. Remember, your top slot is sought after by many and you are only king or queen of the mountain, as long as you can hold it. Every day, you have to earn your rank.

Perfecting on good SEO skills and being in the good graces of Google (and by extension the other search engines) is a daily struggle for all content creators. Brace up for perfection and being the best always! Here are my suggestions for the most powerful SEO Strategies that you can implement from the start.

Authority

The qualitative measure that sees to it you are visible and ranking at the top is authority. You are an authority with quality content and quality links to your site. Page authority will have your site ranked higher while domain authority will also push you to the top with your popularity and age of domain.

Trust

Just like with human interactions, a site has to build an online presence that is trustworthy. Google will only rank your site if they trust you to be legit and competent with your content. Social media will go a long way in pushing for backlinks as this also makes your site trustworthy. You acquire trust when many people want to associate with your site.

Relevance

You become relevant the moment your content commands attention enough to attract backlinks. When Google ranks every backlink, it creates citation flow. They only consider backlinks from sites considered as trustworthy, thus creating a trust flow.

How to Structure your Blog for Easy and Automatic SEO

The above points will be effective if we structure our content well. The following steps show how to structure your blog for easy and automatic SEO:

Shift from using as many keywords as possible and focus on 1-2 quality long tails keywords. The rule is always clear, you are required to sound natural and not sound like you are trying to force keywords. Flow and naturally placed keywords especially with question-based long tail keywords will most likely excite your visitors and make it easy for conversions to take place.

Images are good for your blog post as they reinforce your message. However, you have to optimize images as well by putting the right caption, introducing the image with a good description, and having a short explanation of the image. Now that search engines cannot see an image as we see them, the well-intentioned texts will do the trick.

Avoid Duplicating Content and Giving Searchers What They Want

Be careful with duplicating content for the simple reason that in most cases, it is not usually a duplicated content literally, but using similar tags that can make search engines mistake them for duplicate content. Therefore, making visitors confuse your content for another person's or literally going to the wrong site.

Some ways to prevent this type of confusion is to use a URL structure guide for visitors and making sure that at every point of your site the URL matches the topic or the subtopic you positioned for the particular that link. It helps visitors have an easy time navigating your site. In most cases, they can simply change what they want to read by clicking a key work on the URL. For example, one can click the word 'contact' to 'home' and easily switch from the contact page to the home page.

The next tip is to maximize on the opportunity of using internal links. When writing about one topic in your blog page, it may require a brief intro from another relevant topic you had written on earlier and published on the same blog. You will not only sound repetitive to return visitors on your site by writing content again, but you will be limiting yourself from creating new material. Instead, create sub links that would naturally link back to all other pages you deem necessary for the current page content. This will allow your visitors to choose the topics they wish to review, instead of re-reading past information.

Another suggestion is to go big on Google analytics and trends. Let me explain, many times it is easier for an entrepreneur to solve an existing problem by creating a solution. When you visit Google's console you realize that most people have interests in a particular topic, why not jump in early enough and provide the much needed information?

A bold title with the main keyword will help the reader know whether the post is relevant to their search or not. Keywords in H1 and H2 headers also go a long way in ranking pages. Google will also rank it if it deems it important to the search question at hand. A great blog with not only good content, but with visible, clear titles and subtitles will help a reader have an easy time from point A of the communication process to point Z. Subtitles show a writer who has organized thoughts and points. It makes it easier even for a reader who is short on time or one looking for something specific on the same topic to skim through fast and successfully.

The Importance of the Sitemap
A sitemap is one of the greatest tools to employ for SEO. Submitting an XML Sitemap to Google is not a direct ticket to being indexed as Google is primarily out to crawl your content and rank it. A sitemap will require you to be consistent with your content in line with the issued side map for the following two reasons:

Usability
A visitor should have an out of this world user experience when they visit your site and click the links that you have provided. There should be good flow of information and page speeds should be as fast as possible. Also, your site should be clean and easy to view.

Responsive
A visitor wants a responsive website, whether it is you responding, an administrator, or an auto response, the visitor should be responded to as quickly as possible. When this is primarily factored in by the blogger, then one easily increases their website value.

The Importance of Link Building: Why is linking building so important?
Link building (as we discussed earlier about building credible collabs) is the ultimate process of creating partners online and branding your online presence as it is the only way web pages link to each other. It is critical to build your page links as this makes you an authority according to Google. As well, when someone links you in their page, they are basically inviting their audience to visit your page. In most cases, they direct visitors to you as an expert and one who has something they probably would not do without.

Paying to get Link on Website with Authority
Would you be willing to buy advertising space on that blog? Or would you be willing to pay to write a guest posts on the authoritative site? The two options will see you paying to be featured there. And the visibility is guaranteed. Also, the fact that you want to associate your blog with the ones already setting pace in the market is a great effort on your part.

Paying to get a link to a website with authority is considered as an unethical practice by Google. If you are caught, then the consequences will be dire on your site. Now that backlinks are a crucial part to ranking your site, Google expects a fair ground for all participants.

The greatest question is, why would you prefer shortcuts? We believe the process in every product or brand ultimately makes the whole difference. A genuine blogger would take the long route at least to prove to oneself you deserve the victory that will be preceded by sweat and strategy. You may pay your way to the top and then realize you cannot sustain yourself up there, yet you already lost money paying for the site.

The only way to pay for backlinks from authoritative sites is to pay with your outstanding content. You will agree with me that it is costly to bring out a brainy and smart piece of a read, but use it as needed or as you see fit.

How to Acquire Links and What to Avoid in Link Building
When you become an expert in your niche, you will be offering unmatched content online that others would want to associate with and create leverage on. Naturally, you will attract link building networks your way or have collaboration opportunities with other large influencers in your niche. In the next chapter, we will look at different ways to monetize a successful blog.

Chapter 3: Other Monetization Methods Part 1

Affiliate Marketing

You need to position your blog or website with quality products and services to draw more visitors for greater visibility. The hope is that these product producers and service providers will notice you as you are already standing out with your content. Reach out to your friends, partners, and family to have you on their web pages. Networking will go a long way here to improve your legitimacy and help you monetize your site. The first step in using product and service partnerships to grow your revenue and site traffic is to establish good anchor text. The anchor text points to the product or service links as a backlink. A web page will require an anchor text that is a hyperlink to redirect a visitor to the intended page (of the product or service) with either more information, illustration, or a place to purchase the marketed product or service. You will be compensated by either commission or a cut of the sale price of every sale you generate. More detail is below.

1. What is affiliate Marketing and How does it work?

Affiliate marketing is one of those golden opportunities bloggers have found to make money easily and with little real effort. Imagine yourself as a seasoned blogger with millions of readers per month having been given a product to recommend and refer your audience to the brand owner. In return they give you commissions or cuts of the sale for the conversions from your blog. This is the epitome of the of the term passive income. Affiliate marketing tops the ways an influencer can make money while they sleep.

It is the greatest wish for most bloggers, to wake up one morning and just look at the rising zeros in their bank account. All for placing a link and sending your readers to the brand owner or the service provider. Then as they buy the product or sign up for the service, you earn money for directing traffic and new customers to that particular business.

Affiliate marketing only requires you to identify a company or a business owner whose products you can comfortably recommend in your blog. They just seem a natural fit for your niche. For example, a travel blogger can easily recommend the top and best hotels in a particular area, or a nutrition blogger may recommend meal delivery services. When people use your referral link to book spaces in the hotel or sign up for a month of meal kit delivery, you get a commission.

In most cases there are multiple influencers or affiliates on the web competing to market the service or the product. This is the network that enables the whole process to work as it usually results in a great deal of sales for the business. The influencers that send the company the most sales are retained, while the others are usually cut loose. The top sellers or affiliates are given bonuses and discounts for their readers. This usually results in more sales for both the influencer and branded company.

This is how bloggers or influencers use the system of affiliate marketing to push the products of the business owner. It is these factors that motivate brand owners, knowing that he or she has a sales force of affiliate marketing that earn no salary and are only paid when they produce. The networker will ensure the process is smooth as possible by placing clear referral links their customers will see and will work hard to promote the product, as they get paid to do that.

Now I am going to take you through the journey of becoming an affiliate marketer. I'm going to give you the step to step guide to pick the best products or services for your niche. Even before you start your blog you are probably choosing a niche by keeping in mind what product you will wish to promote. These are the products that will sell easily, or you know you will be able to promote with little effort. So naturally, you will have to find a product that will flow smoothly with your content.

Explore the different affiliate programs that are available and brainstorm the one you would like to pick (or more-you are not limited to just one affiliate partner). We will look at the 10 most popular and most rewarding, then you can be in a position to pick the best. You will even be in a position to explore more from the knowledge that you'll pick up. We are also going to look at the strategies and tactics employed to make your affiliate marketing efforts as natural as your blog. This natural appearance to your audience will encourage more clients to convert to sales by recommending you and the product to others. Here are some reasons why anyone working as a blogger or social media influencer should become an affiliate marketer.

Controlled Competition- Even if we sell the same product as many others, the likelihood of you being put out of business by them is low. The normal scramble for market share is eliminated, as your entire business is not tied up in selling the product or service. Also, your marketing is based on your niche of interest and not the product. The product is simply an extra you offer to your readers, not a requirement. If they choose to buy it, it is because of the value they think they will get from it. Your ability to draw customers or brands is not based on sales, but on the amount of traffic you get to your site. Even if that is unpaid traffic. So, all others promoting the product are on equal footing, except for their traffic numbers. The clients who like your communication techniques and audience numbers will ask you to promote their products no matter how many others they have already partnered with.

Boundaries do Not Apply- A company in the USA will not hesitate to reach out to an influencer that lives in Europe or China as they probably draw an international audience. The American company (or international company) will be anxious to provide the product to a population that may have never heard of it except from the influencer. You sharing with your local and a worldwide audience makes you valuable to them. The product or service you researched and found on your affiliate program will help the company in the USA and yourself, as an affiliate marketer, make sales that would otherwise have been impossible.

Built in Audience- The above points lead us to the ultimate challenge, how to continue to build your audience and seek to maximize the most benefit from them. Once they have all bought the product, then how do you continue to build sales? There are only two ways, partner with another product (new to your audience) or seek new followers. The latter is most beneficial as you do not want to be accused of churning (or bleeding your audience for sales). That could lead to your loss of followers as you are seen to be just a salesperson, not someone giving them useful information. It is best to partner a long time with one or two companies that add value to your audience. That unique value will help continue to earn you subscribers and help the passive income through affiliate marketing to grow.

Most Popular Affiliate Programs
Loosely defined, an affiliate program is a set of systems or network that enables the process of affiliate marketing to be easy and smooth. It is the intermediate program between companies and affiliate marketers. You can imagine a company like Amazon or Loot Crate can have over a million affiliate marketers across the world. The programs are simple and cheaper than the internal employment and sales system, with its payroll, sales tracking, and the taxes that go along with it. Commissions are universal and much easier to account for and credit to the affiliate marketer. The product is drop shipped or the service is provided through established means, which is much easier where logistics are concerned.

Below are the 10 most popular affiliate programs that bloggers with good followings (and some without) can make some money with.

1. ShareASale Affiliates

ShareASale is one of the oldest affiliate marketing websites in the world. It has a heritage and it is known to have even digital paying options aside from the normal standard payment options that almost every other affiliate website has. It is a bit more complex than other programs. ShareASale affiliates does not necessarily require great technical know-how; it's just that it's a bit hard for beginners to figure their way around it.

Commissions vary by promoted products.

2. **Amazon Associates**

Amazon is by far the biggest of the affiliate programs and is the most popular with influencers because there is no limit to the products you can offer and they give up to 10% commissions of the total sale. When I say total sales, unlike other affiliate programs that vary commissions by products, there are always at least 20 items on amazon where you earn a solid 10% on the sales total (minus tax). The other items have varied rates from 5 to 7%. They also give you credit for sales made through one of your links even if the customer doesn't buy the product attached to the link, but purchases something else. This happens when they click your product link, but stay on the site to do further shopping and purchase other items. Amazon has varied payment options, thus making it convenient. Also, you can market and sell your own products from Amazon and keep all the profits minus shipping. This can be passive or not, as you will have to either create, list, and ship the product or ship a bulk amount to an Amazon Warehouse to ship for you for a fee as they are ordered. The fees can be built into the selling prices if you can still keep the prices competitive.

3. **eBay**

We find this to be a favorite for online influencers, because you can find anything and everything under the sun on eBay. This gives most bloggers flexibility and a choice on which product they wish to market and refer their clients. You can also market and sell your own products from eBay and keep all the profits minus shipping. This is not quite passive, as you will have to create, list, and then ship the product. But it can be much more profitable than partnering with an eBay seller to market their products. You can also employ a dropshipper for an additional fee (which you can build into the selling prices) to take a lot of the work off your shoulders. Some popular dropshippers are below and you can find their sites with a simple search.

I. Doba – #1 Drop Shipping Company

II. Oberlo – Marketplace for eCommerce Products

III. Dropship Direct– Wholesale Drop Shipping

IV. Sunrise Wholesale – Wholesale Dropshipper

V. Wholesale 2B – Best Drop Shipping Wholesalers

VI. SaleHoo – Dropship Wholesalers.

If you choose to partner with a seller on the site (rather than market your own product) then commissions are split between you, the affiliate marketer, and the eBay platform. This can be much less profitable than getting commissions directly from the brand company. However, it is still additional income that with enough volume can yield profit.

Note if you choose to use to partner with an affiliate partner that utilizes an auction to sell an item, then there is a possibility you could receive less or no commission. For example, if it takes more than 10 days to close the sale or if the item sells for less than the suggested retail price, then you will lose on all the commission's you had acquired on that particular auction. It is a well known glitch and we highly advise not using auctions but direct sales on all products that are not directly sold by you.

4. **Shopify**

For direct sellers you can earn subscription fees for the first two months you start working with them. To top that, you earn as much as $598 on their standard plans. You also have a 100% share of their enterprise plan. There is a lot of money here that may inspire partners to offer higher commissions to their influencers. Like eBay and Amazon, Shopify offers both affiliate marketing and direct sales with varied payment options.

5. Bluehost Affiliate Program

For a blogger who is doing a niche that addresses other upcoming bloggers who would need a site, or entrepreneurs who are yet to create or own a website, this referral rewards may be for you. The pay or commission is limited to the rate you can convert your followers website owners via Bluehost. Bluehost is currently one of the top recommended WordPress hosts available. With affordable prices, flexible packages and a great customer support team, there's a convincing argument as to why they're so highly recommended. Maybe it's time you partnered with them too and gave your followers a value for their future sites.

Choosing products or a price range for affiliate products

If you go about your business or spend a lot of time shopping, the one thing you will notice is that the products on sale are either very expensive and only a few pieces get sold per month, or very cheap product that sell really fast so when the former sells say 100 pieces the latter sells 10000 pieces.

In Affiliate marketing, high ticket affiliate marketing sees to it that an affiliate marketer sells on average very expensive products and the conversions from the referrals usually come back with high commission compared to the total amount of revenues the company gets. Consequently, you will find an affiliate marketer struggling to make commissions with low ticket affiliate marketing which involves products that are very cheap versus an ebook is going for $50. The marketer may sell less of the ebook, but those carry much higher commissions than a cheaper $10 item, so in the end, quality may outweigh quantity.

So, choose high ticket affiliate marketing because you do not have to sell huge amounts to make decent money. This is very beneficial if you have a smaller following that has disposable income or just a smaller following in general. Whereas, if you have a larger following then a lower ticket might work as well. The best thing is to make the most out of an opportunity and vary the items or services you promote. Another thing, people are more likely to shop for expensive products online nowadays, because online is often where you get the lowest price relative to the product or service. Shopping online sees to it that at least one gets a chance to compare prices and get the most out of something. Shoppers will check for the best price and the best reviews on items or services.

Blogging is not just a game. It is an industry just like any other. All the necessary work ethics that will propel a company to the top, make the highest of profit, and command the largest share of the marketplace are the same efforts and factors needed for a successful blogging career. There is no single business where one can just pick a random product without having a clear understanding of the market, the needs, the problem, and the solution that will bring revenue to the solution provider.

So bearing that in mind, why would a blogger just pick a niche for the sake of it without having the end goal in mind? From this guide you will get to know all the facts and expectations in the field of blogging so that when you start off you are equipped. If today you were to go on a road trip into some interior region the wisest thing to do is get a rough idea of the distance you will cover so that you budget for enough fuel to and from your destination.

It pains me to see the number of projects and businesses people pour money and effort into only for the projects and businesses to be left hanging and undone. It is a waste of resources. Why would you even waste your time studying all these materials we provide and others only for you to start a blog and pour your heart and content into it only for you to get tired in the middle and never even get to monetize or earn money from it. We have highlighted the above scenario so that we get to the serious part of blogging. Yes, you need to select a niche and at the back of your mind you need also to be clear and have plans on what products you will engage with in your affiliate marketing processes. The following are the best pointers to selecting the niche of your blog first looking at the best products on the programs:

What is available on your affiliate marketing program-

Do not pick a product that is not related to your niche or that no one else in your niche is providing. A nutrition blogger would not necessarily offer a traditional processed cake mix, while a baking blogger might. A product has to be there in your niche, You have to check on its features and how fast it is selling, and you have to check what it will be worth to your followers.

Now that we have talked about high- and low-ticket affiliate marketing strategies, pick your side. Will you rather sell a few affiliate products and get high commission, or will you go for products that are cheap in value and move fast? The most important thing is, among all the available products, what will you be most comfortable offering to your followers and incorporating into your content? Finally, does the value in commissions matter to you? If yes, go for the highest of figures that will motivate you to be creative and think and work on your blog around the clock without getting bored. After all, money should be enough motivation for effort and hardwork, even if you are tired.

Your strength and the opportunity to train from the best- My growing pursuit for knowledge is motivated by the person I am becoming each day. Mental and intellectual growth is fulfilling and making me want to share it with others. You will continue to work hard, and your blog will thrive. The many clients that I have gotten the opportunity to serve are more than grateful and have benefited from the information I provide. So make sure any brands you partner with fits in with your brand and bring that benefit to your followers. Never compromise your morals or reputation to make a quick dollar, if you choose carefully people will buy the product to get its benefit. Your job will be easy in the terms of sales.

Have a heart for leadership by serving Lead naturally and with the idea of serving those you lead. Strive to see a team of people using the resources at their disposal efficiently. Your work ethic and work delivery has to be excellent and exceptional. with the goal of educating your audience. Choose brands/companies that mirror your objectives. Make sure they mirror the leadership through service model by having a quality/useful product/service and having hands on customer experience. If the brand mirrors your own, then you should feel confident in partnering with them and leading your followers to them.

Stay passionate about research and learning- Your writing stays up to date with world research and top business trends that affect your niche. You constantly read, watch videos, and keep informed about the latest information that your followers will need to effectively participate in the niche. Your knowledge is why people seek out the advice of a professional blogger and ensure your blog's success in the future. Make sure your partner brands also keep up with those same trends and constantly improve their products.

You provide a wealth of network relationships- After months or years of producing a quality blog you build a network of other niche influencers or entrepreneurs. that operate in the niche. You will keep abreast of what they are doing and promoting. You should use that as a way of discerning between brands. I am affiliated with various blogs and organizations that are quite resourceful. I use those relationships for the purposes of learning, networking, sharpening my wits, and giving back to society. Being influential in an industry is a huge responsibility that should never be taken lightly. Association with any brand means you will make it visible to a greater audience than just yours.

The World is a Village- The internet has made the world a village. You have to take time to study and understand people. You have to be very multicultural thanks to current global economy. Make sure to appreciate all people and try to serve everyone from every walk of life by giving the best information possible. Personally, I had an encounter with a handicapped blogger who was making over 20 million USD annually and that changed my life. The encounter left me better and excited about life. From that one session, I purposed in my heart to serve society through it. My mission in life is to see people have the best online experience possible for them to fill fulfilled in life. Make sure both your niche and affiliated products hold up that standard.

You should always be grateful for the opportunity to present yourself to a potential global audience. Write well always, you never know who is reading. A potential client would be in your blog reading, see something that inspires them, and then later pour a lot of money in your endeavors. Always write for this kind of client. Focus on not disappointing them but exciting them then later getting the best from them no matter where in the world they are.

Choose a few related products-services for cross and down sell-Excellence is the act of making the most out of available limited resources. As a blogger, you wear the heart of a salesperson and teacher. Once someone visits your site and the client becomes convertible, it is your duty to ensure that the client is in a shopping mood. Make sure you not only sell the item the client came for, but you suggest more products related to what the client is buying - this is called cross selling. If at any point the client falls back due to cost constraints, you take the opportunity to downsell and sell cheaper available substitutes.

The above case scenario will only play out successfully if you as an affiliate had already done your homework. The homework is picking a product that you will use for your affiliate marketing and understanding all the other related products that you can sell to a potential client. Have other products available that are of the same value in terms of content, information, satisfaction, need solving capacity, but for a cheaper price so that you'll be in a position to sell either way. In short, choose products and services that are related to your core product or service in a range of prices.

How to pick up the products-services that sell the most

The following is the smartest strategy to employ when seeking to find the products and services that sell the most through affiliate marketing. Do your research. You can know what product is selling fast in the market by watching trends and sales on larger retail websites or on the brand sites. The best-selling product and the best service companies in the world are what you should focus on. Search for it and pick what will interest your readers and move fast and consistently. You will never go wrong with either fast-moving consumer goods or home appliances that we use every day, or we need to replace often.

Packaging your blog with ebooks that offer more value is one of the shortest ways of identifying what moves fast. This is because people are in your blog already seeking information concerning the niche you are in so offer more on that at a price. Most importantly visit those blog sites that are doing well and are even being published in successful magazines or as top companies in the world. Check out what they're selling to earn big commissions and follow suit. Follow the money.

How to be the best-selling affiliate-Many people have had their paths cross with rogue and unqualified "professionals" and the results can be devastating to say the least. I had a friend that had an unpleasant experience with this type of "expert." As a young adult, my friend and his sister were mistaken for some troublemakers near my high school and were arrested for trespassing at a Subway restaurant. His parents hired a lawyer that was affordable at the time, but unfortunately the results were disastrous. The attorney was not fit for the job and the case concluded with a plea bargain. I remember the judge asking the attorney if he knew what he was doing. I am certain that if my friend had a competent defense, he wouldn't have suffered the agonizing experience of clearing up his reputation after it was over. Imagine how many lives are affected because of incompetent legal representation. Thereafter, a strong passion and desire was birthed in my friend. He decided that whatever field he choose he would be excellent. This motivation makes me question anyone who just lives life just for the sake of financial benefit only. Don't be an example of a singular money chaser.

You should aspire to want to change people's experiences online. Why would you refer your loyal readers to a product that yourself would not spend money on? It has to be different and it has got to start with you. Be industrious and open-minded. Believe that success is a sweet gift to be enjoyed by everyone regardless of status and race. And is paramount when it comes to people spending their money on genuine products.

You need to have hands on experience on entrepreneurship, branding, sales and marketing. This are things you are supposed to acquire from the general school life. A cousin of mine first launched himself in the music industry by playing local media houses with his twin brother. It was smooth, fun, but not as profitable as expected. He took a sales job to make ends meet and in the middle of his music career, he grew successful in sales and quickly grew over the ranks as a salesman at one of the largest cruising companies, Norwegian Cruise Line.

He was able to successfully grow a sales resume working for various companies which finally lead him to create a travel agency, Executive Roadside & Travel. He decided to go into business for himself and quit the sales job to operate his roadside and travel business. Through consistency and focus, he was able to sustain a modest income and attract the attention of my roadside service provider, National Motor Club. In less than a month, he ran the fastest growing division and took home the coveted award of divisional manager of the month during his first month. At the moment, he is now running a travel blog that has is popular for the information offer travelers and allowing them to purchase services/products needed on the road. Yes, it wasn't his original plan, but he made a great passive income and is able to travel to pursue his music as well. So if life gives you lemons make lemonade; it is just as sweet, even if it wasn't your first flavor of choice.

Using affiliate links in the most natural way as possible-No one in the world wants to feel sold. Remember a bloggers primary task is to provide quality content that informs. When you compromise your good content for sales then you deserve to be left by your readers. This is because the principal stands, people over profit. Why can't you first serve the needs of the people who are visiting your blog and after you have satisfied them go ahead and lead them into your sale strategies? It is not wrong to sell but when you sell just to sell you are breaching the contract of why those people visited your blog in the first place.

That said, there is a need to include affiliate links naturally into your content. That is the very reason we firstly recommended that you pick a niche and a product that will work together naturally. For example, if you're still working on a travel company it will be very hard for you to recommend a product like kitchen gadgets. That is better placed in a blog or website about cooking or nutrition. But, a gas discount card or roadside assistance plan would fit naturally in a travel blog. When you use affiliate links naturally people will be more motivated to checkout your offers because the leads to the offers will be smooth.

Giving quality contents before affiliate links (create captivating and interesting contents)

Giving quality content before affiliate links is just going back to your roots of good writing and information. Bloggers are primarily known as people who provide good content concerning the different desires of the public. Affiliate links are simply secondary introductions to a blogger finding a way to earn while serving the needs of the people. It goes without saying, if one prioritizes affiliate links over good and quality content then you are as good as done in the business of blogging. You won't stay long. Put your house in order and prioritize first things first. In most cases, if you do what is expected of you to be successful then success will follow in its path.

Chapter 4: Other Monetization Methods 2

Direct Email Marketing

Gone are the days where bloggers were easily countable around the globe and they would just request readers to send them their email. After a steady rise of bloggers in the market, there have been a series of smart ways identified of getting the emails from clients without directly asking. This enables for you to not only let them know about new content, but to market products and services for pay. This is a great way to make sales without littering your site with links or ads (we will cover this a bit later). Also, it is a great way to keep your name on your readers' minds by staying in their inbox. However, most people will not just give you their email address, so we have to use alternate methods to get them. Here are some of the best I have found.

Lead magnets are the strategies that bait readers on a blog with a worthwhile product to have them send the email so that the product is in turn sent to them via email. Lead magnets require you to go a notch higher and know for sure what exactly you would need to offer visitors and get the desired response. The following steps will surely make your efforts bear fruit:

1. Conduct research and get to know what is that one thing that people would love to have in their emails and make a difference in the lives of businesses. The best way to the answer is to ask. You can start with the smallest of email contacts you already have and can also use your social media to ask friends and followers what do we want most to get from you for free. It is good to know also that following up on your platforms comments from people who follow you religiously with questions will be a good place to start because simply you'll be giving them what they have already requested from you. Existing followers will be happy that at least you listen to them. This will be a plus on your reputation

2. You also have to be outstanding, because as a reader yourself you know a reader can never have enough on the shelf to read. Even when the available written material would take a million lifetimes to accomplish. We are always enticed by new material. Because we are more inclined to the now and the future, so make sure your material and content is enticing.

The Importance of Email Marketing: create lists and advertise related products

Since the email mode of communication has become mainstream, email marketing has always been a classic way of doing top notch and targeted marketing. When a client gives you his email or subscribes to your emails it means they are attracted to your keywords and blog placement. So they are more likely to read and respond to your email messages. The following are key thoughts to remember when creating an email list and advertising related products there.

1. An email is a direct message to a particular recipient who had proven to be on the same niche with you and is interested in your particular keywords.

2. When sending an email to such specific audiences is more likely to create more conversions to your advertising materials that are sending their way.

3. Online, Comparison, or direct shopping is a trend for many people and getting an email with a suggestion of potential items one can buy is a great opportunity for many.

4. The email should provide direct links to products on sale, so the process of conversion is easy and you do not get to lose a potential client who postponed to go and check a site later because they were not really available. This happens when one is seeing an ad anywhere else but, on their computer, or phone.

Most email lists will be gathered from your blog directly, or through emails sent from your blogs to those requesting information or to those referred by other visitors. However, you are limited to only your direct traffic. There are many other ways to both attract others to your site or generate sales off your site.

Creating an email list outside your blog.

Make use of sites, like forums, that are outside of your blog. You should be a regular contributor or poster on free open forums that discuss your niche. This is a great way to leave links to your blog, email list, or products. Many people Google a niche and start on a public discussion forum rather than an individual blog. But, that doesn't mean you can't be on the forum as a fellow discusser. This will show people your expertise and they will seek you out. An effective placed link will bring them right to you and your email list.

Also, social media is a great place to start. You can use both your pages or accounts or a forum/group. You can place links or advice on the forum or group (as long as the admin allows it). This will be a post by post type of strategy. Another way, especially on Facebook is to pay them to advertise your lead magnets. This a process known as social media targeting and it is an effective way to generate email leads. You can choose to run advertisement on Facebook (or other platforms- we will discuss how it works later in this guide) and pay to reach people (based on interests, location, or personal factors) to get your free lead magnets. The ad or promotion will only reach those persons who will be interested in what you are selling or the information you are offering. All of them will be of the mindset of "I want to be part of what you discuss in your blog" indirectly. In other words, you are more guaranteed an audience of your choice on social media, than any other platform. You ask why? This is because this is where everyone is spending their time on. You will find potential clients on Facebook, Instagram, YouTube, and Twitter enjoying their social time.

Secondly, now that you are running a blog on the internet, you are bound to get more conversions if you advertise on social media than on any other media platform. No One really watches traditional TV or listens to radio anymore. There are limited opportunities for leads on streaming services and online radio, but they are expensive. There is no better way to get people clicking on your lead magnets than creating catchy captions on Facebook and putting the headline of the lead magnet in bold. I guarantee that you are more likely to get instant visits to your site if you advertise it on social media as the lead to your blog is only a click away. This is a far better option than advertising on television or radio and someone needing to go either on phone or PC to look out for you.

Facebook can tailor your ad to reach the right audience for you. You only reach who you want to reach and pay for just that. While running your adventure blog, you might want to write about hiking events at a site of your choice. If you live in Dallas, most probably you know people in your community who love travel and you will want to advertise to them while promoting local tourism. As well, the fact you will be writing about them is enough for them to give you clicks. Also, depending on your content, you can, go beyond targeting a particular location, even going as far as pinpointing what mile radius your town of choice should reach. You can specify gender, age, hobbies and interests of your target audience. Here, you get more value for your money. Go ahead and target that audience from anywhere in the world that you feel are likely to be interested in what you offer and in turn, their emails will make a difference in your traffic and sales.

With social media, you are sure to create an email list faster than you would in any other way. You not only have to advertise on social media but be active there and interact with potential follower and fellow influencers. You could also pay or strike collab deals with other bloggers outside your niche to advertise/shoutout you in their space. In this case, you will tab into a more diverse audience that may not have the same interests but may have a need you can fill.

What should your email send include?

Most subscribers to your blog visit it regularly, so what should you include in your weekly emails? Take that golden opportunity to send your new posts directly to them along with partners or affiliates that easily relate to those posts. You might also want to send special posts (not available on your normal blog) to your subscribers. This will be an inducement to remain on your email list and give them a feeling of being in an elite class of follower. Do not just push sale only emails to your subscribers. Just remember generally if you do this, most of them will either unsubscribe or mark you as spam.

Keeping Subscribers engaged

It doesn't matter to the world what you do to make ends meet or if you are making money from your blogs, all people want is to get their needs met. Are you capable of meeting them at their point of need? Yes, you can only do that by offering the best of content and information. If you are then you will keep the quality content coming and anyone will be to continue reading your blog or opening your emails. Blogging has no age limit. You can blog as young, old or in between and get the same opportunity to make yourself great! Would you be willing to take that risk and do whatever it takes to make it at the top?

This point reminds me that blogging welcomes everyone from every field in life. Whatever interests you or whatever lessons you have learned in this life can be shared with others for you to make a decent income in return. Blogging will give you the chance to awaken all your dreams. Which may have either been buried because of lack of money or lack of a flexible time that would allow you time to pursue your dream. Imagine you can your use laptop and work from anywhere in the world! Imagine being a travel blogger and actually traveling to blog or a pet care blogger than fosters animals and documents that experience. This should be motivation to find ways to make as much great content as you can and live the best life on your terms.

Blogging embraces everyone no matter what their situation is. In fact being "different" can be an advantage while blogging, as most people want to read about a life unlike their own. People can write about life in a wheelchair, having physical impairments, or other limitations that may seem difficult and inspire others. While certain disabilities my not work (easily) in other industries blogging and writing good content is all inclusive. It will require you to dive in with everything you are. It is known that the best writers, artists, and comedians have proven to have operated from their worst point of sorrow, but still empowered others. Some have been depressed to the edge of suicide and actually left us with masterpieces of their genius brains. They proved to the world that despite life being how it is, they were willing to excel in their craft. No betrayal, no pain, no fear, should make you hold back your writing talents. Write your pieces every day like they are your last or a measure for a Nobel peace prize or some other international award!

Can you write unapologetically well? Can you give your all without trying to fix your imagination to fit our usual confines of society? Let people read your work and experience life in totality. Readers sharing in your deepest joys and your wildest dreams. Write and let them walk into your life every time you publish yourself and leave them longing to read and live your life again. The only limitations of writing are the ones in your head, and they are not real.

Remember that Google (and other search engines) have set standards and they are on the radar to check if your content is great and helpful to their users. Therefore, you must be trustworthy and do what needs to be done to stand and be counted as a top blogger. With the above in consideration every day, why should you fail to deliver content. Write to impress, and give your best shot each round. Make sure this comes through in not only your blog, but in the marketing emails you send.

Chapter 5: Other Monetization Methods 3

Advertising on your Blogs

Blogging and media work for money is the agenda here. You create a mass of audience by giving them information they need, education, entertainment, or a combination of all these items. You lay out your life for them to see so their minds and emotions are refreshed. In turn, the audience you gather behind you can be used to create income or generate money. This process is called monetization and so far, we have talked about affiliate marketing and email marketing and sales. Affiliate marketing and Email Marketing are both great as seen above, but it is not the only monetization process. There are many ways to generate an income using a blog as the anchor. The information below is an overview to the world of Direct Blog monetization.

As a blogger, you have worked hard to build a loyal audience and fanbase for your blog, as well building a readership with thousands of readers daily. For example, your travel blog is having 3000 visitors a day and that pet care blog is generating daily traffic of 5000. These are a good number to start converting to money. How do you do it?

You can place ads directly on your blog. As your visitors read your postings, there can be strategic adverts in the site, usually appearing on the sidebar of the site, but they can pop up over the text. Therefore, be careful about the types of ads you use on your blog, as you do not want to drive readers away. You can either sell that space directly or link your page with Google AdSense that will channel ads to your site. The two styles will be discussed later in depth.

As an authority, you can write recommendations and reviews of products and services and receive money from the mentions (affiliate links). But some useful products may not have affiliate programs or not allow sites like Amazon to make them part of theirs. So, using straight up ads are the only way to integrate those products into your blog. The best products and services to advertise are the ones directly connected or related to your niche. In this case if you are a travel blogger, you can do recommendations of hotels, airlines, tours and travel companies, tourist attractions sites and cities, unique wear and fashion from the different areas you cover. The Pet Care blogger can advertise pet food, pet accessories, adoption, foster, or rescue programs. You are already trustworthy and respected enough to be an authority, so be careful when choosing those products. Below is an overview of the types of ads that are regularly on blogs.

All of the following methods and types of ads have two avenues of achievement. The first and most profitable is to be your own agent and broker by negotiating with companies and other bloggers for advertising on your site. This takes a lot of work up front, but once done, it becomes a very passive way of making money. The second is to partner with either Google AdSense or AdWords (Google, Reddit, and YouTube), Facebook/Instagram, or Twitter for targeted ad placement on your site or Social Media for money or for targeting advertising of your site, blog, products or services to increase your audience and sales. It is definitely a circle of life, so to speak. In an upcoming chapter we will look at all these methods.

Types of Ads and Methods of Using Them

Publishing Contextual Ads

Contextual advertising connotes the word context. Context involves keywords. This is a smart way for a client to pay for a specific targeted audience to get their ads. A blogger is also guaranteed more ad clicks with the right audience landing the related ads. Here, search engines are smart to channel advertisement where the context displayed matches the industry of the product or service. Search engines are also in a position to categorize and reach the intended users of the contextual messages.

The best example for Contextual ads is Google's AdSense. This is how Google knows what traffic they can channel a particular ad for maximum click on the ads. The ads also can be URL specific If you choose to skip AdSense and sell your space directly to companies, they usually have a similar system using search engines to do the same thing.

As a blogger, you are paid by impressions (the number of times and ad is viewed, it is measured by the pause and reading of it. Click through Impressions are the number of times someone clicks on the ad and visit the advertisers page) any additional can go in your blog. The advertiser pays for each Click Through Rate (CTR), and it can be profitable, so consider publishing contextual ads only. However, remember you must not overwhelm your readers with ads, so the make sure all ads are of the most related product or service to your niche or blog.

Using text link ads

As the title suggests, this is an ad placed as text in the normal context of your writing, but then it is highlighted and hyperlinked (very similar to you placing affiliate links yourself). A reader who wishes to click on the ad may either be redirected to a new page with the host advertiser or the blog may redirect him to the advertiser on the same page. For a reader who was no interest in the ad, the redirections may make him lose interest with your blog and you may lose the reader. Many a times, they are too annoyed to return, so make sure to make wise choices or make sure these ads are easy to spot for those who do not wish to click them.

Yes you are selling to people, but you should not make anyone feel sold. That's the name of the game. In-text ads usually have the advertiser pay a blogger pay-per-click. This is the most common, but sometimes a blogger may be paid a flat rate fee for advertising in their blog. It is purely negotiated by you up front with individual companies or outlined in the Terms of Service on Google AdSense.

Placing Impression Ads

Companies can also pay to place impression ads that appear when people are searching a particular niche or pay you for the same status when people search a term on your blog. You can also pay to advertise your blog to others using the same system. Placing ads impressions work with two factors; placements and keywords. You can use either of the two or combine the two to get outstanding refined results. You have the power to decide if you wish your ads to be featured on all selected Display Networks (the sidebar of the Google search page where the ads remain static and never change, since the advertiser has paid to be there whenever the keywords are searched) and you also decide the budget to go into the same, whether you are paying or being paid.

When you use both factors to zero in on your audience, you enjoy having refined audiences who are likely to click on your ads and convert with great sales. You also are in a position to earn more as a blogger if the two factors are applied. Placements make it easy for you to play with your bidding chances for higher wins on your end as an advertiser. Placement can also help you to place bids on the exact URLS of your taste.

In addition, you can pick keywords and direct ads to websites which only focus on the industry you are in. You are better placed when you are in control of who sees your ads. What you pay as an advertiser for clicks will eventually convert to sales or traffic (to draw more paying advertisers) with reasonable rates.

Publishing Sponsored Reviews and Paid Posts

An advertiser may choose to write a very good review on his product or service then approach you to publish it on your blog. Or, they may even pay you as a blogger to write and publish a review on the product on your blog. This is direct advertising and it pays well since there are no intermediaries. However, this is an ethically gray area as you do not want to endorse a product or write essentially an unfounded review on a product or service, you have not used. Proceed with caution and make sure you give the product or service a whirl and be honest in your endorsement.

Advertisers can shy away from doing a direct review of his product and prefer some mentions and endorsement on a post. The post might be talking about touring Mt. Kenya while the blogger chooses to focus also on the accommodation he had at the client's hotel. The blogger ends up selling both Mt. Kenya as a tourist site and the client's hotel as the best choice while at it. Just make sure you have actually stayed at the hotel.

Guest Posts

Guest posts are the shortest route for a blogger to make their brand or blog known to other readers in another influential blog. For beginners and newbies, guest posts will skyrocket you to greatness. Here you tell people, "hey, I have not been around for long, actually I just started blogging, yet I am so resourceful you should check me out". If the guest post is likeable and informative to them, then you will easily win yourself followers. In some cases, you will pay the bigger blogger for the chance to guest write for them and in turn once established smaller bloggers and influencers will pay you to do the same.

Guest posts benefit your blog in three ways:

1. You earn from someone by simply taking the time and writing for your blog.

2. You earn time off your weekly schedules because your loyal readers will find something to read that is informative, while you took some time to rest from your schedule or get ahead on your posts for later.

3. You prove to your readers that you are influential enough to attract guests to your blog. This helps seal your value and makes you a leader in your niche.

Placing your own Ads selling your Products-services

Oh, this is beautiful, and it is my favorite. This is where you reap the fruits of your efforts. Imagine having a blog with a monthly traffic of 2 million readers and going ahead to run a business that will directly benefit your audience! It sounds fun. So sometimes it will become necessary to pay for ads to sell the product or service you offer. Personally, why I choose to endorse this mode of advertising more, is because of the rule of reciprocity. Today if my favorite blogger decides to sell some jewelry or perfumes, I would definitely want to promote them. Even if as a way to say thank you for keeping me on my toes for their next publication.

Loyal readers are more likely to promote your business if they see it outside your blog. This can be either as a legitimate business person, product inventor, or being advertised as an expert. If they see paid promotions from other influencers or ads on Google, then it established your validity a more than a blogger. This will make them feel more at ease in promoting you and they will share your content or product/service. You may be out 200 dollars in paid ads, but you may get 500 dollars in sales and free advertising through shares and shout outs, because of the perception of being legit.

Now what can you sell? I mean the possibilities are limitless, but make sure whatever it is it relates to your niche and blog in a natural and fluid way. If there is not an existing product you can sell, then create your own. The most obvious is putting a very detailed and expanded niche advice or information into an ebook. You are already a writer, so why not write manual or informative book, beyond your blog? Being a published author carries a huge amount of weight, especially if your niche and blog are mainly information that would not easily tie to any other physical product. Your business does not have to involve anything else other than writing or it can be an actual product, service, or gadget. Just find something valuable to sell. You will do well, especially if you have created an audience for yourself already. It is only fair you do yourself some a favor and take advantage of the ready market. Why create influence to help every other person sale their products yet deny yourself the benefits?

Don't be worried about how to get your product out there. In the case of a book you can self-publish through Amazon Kindle or Audible, as well as many other sites. Then you market it to your built-in audience and possibly others. Remember we are going for 500 hundred people giving you 20 bucks a month to reach 10k a month. This is just another way to hit that average. So, no book deal is required. Though that is a possibility, you can write a chapter or two and send (along with complete information on your brand, blog and reach) to an existing publisher. They may have the systems in place for marketing beyond your means, and they may offer you money upfront and a cut of sales to put it out or buy it outright. The possibilities are endless, just make sure you crunch the numbers and do what is most profitable.

In the case of a product or gadget, there are many companies (just Google ghost or 2nd party manufacturing) that will work with you on developing things like skin care, cosmetics, supplements and gadgets to your specifications and produce them under your brand. Just make sure once you know what you want you put together the blueprint or formula and get a patent, so the idea is yours. There are many websites like LegalZoom that can help you file for a government patent if it is needed. There are fees involved, but to start your own business, it is worth it. The same is true of a service. Put together a game plan and perhaps offer it free or discounted to a few people to get good reviews. Then market it to your audience.

Displaying Ads in your Blog's Feed
There are many companies will pay you to channel traffic to their site at a fee. A good example is Google's AdSense. You will need to sign up for an account with them and give your full details including payment ones. On your WordPress website, assuming you are using WordPress, click on the WordPress widget, then click on appearance, then select widgets, pick custom HTML and drag it to the best location on your site then drop it there. Remember to paste the Google AdSense code. From this point, you will be golden, waiting for advertising money to reflect in your bank account.

With Google AdSense, you do not have to worry about finding individual advertisers yourself. Although you will have to part with half of the ad revenue due to Google AdSense pay model. This is simply because you did not broker your own deal with the advertiser, but Google did. Google acts as a middle man and brings advertisers to your site for a cut of the fee. This brings us to our last option for now. Read on.

Selling Ad Space Directly
You can have such a great blog that advertisers will be either be approaching you directly to feature ads on your site or responding when you reach out to them about a deal. So you will find yourself booking sales meetings with potential clients to sell them advertising space. Whether you go fetching for them or they come, the bottom line is you have advertising space up for grabs. Here, you make a lot of money and you pocket it all.

Apart from writing great content, selling as space should be another priority. It pays well. Have fun selling it. Just note somewhere, you will have the added job of finding and brokering deals with clients, along with managing and creating for your huge visitor traffic to your blog or site. Let traffic building motivate you to increase the worth of your advertising space. Again, just like other forms of advertising, make sure you are choosing relevant and helpful companies to partner with.

Chapter 6: Using Google and Social Media for Profit

In this chapter we will explore the uses of both Google AdSense and Google AdWords for both getting paid advertisers on your site and social media, as well as advertising to grow your own audience. We will also cover the basics of using the various forms of Social Media to grow your brand and advertise.

Google AdSense

To first get started you must create a Google Account, this is as simple as creating a Gmail account. Go to Google to do this. This is what will allow you to use the service, which is an advertising brokerage site. Basically, companies pay Google to place their ads on busy or related sites that will cause people to click on their ads and buy products.

Companies trust Google and their algorithm to do their best for them. Google has reach and reputation that you and I do not have, so partnering with them is a great way to go for generating ad revenue.

To create your AdSense account, follow these steps:

1. Visit Google AdSense

2. Click Sign up now.

3. Enter the URL of your website or blog that you want to show ads on. This could include both a YouTube Channel and Reddit Account. You can also set this up directly through YouTube (Google owns YouTube) and then it will link to AdSense.

4. Enter your email address.

5. Click Save and continue.

6. Sign in to your Google Account.

7. Select your country or territory.

8. Review and accept the AdSense Terms and Conditions.

9. Click Create account.

You are done.

For most sites the approval is pretty easy, especially for WordPress, which is a reason we suggested it. Smaller sites like Wix may have some issues, but as long as the site is written in a basic HTML manner it should be fine. For all sites (except YouTube-which requires 4k watch hours in a one-year period and 1k subscribers to qualify) you do not have to have a certain threshold of traffic, but it helps to speed up the process. Bear in mind that you must reach Ad Revenue balance of at least 100 dollars to be paid, so if you have a small amount of traffic, it may take a while to get paid. Once the account is approved, you will tell google about your niche and demographic, so they can choose appropriate advertisers.

Google AdWords

Different from AdSense, AdWords is a way for you to advertise your blog, site, product, or service to others by being placed on relevant sites and pages. Just like you are paid by clicks and impression in AdSense, you pay by them on AdWords. Think of you being one of the companies that is paying to be on your site, but instead you are paying to be on someone else's. You trust Google to place you based on what you tell them about your site. Basically, it is the polar opposite of AdSense. To apply you go to AdSense and fill out an application, and you will be contacted. Rates and programs very, so the application must be done first.

Using Social Media

In this chapter we will learn how to harness the power of the various social media sites to both promote your blog and generate sales. Social media should be a passion and a hobby for everyone who wants to succeed in the online world. In the media industry, it has been being called "the new media" and is replacing traditional sources of news and information at a rapid pace. It is a phenomenon in the market that is still new despite a decade having passed since it is emergence. Researchers are studying it day and night as it has proven to be impactful, fast, and phenomenal in the hands of one who knows how to use it. Social media has changed the rules of the game completely. It has combined the powerful social world with the economic part of it and the results are fireworks!

For the first time in history, a brand has an opportunity to create an audience around it without using mainstream media for publicity. The latter was expensive and remained a luxury for the rich. Today, social media is so affordable, yet you can have the same and more rewards one used to get in the past through mainstream media after paying a fortune for a few seconds in front of an audience. People spend so much time on social media that you can get a lot of time in front of a targeted audience, instead of a mass random audience.

How wonderful that you can create an online presence that can spark emotions as intended, attract likes for instant endorsement and reactions, openly invite people across the globe to comment and debate around the issues you have raised openly and instantly, and attract people to share your message to their circles. The last point requires some time, but it is what every blogger should dream of. In social media, when almost everyone seems to share your post or video, the shared content is referred to as one "going viral".

Remember the audience we said earlier that you now have power to create? Yes. That audience takes time to grow. With good effort and great content, you can grow it into millions of followers. When you share content, most likely it is visible to the community you have created around yourself, in this case, your audience. When someone decides to share your work, it means they have taken a deliberate decision to share your content to their circles and audience. It is the best thing; if you have 2 million followers, you are only guaranteed that many people accessing your work. But when say 10 people with 2 million followers each shares your work to their circles, then we are talking of up to 22 million people seeing your work! Isn't that impressive! Google will take note of your impact and definitely rank you at the top. You are now an influencer and your work will be pushed more for more to see.

Social media has the potential to build your brand. A brand requires creation of awareness to a potentially large amount of people. The more the people know your brand, the better your position to your competitors. There are no shortcuts here. If you are good and have great content, the results can be quick. The masses will like you, celebrate you, and share you. If your work is below average, then you will go unnoticed or even be ridiculed for years. It is a great platform to help sharpen your teeth but be sure you share only accurate or useful information. Progress and growth will attract a steady flow of people looking at your content and recommending it to others.

Social media is relatively cheap compared to all other media. Yes, you will have to work with a budget, but at the end of the day, it is thousands less than any other media channel. The mind-blowing fact is, you spend less, for even more guaranteed conversions and impact! Google appreciates and recognizes backlinks from social media. They will rank you higher from your effort there. Ultimately, you will be on top of the SERP (search engine results page) if you crack social media success with you blog!

The above are reasons that would make anyone want to jump in social media with both feet! But, below we are going to discuss the nitty gritty details of how to launch yourself on this massive platform. The fact that almost 80% of the world's population is on social media and almost 50% are active users should ring success bells to you.

We are going to learn the step-by-step guide to launching and running social media platforms. Last but not least, we will look into how to achieve success in all platforms, creating harmony.

Create a profile on the main social Networks

Blogging takes a leap higher when launched on social media and we are going to zero in on the major platforms; Facebook, Instagram, Twitter, YouTube, Patreon, Reddit, and Quora. All are social media platforms, but they work differently to achieve more or less the same goal. Below is a roadmap to each of them.

Facebook

Facebook is undoubtedly the most popular of all social media platforms. Actually, most people think the term social media and the term Facebook are one and the same. 2018 statistics showed that despite having over 4 billion registered accounts, it has an impressive 2.27 billion active users! This is massive!

How it works

Facebook allows you to create a profile as a person or business. You will have your profile and cover photo to put a face or any identity you may wish with your name. It allows you to share as much about yourself as possible. Your location, education history, contacts, family members, hobbies and interests, books and movies you have read and watched respectively, your favorite pages, your public groups on the same platform. You can answer random social questions your friends might be interested in, places you have visited, and so much more. Basically, others can live your life with you.

In addition to the above, Facebook allows you to have up 5000 "connects" referred here as friends. Beyond 5000, all others who wish to link up with you automatically become your followers. Here, you can have as many numbers of followers as you possibly can.

On the business side of the platform, Facebook prompts users to "share what is on their minds". Here people will create content and write about anything and everything. One can write content and/or back it up with an image, a video, or a shared link to a blog post. Basically, you can write content, share captivating images or informative illustrations, share videos, and best of all for you, share your blog posts with your audience/friends.

Facebook will give you an opportunity to create a page independent of your personal account, if you wish. You can run your page as a brand name based off your personal name. You can be either an independent publisher of your blog or the face of your blog if you work as a team. In most cases, it is more rewarding to work with the brand name of your blog. Remember, you are here to build a brand for your blog. A page will allow you to specify your niche and give a brief description of your blog. For example, if you run a travel blog, you will indicate travel as your main agenda. You will also go ahead and describe the extent of your adventure and content. This way, you will attract an audience that is interested with the same things as your blog. You will realize you will attract a lot of travel enthusiasts and all other matters related to travel.

Below is a step-by-step guide to winning on Facebook with a page already in place

Make clear your intention. Unless you are a news blog, more often than not, you will want to confine yourself to a niche. Remember news is a niche on its own. What is my point? Be a master of one niche. Let people know what niche you specialize in. Be a resource for good content on one particular area of life and create Audience on it. This will see to it you create a steadily growing number of Audience who are likely to stay loyal to the blog. You don't want to attract someone because of travel matters only for you to jump ropes and start engaging on totally different matters like religion and politics. In most cases, this will be a put off to the people who followed you for travel. In the end, you will have very unpredictable followership as people come and go.

Rarely will anyone invent a wheel in this day and age. That said, there are many people running blogs like you do and doing the same niche as you even on Facebook. How do you stand out? Your competitor may have 10 million followers. You can equally match him and have 10 million followers. It is possible to run a page that has hundreds of millions of followers while your competitors have tens of millions of followers. We all know what is great stands out. These are not figures you fantasize about and they appear. You work for them and your content will have to be top notch.

Accompany most of your shared blog posts with captivating captions. Bait Facebook users to want to read more. You are more likely to get clicks on your blog with either a very catchy caption or a very catchy headline. If you have both you have massive chances already.

You cannot open a page to only share blog posts. Wrong move. You will have to do other independent things to create a life and presence on your page. Actually, if you run a page that only shares blog posts, you are more likely to lose big time. I believe in the thumb rule of reciprocity in the universe. Choose either to be informative, educative, or entertaining. Let people follow you for the above. You will keep them coming. Then once in a while, share your blog posts, and as a rule of thumb, people will want to reciprocate your good effort in their lives for the above three and promote your blog. Or, if not for that reason, they will always be curious if your blog post is a greater version of the value they get from your other offerings.

Marketing and Advertising on Facebook
Any brand worth its name today has advertised to get there. Advertising is the process by which you pay a media channel to push you to their mass audience. Say Facebook has a potential of 5 billion people on their site. You pay them to reach that number of audiences. But if you pay to reach 5 billion people, you will have to cough a few more thousand dollars unlike one who will want to pay for only 20000 people, consisting of only women, age 28-35, located in say, California only. You realize the latter cluster of Audience will achieve more for less. This is what you get when you pay Facebook to advertise your blog.

Today if you advertise yourself on a daily newspaper, you are sure that your target audience will be localized, since daily news in USA cannot really sell in Japan. While on Facebook there is a guarantee of more audience on social media than on dailies. What we are trying to say is you are more guaranteed of an Audience of your choice online, and on social media, than any other platform.

Secondly, now that you are running a blog on the internet, you are bound to get more conversions if you advertise online than on any other media. Say you own The Washington Post, you are more likely to get instant visits to your site if you advertise for it online as the lead to blog is only a click away, rather than advertising on television, requiring someone to go either on their phone or PC to look out for you.

Facebook can tailor make the right audience for you. You only reach who you want to reach and pay for just that. While running your blog, you might want to write about hiking events at the second tallest mountain in the world, Mt. Kenya. This is a global destination. If you live in Texas, most probably you know there are people in your state that love travel. Most likely, you will want to advertise to them and at least advertise to Kenya, the hosting country while promoting local tourism. As well, the fact you will be writing about them is enough for them to give you clicks. Also, depending on your content, you can go; beyond targeting a particular location. You can even go as far as pinpointing what mile radius your town of choice should be, or you can specify gender, age, hobbies, and interests of your target audience. Here, you get more value for your money.

Instagram

Instagram is popular and has a specific kind of audience. Here, images are everything. Images precede captions. If you miss it on imaging, most likely no one will bother with your great caption. We are talking of 1 billion monthly active users. For a brand that depends on people and viewership, this number is mouthwatering, and you would want to make the most out of it. Instagram was purchased by Facebook last year, so the same targeting opportunities are possible.

Remember our travel blogger. What is travelling without pictures? You are more likely to thrive on Instagram than on any other platform. Besides great content, photography skills are needed here. Whether you perfect the art of photography, or you pay an expert to do it, or you buy images online, the choices are many and all are great. Do what you may, to win an audience with simply good photography. I cannot emphasize this point enough. Photography is king here. Instagram should motivate you to also win at photography even in your blog posts. A blog is beautiful with a picture here and there. For a travel blog, pictures could be enough for a blog. You might need only minimum captioning. Pictures should be unique and high quality, do not just post downloads or screenshots. Make Instagram the album of your life.

On Instagram, the same rules on marketing and advertising applies as they do on Facebook. It gets better since they are under the same umbrella company. You can cross-advertise the same item on both Facebook and Instagram. How wonderful! You know, you might want to target Texas audiences only, just that, and you might find a very active user on Instagram who does not either own a Facebook account or has one but hardly checks in there. To get this person, you will have to advertise on both platforms to be sure of getting as much attention to both Facebook and Instagram lovers.

Twitter

Twitter is uniquely different. It doesn't have as many users as with the other two mentioned platforms, but twitter followers tend to be very loyal to twitter. We are talking about around 326 million daily active users. Twitter is the debate center of the world. People who are more into intellect and conversations over images and social fun. Your captivating blog posts will do well here. People are most likely to read and follow links here. This is because they are inclined to seek out more information and evidence for the discourse they have been following here throughout the day.

You can easily make yourself an authority in blog matters here. Besides sharing your blogs and interesting tweets here and there, the biggest task on Twitter is to follow conversations. Engaging on developing and current topics on trending hashtags is more likely to make you visible than creating just content in your own space.

Engaging someone on twitter will most likely invite them to want to know more about you, and if and when they visit, find you specializing in an area of their interest, then they are likely to stick with you for life. First by following you. Twitter will also give you an opportunity to advertise and feature your ads on their platform. It is a very effective tool for anyone who is keen to invite new readers to their space.

YouTube

YouTube is the second largest search engine in the world, reaching 10 billion people daily. As you probably know, it is video based, so you will have to adapt your strategy a bit here. Instead of just sharing things relevant to your blog in the form of posts or pictures, here you will need to adapt your blog for audio/visual audiences. Videos are a great way to market yourself as people get to actually see and hear you. Also, the interaction on YouTube, as well as the opportunity for the AdSense money is second only to Google Search. In addition to AdSense, there are several Google Partners which we will list below that can market your channel videos on third party sites. YouTube can really help gain you a following.

Making video content of your blogs (VLOG) or content related to your blog is the best option for YouTube.

You can link your blog, place affiliate/sales links, or links to your other social media in the videos or video descriptions. It is a chance to provide another type of content for your followers and engage with them. In addition, you will get a whole new audience that does more listening or watching, than reading. Not because they are lazy, but they are busy or just prefer to hear and see their information. Your followers who find you there will also be able to see and hear you, which gives your blog a whole other dimension.

Also, YouTube is a way to get extra ad revenue from AdSense by allowing Google to place ads on your videos (once you have 1k subscribers and 4k watch hours). Furthermore, you can advertise through AdWords to get your videos in front of a targeted audience, thus increasing traffic to all your sites. In addition to AdSense there are some other services (Google Partners) that can market your YouTube content and blog for a small fee. This list is courtesy of Google. Some of them are:

Product Name - *Company Name*	Vendor Type
A9 *A9.com, Inc., Amazon Europe Core SARL*	Vast Provider
ADTECH GmbH *Oath*	Vast Provider
ATK Media GmbH *ATK Media GmbH*	Ad Server Advertiser
Action Allocator *Explido Webmarketing GmbH*	Research - Analytics
Ad VRF (Compete Pixel Study) *Compete, Inc*	Research - Analytics
AdAction *Delta Projects AB*	Vast Provider
AdAction *Delta Projects AB*	Vast Provider
AdGear Technologies Inc. *AdGear Technologies Inc.*	Vast Provider
AdMotion USA Inc. *Admotion USA Inc.*	Vast Provider
AdTraxx *Explido Webmarketing GmbH*	Research - Analytics

AdVentori SAS *AdVentori SAS*	Vast Provider
Adap.tv Inc. (AdWords/YouTube) *Oath*	Vast Provider
Adform *ADFORM A/S*	Ad Server Advertiser
Adfox *Adfox*	Vast Provider

Adition *Virtual Minds*	Vast Provider
Adloox *Adloox SA*	Research - Analytics
Adluxe *HyperAdvertising Ltd*	Vast Provider, Ad Server Advertiser
Admetrics GmbH *Admetrics GmbH*	Vast Provider
Adobe Scene 7 *Adobe Systems Inc*	Creative Agency CDN
Adometry by Google *Google, Inc.*	Research - Analytics
Adrime *Weborama SA*	Vast Provider
Adssets AB *Adssets AB*	Ad Server Advertiser
Advertising Technologies LTD *Advertising Technologies LTD*	Demand Side Platform

Alphonso *Alphonso*	Research - Analytics
Aperture *PulsePoint, Inc.*	Research - Analytics
AppNexus Open AdStream *AppNexus Inc*	Vast Provider
AppNexus Open AdStream *AppNexus Inc*	Vast Provider
AthenaHealth *athenahealth, Inc*	Ad Server Advertiser

Augur *Augur Technologies Inc*	Research - Analytics
Barometric *Barometric, Inc.*	Ad Server Advertiser
Bluestreak *BlueStreak*	Ad Server Advertiser
BridgeTrack *Publicis Media GmbH*	Vast Provider
Campaign Monitor (YouTube) *Integral Ad Science, Inc*	Research - Verification
Celtra Inc. *Celtra Inc.*	Vast Provider
Channel Intelligence *Google, Inc.*	Research - Analytics
Cheq.ai *CHEQ AI Technologies Ltd.*	Vast Provider

ClickTicker, LTD *ClickTicker, LTD*	Ad Server Advertiser
Clinch.co *Clinch Labs LTD*	Ad Server Advertiser
Collabo LLC *Renegade Internet, Inc*	Ad Server Advertiser
ComScore (AdXpose) *comScore Inc.*	Research - Verification
ComScore vCE (YouTube) *comScore Inc.*	Research - Verification
DEVK *DEVK*	Research - Analytics
DeltaX *AdBox Software Pvt Ltd.*	Ad Server Ad Network, Vast Provider
DoubleClick Bid Manager *Google, Inc.*	Demand Side Platform
DoubleClick Campaign Manager *Google, Inc.*	Ad Server Advertiser, Vast Provider
DoubleClick for Publishers Premium *Google, Inc.*	Vast Provider, Ad Server Advertiser
DoubleVerify Inc. *DoubleVerify Inc.*	Advertising Option Icon
DoubleVerify Inc. *DoubleVerify Inc.*	Research - Verification
DoubleVerify Inc. (BrandShield): Ad Swapping *DoubleVerify Inc.*	Ad Blocker
Duepuntozero Research SRL *DUEPUNTOZERO RESEARCH SRL*	Research - Brand Lift

DynAdmic Corp. *DynAdmic Corporation*	Ad Server Ad Network
E-Plus Mobilfunk GmbH & Co. KG *E-Plus Mobilfunk GmbH & Co. KG*	Ad Server Advertiser
EUROZEST MEDIA LIMITED/Avid Ad Server *EUROZEST MEDIA LIMITED/Avid Ad Server*	Ad Server Advertiser
Extreme Reach Digital (ER Digital) *Extreme Reach, Inc.*	Vast Provider, Research - Brand Lift
Extreme Reach, Inc. *Extreme Reach, Inc.*	Vast Provider
EyeReturn Marketing *Eyereturn Marketing Inc.*	Vast Provider
Eyewonder Inc. *Sizmek Inc.*	Ad Server Advertiser, Vast Provider
Flashtalking *Flashtalking, Inc.*	Vast Provider
Flite Inc. *Flite Inc.*	Vast Provider
FreeWheel *FreeWheel*	Vast Provider
Gigya *Gigya*	Ad Server Advertiser
GoldSpot Media *GoldSpot Media Inc*	Ad Server Advertiser
Google Zoo *Google, Inc.*	Research - Analytics
HLEB *Blueworks Commerce Inc.*	Ad Server Advertiser

HRB Digital LLC. *TruEffect*	Ad Server Advertiser
Hindustan Times Mobile Solutions Limited *Hindustan Times Mobile Solutions Limited*	Vast Provider
IBM Experience One (Unica) *IBM*	Research - Analytics
Ignite Technologies *Ignite Technologies, Inc.*	Research - Analytics
Innovid Inc. *Innovid Inc.*	Vast Provider
Insight Express (AdIndex) *Kantar*	Research - Brand Lift
Insight Express (Mobile Ignite) *Kantar*	Research - Brand Lift
Internet Billboard, a. s *Internet BillBoard a.s.*	Ad Server Advertiser
Jivox Corporation *Jivox Corporation*	Vast Provider
Kreditech Holding SSL GmbH *Ingenious Technologies*	Research - Analytics
KuaiziTech *KuaiziTech*	Ad Server Ad Network
Leadcapital *Leadcapital Corp*	Ad Server Advertiser
Liverail Inc. *Facebook, Inc.*	Vast Provider
Local Marketing Institute LLC *Renegade Internet, Inc*	Ad Server Advertiser

MASSMOTIONMEDIA SARL *MASSMOTIONMEDIA SARL*	Vast Provider
Mashero GmbH - VAST *Mashero GmbH*	Vast Provider
MeMo2 / Hottraffic *Hottraffic BV*	Research - Brand Lift
Metro Parent *Renegade Internet, Inc*	Ad Server Advertiser
Miaozhen Systems *Beijing Miaozhen Information Consulting Co., Ltd.*	Vast Provider
Mixpo Inc. *Netsertive, Inc.*	Vast Provider
Moat Inc. *Oracle Data Cloud*	Research - Analytics
Monsoon Ads Pvt. Ltd. *Monsoon Global Ventures Inc.*	Research - Analytics
NET-Metrix-Audit *NET-Metrix AG - Switzerland*	Research - Analytics
Nextperf *Rakuten, Inc.*	Vast Provider
Nielsen (Brand Effect Extended View [BEEV]) *Nielsen*	Research - Brand Lift
Nielsen (Sales Effect) *Nielsen*	Research - Analytics
Nielsen (Watch Effect/Net Effect) *Nielsen*	Research - Analytics
Nielsen Digital Ad Ratings *Nielsen*	Research - Analytics

OOO GPM-Digital *OOO GPM-Digital*	Vast Provider
Omnibus co. Ltd. *Omnibus co. ltd.*	Data Management Platform
OpenX Ad Server *OpenX*	Vast Provider
OpenX OnRamp *OpenX*	Ad Server Advertiser
Platform IQ *Platform IQ*	Vast Provider
Pointroll *Pointroll*	Vast Provider
Proquire LLC - Accenture *Proquire LLC - Accenture*	Research - Analytics
Rakuten Attribution *Rakuten, Inc.*	Research - Analytics
Reamp *Comune SA*	Ad Server Advertiser
Reddion *GroupM*	Research - Analytics
Renegade Internet Inc. *Renegade Internet, Inc*	Ad Server Advertiser
Republic Project, Inc. *Sizmek Inc.*	Ad Server Advertiser
Research Horizons LLC dba Phoenix Marketing *Research Horizons LLC dba Phoenix Marketing*	Research - Brand Lift
Research Now (YouTube) *Research Now Limited*	Research - Brand Lift

RevJet LLC. *RevJet LLC.*	Vast Provider
SPACE ADSERVER *SPACE TECNOLOGIA E INTELIGÊNCIA LTDA*	Ad Server Advertiser
Samba.TV *Free Stream Media Corp.*	Research - Brand Lift
Sizmek *Sizmek Inc.*	Vast Provider
Skillup Video Technologies Corporation *Skillup Video Technologies Corporation*	Vast Provider
Smartstream.tv *SMARTSTREAM.TV GmbH*	Vast Provider
SpongeCell, LLC *Flashtalking, Inc.*	Vast Provider
SuperAwesome *SuperAwesome*	Ad Server Ad Network
Symphony Advanced Media *Symphony Advanced Media*	Research - Analytics, Research - Brand Lift
TF1 - FR *Groupe TF1 S.A*	Research - Analytics
TUI UK Limited *Flashtalking, Inc.*	Vast Provider
Target.com *Target.com a division of Target Corporation*	Research - Analytics
Telemetry Limited *Telemetry INC.*	Vast Provider
Telogical Systems, LLC *Telogical Systems, LLC*	Ad Server Ad Network

Tender Industries AB *Tender Industries AB*	Vast Provider
Teracent Corporation *Google, Inc.*	Ad Server Advertiser
The Walt Disney *The Walt Disney*	Research - Analytics
Treepodia *Treepodia*	Ad Server Advertiser
Tremor Video *VideoHub, a division of Tremor Video, Inc.*	Vast Provider
TruEffect *TruEffect*	Vast Provider, Ad Server Advertiser
TubeMogul Inc. *Adobe Systems Inc*	Vast Provider
TubeMogul Inc. (AdWords/YouTube) *Adobe Systems Inc*	Vast Provider
Unica an IBM Company *Unica*	Research - Analytics
Unicast *Sizmek Inc.*	Ad Server Advertiser
VideoHub *VideoHub, a division of Tremor Video, Inc.*	Research - Analytics
Videology *Videology*	Vast Provider
Videoplaza *Videoplaza*	Vast Provider
Vindico *Broadband Enterprises*	Vast Provider

Visible Measures Corp. *Visible Measures Corp.*	Research - Analytics
Weborama Campaign Manager *Weborama SA*	Vast Provider
Yahoo! *Oath*	Research - Analytics
YouTube, LLC *Google, Inc.*	CDN Provider
ZEDO Inc. *ZEDO Inc.*	Vast Provider
ZEFR Inc. *ZEFR Inc.*	Vast Provider
b34106183_test *b34106183_test*	Ad Exchange
dbupdate1 *dbupdate1*	Ad Exchange
gemiusDirectEffect *Gemius SA*	Vast Provider
iBillboard, a.s. *Internet BillBoard a.s.*	Vast Provider
mov.ad GmbH *mov.ad GmbH*	Ad Server Advertiser
uSwitch *uSwitch Limited*	Ad Server Advertiser

Patreon

Patreon is a social media site that allows followers to "subscribe or pledge" different amounts of money to their favorite influencers. Each influencer creates several levels of support at the site ranging from 1 to as high as they wish. At each level they offer different types of rewards based on the pledge amount. These vary from creator to creator and must be tailored to the things the creator can do consistently. Some examples are private patron only live chats, t-shirts, autographs, exclusive blogs or vlogs posted for patrons to the Patreon site. Basically, just get creative and people can sign up for as little as 1 buck a month. The donations are taken monthly and sent to the influencer.

Reddit & Quora

Reddit and Quora are discussion forums where users discuss and share various types of information. What makes them different is the fact that on those sites users can both upvote information to get more views for it and ask direct questions on various topics. The answers are cataloged and can be shared with others asking those same questions. These are great places to show yourself an authority in your niche and help drive people to your blog for more information. Finally, you can advertise on both platforms using Google AdWords to drive people to your answers over others.

Social Media Strategy

Social media may appear to require a larger work schedule than you anticipated but having weighed all the economic value you get from social media; it is only fair you seriously think and work toward creating leverage on the platforms.

Create weekly or monthly schedules for your special media platforms. You have to have the end in mind. Write down smart goals and objectives. When you start, you have to have goals like, having 1000 followers weekly on each platform. Create themes for each week. With the themes in place, it is very easy to create content around your theme. Prepare images for each content. Set a specific time of day for doing uploads. It can be a morning routine. Say post on Facebook three times a week, then share a blog post weekly if you write your blogs weekly. You can decide to be doing two Instagram posts per week and one link to your blog weekly. You can then have daily twitter uploads and engage conversions there whenever possible. You can make twitter your hobby and go to place to unwind while indirectly creating an impact on your brand.

From the above, it is clear that planning is everything. You do not just wake up and rush to upload items. Then when you are lazy you stay for even a month without updating your pages. Audiences should have some anticipation that their favorite blogger is going to share a blog post every Tuesday 6 a.m. for example. You are the leader here. You set the pace. Whether or not readers keep up, you cannot afford to be the one failing them. The good thing about you being ahead is, as long as the post is up, even if your readers read and engage a week later, the job is done.

Now that you are running the same brand on different social media platforms, it is important to keep a certain sense of identity and personality around you. It is also important to keep it professional and use the same enthusiasm across all platforms. Ok, I realize you may prefer one platform to another, but you have to keep it consistently positive on all of them. This is because the Audience you will get on Facebook will not be the Audience you get on twitter, so you must appear the same on all. Basically, be open and welcoming to all followers. As well, let the ones you impress on Facebook not be disappointed when they follow you on twitter. One thing, you will have a group of followers who love you so much that they follow you everywhere. With this in mind, you need to keep your A-game anytime anywhere.

One trend that is picking up well on social media is building a following based on controversy. You ought to be careful though what you want to be controversial about. For example, you can be safe being controversial with matters of social ethics, yet put yourself on the line with political controversy. If you are in it for just likes, angry reactions do still add the count of the reactions, commentating, and going viral, but be cautious and pick your battles. Champion something important to those in your niche and try not to rattle too many cages. Let it be just social and not anything that can put you in trouble. Remember, we are blogging for fun and money. However, if you must choose something more controversial than pick a topic that most people can get behind.

A good example would be the problem of society labeling certain people as immoral yet those who engage with them to complete the process are left out of the label. You can post something like this on social media,

"The unending debate is a perfect mirrored image of what society is and perceives of power or money. Certain people have a free ticket to doing what they want, when they want, but others are demonized for it. You cannot eat your cake and have it; always being held in higher esteem and allowed to practically do as they wish, while others will be chastised for the same behavior. Such as the difference between sexual mores of men and women, or the legal system for rich vs poor, or the politician class (no matter the parties)." These are issues most people can understand and not get too ruffled over, but other than that, try to avoid controversy. Yes, it is good for social media follows, shares, and reactions, but may not be good for building a blog following.

The above illustration is an example of how to use controversy without being too controversial. By talking about things that most people can get behind you will be riding the fence to a certain extent, which will get people on your page without raging against you. People will share their own perspective and respond to you. Others will tag their friends to come and share their opinions. Such social media practices led to easy fame for many, and it can work for you if you use the right mix of information and light controversy. The primary lesson here is do something out of the ordinary and the comfort of your imagination. You have to get people talking about your blog. The goal is traffic and conversion. Do whatever you what you can, as so long as you do not slander anyone or do not commit any crime. The call here is for you to be proactive. Always be ahead of the pack. You cannot just afford to sit there waiting for other bloggers to set the pace for you. By the time they have employed a creative tactic on their blog, they have already converted the traffic to money and by the time you are copying them, the Audience is already aware of the trick. You want to get them before the practice is common knowledge.

Chapter 7: In Conclusion

Blogging is not a walk in the park, it is a job and can be a rewarding one, but it takes dedication. Please do not enter into the career with expectations of only doing a very light workload for a great living. In truth, it takes many hours of research and writing/rewriting to produce a great blog post that people will read and share. But as well, it is one among the most rewarding ventures out here. Jump in with all you have, dare yourself, and see how much you can pour into a blog and how much great information you can centralize and give to people in a concise manner. It is a system that rewards hard work, dedication, and creative endeavor. But what are some good strategies you can employ from the start to help keep your blog and the information it gives on top of your niche? This will also keep you on the top of the desired sites for advertisers and make sure people think of purchasing your product or service above all others. So, Let's wrap up by looking at some of those.

Staying on top of your niche and popular with advertisers

Growth and progress are key in every field, whether blogging or a traditional job or business. If you start on your own, as your audience grows, so will your needs and possibly theirs. The following are pointers on keeping up on top of your niche and on a good footing with your followers.

You will start to see a lot of messages from your audience that require feedback. This is a side effect of growth and being a good blogger. Remember the customer and follower is king. Keep in mind that even though you have to make a living by converting your audience into money, you know far too well that each one of them matters and you need to keep them happy. This is regardless of whether they purchase things from you or click on ads. You cannot neglect your fan base and that is the measure of your business. When they have simple demands like asking questions concerning your blog posts or having further queries, you will need to answer those question yourself or have a trusted person do it for you. When there are a lot of requests for you to supply more of what you give, such as responding to comments and emails it will cut into your normal writing and social media posting time. This is true especially if you use multiple social media platforms, in addition to your blog. The more places you are will equal more comments and inquiries that cannot and must not be ignored. Doing these tasks will inevitably detract from your normal tasks (the ones that got the blog started). You may be motivated into doing less or shorter researched posts per week, but this is not good for your blog or reputation. So, it may be time to get some help. Just like if you owned a store or cafe, you can't do everything, and a blog is not a small task. Whatever energy you put into creating a superb post to last your audience a week will also be required for daily output and interacting with followers. At this point, you will need a team of support staff or at least a contractor to help with daily tasks. The key here is to carefully choose and train someone or some people who will work to achieve the vision and mission you had in the first place. You need to multiply yourself in others, as you have an intense type of job that starts far before and goes well beyond the creation of a post or article.

You have not just a blog, but a community of peoples, across many platforms that requires your input and direction. I know, "I can't afford help", but you can use websites like Upwork or Fiverr with a multitude of freelancers that work for reasonable prices. Also, you cannot afford to let things fall behind, that will cost far more than the couple hundred dollars per month it takes to hire help. You have to develop a workspace that will churn out work that is needed, but that will not make your audience feel the shift. They have to think it is you answering them and writing your blogs, so to hire carefully is paramount. At the end of the day, the goal is to offer the same great value they come for in your blog in your daily interactions.

Your work and salary now match the many years of creativity and good writing. As the company expands, a team of creatives and general helpers will go a long way in ensuring you keep your edge in the marketplace. You will have to let go of the "I got this" attitude and learn to delegate; this is true of any business that is successful.

That said, in all you do, aim at your original goal of providing great information. Make your every effort count. Make every interaction as creative as possible to give you a good and profitable/fulfilling life. Do not waste it by either a lack of knowledge on how to monetize or for a lack of wisdom on how to navigate the bridge when you get there. The fact that you write well is only the beginning, but your ability to adapt will prove you are capable of earning much. Know that it takes work to translate talent to money. Only a few cracks the code, I think you will be among them. Rise up and take up what you deserve.

I cannot end this book without commenting on the art for art's sake person. I have a great admiration for that worldview, but it can cloud real world realities. Some people only want to blog for the love of writing, but never take into account the money and income possibilities that are available to them from their art. The challenge I pose to the purists is, what is the best way to make money other than from your hobby and passion? In the real world, these kinds of people end up winning more when they learn the art of monetization, even if making money was not their end goal. They can still honor the process of writing well and passionately, but yet get rewarded for it. This will allow them to write for longer and not have to share their time with a "day job". The fact you get paid to do what you love does not discount the art or make it less fulfilling. Quite the opposite, it allows you greater freedom to practice and excel at it. The time you get because you are taking the worry of earning a living will equal greater opportunity to study and get better at your craft. There is no honor in poverty or stretching yourself too thinly, so please let go of that adage.

In conclusion, blogging is a multi-billion industry that is largely untapped. Those already in it have barely scratched the surface. Blogging is the future for most advertising and news/information sourcing. The fact that we are seeing a global downturn in mainstream media sources and more people turning to independent media (blogging is one of these) proves that the market for advertising will continue to rise for bloggers. It is a noble call to invite people to join the profession and tell them for a fact, if they work hard and play smart that it will work out well. Their art and craft will then yield the joys of passive income for now and forever. A life spent doing what you love is the best kind of life.

Resources for Bloggers-as suggested by award-winning Blogger Raelyn Tan. You can find her at her blog

Time Management and Daily Organizing

1. <u>Evernote</u>: use it to keep screenshots of my competitor's offerings with the Evernote Web Clipper chrome extension, organize information from market research for future blog post ideas, as a notepad for the things I learn or want to remember, personal organization of my life and more.

2. <u>Momentum</u>: free chrome extension that replaces your new tab page with a personal dashboard featuring a stunning photo backdrop, the time, and your personal to-do list.

3. <u>Mindmeister</u>: Mind Mapping software to create amazing mind maps and organize your mind.

4. <u>Meistertask</u>: Great for getting things done, displays to-dos and projects in a kanban style dashboard which I find really useful.

5. <u>Trello</u>: An alternative to Meistertask.

8. <u>Google</u> Calendar: Free calendar by Google to schedule your time wisely.

9. <u>Focus Booster</u>: Based on the Pomodoro technique, focus booster will empower you to maintain focus and manage distractions.

10. <u>My Hours</u>: Helps you to keep track of where all your time is going for free.

11. <u>Unroll.me</u>: Easily unsubscribe from multiple mailing lists you are currently subscribed to and go on an email inbox detox today.

12. <u>Sidekick</u>: Sent an email to someone and wonder whether they opened it? Use sidekick and you'll now be notified when the person has opened your email.

13. <u>Dropbox</u>: Free 2gb cloud storage of your files. You can also use Dropbox to store your freebies/ pdfs/ videos and send the link to your readers to access it.

14. <u>Google Analytics</u>: If you aren't using Google Analytics to track your website stats you need to start. The best analytics tool for website owners, hands down. Get data on your website visitors. It's 100% free too! I highly recommend this.

15. <u>Sumome Heatmaps</u>: Because it's fun to see what people are clicking on at your blog.

16. <u>Statcounter</u>: Great for small blogs, as it allows you to see who has visited your website, where they've come from for each and every visitor in chronological order.

Branding, Video Creation & Visual Marketing

17. <u>Screenflow</u>: Highly recommend for every Mac user to use ScreenFlow to record your screen and edit your videos. It is very intuitive and edits videos really nicely

18. <u>Camtasia</u>: Similar to Screenflow, this is a video editing software as well, but for PC users. It is pretty pricey though.

19. <u>Logitech c920</u>: Looking professional on video is a must for me. This makes a world of difference when I'm filming video trainings or holding webinars – from dark and grainy to HD and superb quality! Bonus:

When I'm overseas my loved ones get to see me in HD.

20. **Blue Yeti Mic**: It looks super cool, and the sound quality is awesome! Great mic for entrepreneurs.

21. **Lighting Kit**: I recommend this lighting kit when filming videos so that your face isn't dark and it looks professional.

22. **Canon t3i**: My camera which I use to film all videos that do not involve me sitting by my computer.

23. **Society 6**: Coolass video tapestry backdrops that aren't as ugly as the dreaded green screen

24. **Picmonkey**: Mad love for creating beautiful graphics for free! Super simple to use too.

25. **Canva**: Allows you to create beautiful graphics for free too, has nice templates but less flexibility than Picmonkey.

26. **VSCO Cam**: An amazing free app for editing your Instagram pictures to get a uniform look for your instafeed.

27. **Adobe Photoshop**: The best tool (and unfortunately the priciest) to create graphics.

28. **PDF Escape**: Create fillable forms on your PDFs for free.

29. **Tinypng**: Compress png & jpg pictures without losing picture quality before uploading onto your blog to reduce your site speed.

30. **Dimpleart**: High-quality caricatures

Writing & Content Creation

31. **Coschedule Headline Analyzer**: Amazing headline analyzer that tells you if you've a good blog post title or not. Great for writing better headlines!

32. **Portent's Content Idea Generator & Tweak Your Biz Content Generator**: Ran out of ideas for content creation? These title generators will come up with whacky, amazing titles for your blog posts that will appeal to your audience.

33. **Grammarly:** Especially great for bloggers whose native language is not English. It finds and corrects grammatical errors, suggest better words for your articles to enhance clarity of your writing and eliminates 250 types of writing mistakes from your blog posts.

34. **Open Live Writer**: Open Live Writer is a free powerful, lightweight blog editor that allows you to create blog posts, add photos and videos then publish to your website.

35. **Getblogo**: Powerful desktop publishing tool for Mac.

36. **Transcribe**: Audio to text transcription service.

SEO & Keyword Research

37. **Google Keyword Planner**: Nothing like searching for keywords using the tool created by big G himself.

38. **Semrush**: The very best SEO tool available. Research on your competitors, do keyword research, and much more.

39. <u>Long Tail Pro</u>: Find Long-tail keywords with this software.

40. <u>Ubersuggest</u>: Google suggestion on steroids – find lots of keyword suggestions for a given keyword!

41. <u>WordPress SEO by Yoast</u>: Best SEO plugin for WordPress users.

Social Scheduling & Autoposters

42.. <u>Buffer</u>, <u>Hootsuite</u> & <u>Edgar</u>: Social scheduling tools to schedule things onto Facebook page/ groups, Twitter and more in advance.

43. <u>NextScripts: Social Networks Auto-Poster</u>: When you publish something new, this free WordPress plugin will automatically publish it onto multiple social networks.

Site Management

44. <u>Uptime Robot</u>: Monitors your website and informs you when it is down, for free.

45. <u>Filezilla</u>: My favorite FTP client that's 100% free.

46. <u>Gtmetrix</u>: Analyze your website's speed and performance and makes recommendations on how to improve it.

47. <u>Google Alerts</u>: Get alerted when your keywords/ website name is mentioned on the web.

48. <u>Updraft Plus</u>: <u>Backup your website</u>.. don't take a risk that you should not be taking.

49. <u>Google Webmaster Tools</u>: Mostly allows you to see what keywords you are ranking for, add your sitemap and to be notified on anything Google wants to tell you with regards to your website.

50. <u>PopupAlly</u>: Craft free and beautiful popups for your website.

List of the <u>top blogs</u> from 2018

What are the <u>most profitable blogs</u> thus far this year.

How to Start a Small Business:

10,000/Month Ultimate Guide - From Business Idea and Plan to Marketing and Scaling, including Funding Strategies, Legal Structure, and Administration Tip

By

Ronald Roberts

Chapter 1: The Basics of Getting Started

Many people dream of being business owners. There's an apparent allure to being your own boss, changing the lives of others while making money and charting the course of your life and fortune. Unfortunately, very few ever actualize this dream. For most, it remains a distant daydream that comes alive when the boss is being unbearable, or when the paycheck is stretched thin by what seems like a million bills. Whether you are employed or in between jobs, you can turn your life around with just a dream and a strategy. That is how most businesses start and it is definitely how many fortunes have been made.

The truth is that while many people wish they could run their own businesses, very few know where to begin. Starting a business can be exceptionally daunting, especially when there are naysayers at every corner bombarding you with stories of failure. It is even worse when you have a job which you are considering leaving to start your own business. You'll find yourself having to deal with a lot of criticism for this less-than-ideal decision. How dare you leave the comfort and stability of a regular paycheck to chase the pipe dream of entrepreneurship? If you are doubting your ability to become and thrive as an entrepreneur, it should comfort you to know that everyone has the potential to become an entrepreneur. There are over seven billion people on earth and every one of them has the ability to create something and sell it for profit. You might not succeed immediately, as many successful entrepreneurs have learned, but there is profit in commitment.

Every good entrepreneur begins their journey with a vision. Merriam-Webster dictionary defines vision as 'a thought, concept or object formed by the imagination'. As an entrepreneur, your vision has everything to do with what you hope to see your business evolve into in the long term. This vision will serve as the guiding light in your entrepreneurial journey, always reminding you of why you got started and what waits on the other side of hard work and commitment. Your vision is what you will sell to potential investors and yourself on those days when you feel like quitting. But not so fast--if a vision is powerful, a verified vision is even more so. Verifying your vision means checking to see whether the idea in your mind is something that can take off in the real world. Often times, even the most brilliant ideas are not ready for launch yet. A wise person once said that nothing can stop an idea whose time has come. As a hopeful business owner, you have to ascertain that your idea's time has come, because the goal is to be unstoppable. Research, networking, and piloting are all great ways to go about verifying your vision. You should never get started on a business until you are confident that you have used all sounding boards at your disposal and found it to be worth the investment.

So, what happens when you want to start a business but don't have a vision yet? How do you proceed from this quagmire? The process of arriving at a vision is not a one-day affair. For some lucky people, it will be a light-bulb moment where they encounter an inconvenience that they feel they can solve for everyone else, at a profit. For others, the development of a vision is a journey of many months and years. You will not be able to sit in your living room and command a vision to come to you. Sometimes, you'll be required to seek some inspiration. Entrepreneurship events, seminars led by established business persons, publications, TED Talks, and online tutorials are places you can look to for inspiration. Going about life while alert to the opportunities presented by everyday transactions and interactions is yet another way to find your vision. Trusting the process is one major ingredient of arriving at an actionable vision.

Once you are armed with a verified vision, you can proceed to look into whether you have everything else that is required when starting up a business.

Business Name and Legal Structure

If you thought choosing a name for your kid was hard, try choosing one for your business! Unlike kids, where you can name yours Madison even though there are several Madisons down the block, business names are protected by copyright laws. You cannot choose a name that is already in existence, however appropriate it seems for your business. Choosing the right business name for your company can make a whole lot of difference for your brand. A good business name should communicate the value and promise of your brand. It should be memorable and not ambiguous. It is not mandatory that your business name carries an exact description of your products or services. In fact, a seemingly non-informative name can carry your brand to success if it is followed up with a thorough and solid marketing plan. Stay away from names which are puns, as the joke might be lost on your audience. If you have a catchy phrase that you are considering as a business name or tagline, do your homework to ensure it is not offensive in particular regions. This can be especially awkward should you decide to expand into said regions. Car manufacturers know this probably better than anyone else. For instance, the Mitsubishi Pajero had to be renamed to Montero for the Spanish market so that it could be more acceptable. While the Pajero was initially named after a pampas cat (Leopardus pajeros) it turned out that the name meant something entirely different in Spanish-speaking regions.

Your business' legal structure is the other item that you should check off the list. Chapter 2 delves deep into the different legal structures and the considerations you should make before settling on one.

Business Plan

A business plan is a document that will be useful for you as a business owner, and potential investors as well. A business plan clearly articulates the direction of your business and demonstrates your knowledge in your market of operation. It is a document that will come in handy when you want to remind yourself of what is at stake and show investors what value you propose to bring to the market. If your business plan is created well, it can be leveraged to win you all the rewards you wish for as a new business owner. Chapter 1 focuses on the business plan and provides tips on how to go about creating a winning business plan for your new company.

Permits and Licenses

Most jurisdictions require business owners to obtain various permits and licenses before they can be allowed to operate a business. The specific type of permits required vary depending on the type of business you will be operating. For instance, if you wish to open a restaurant, you will be required to have a food service license, which is not necessary if you intend to open a bookstore. Generally, the permits and licenses needed for most businesses include a business license, which allows you to run a business in your particular city. You might also require a fire department license if you will have physical premises that are open to the public and an air and water pollution control permit, especially if your work involves discharge of waste materials. It is important to check with your city's council offices for a comprehensive list of permits and licenses that are mandatory for all business owners, and for your particular type of business.

Employees

If your business is relatively small, you might be able to run it as a one-person show. However, most businesses will require at least one helping hand to ensure that operations are smooth and uninterrupted. Before you open your business to the public, ensure that you have the right team on board to help you take care of day-to-day tasks. A team could be composed of permanent employees or consultants and freelancers who are available on a need basis. In the beginning of your business, you might want to outsource as much of the work as possible instead of hiring permanent employees. This way, you can cut down on start-up costs, as hiring full-time employees is likely to cost you a lot more than pushing work to a freelancer would. Either way, you'll need to know that you have people who will help you implement your company's vision. If you are selling a product that will be dispatched to customers within your city, have a delivery service or at least one delivery guy on stand-by. If you intend to engage with your customers on social media, get a social media manager on board to interact with online customers when you are up and about looking for investors. Assemble the right team early on and be clear about their roles and job descriptions. Once your company is up and running, you'll be glad that you have one less thing to worry about because someone else is worrying about it.

Business Insurance

This is not something you want to think about when starting your business, but things actually do go wrong at the most unexpected of times. If and when this happens, it helps to have insurance to cover you for any losses incurred. For a small business, general liability and property insurance are ideal. General liability insurance, sometimes referred to as business liability insurance, protects you from claims that arise from your business operations. These claims could range from bodily injury to personal injury and even property damage. If customers lodge complaints that they have suffered any harm from your products or services, you can use funds from your general liability insurance to settle the costs of the claims. On the other hand, property insurance protects you in the event that your business premises are damaged, or the contents of the premises are stolen. Property insurance includes homeowners' insurance, which means you can still insure your business property even if your company is based in your home.

Branding

Once you have gotten all your ducks in a row in terms of a business name, plan, and business permits and licenses, you should embark on creating an identity for your business. Do not just tell people about your company - show them too. A well-done logo and business website will do wonders when it comes to pushing your business out there. Hire a good designer and printer to create some professional business cards for you, that you can hand out at networking events and to potential customers. Invest in promotional material such as brochures and flyers as well. While your marketing efforts will involve a little more than printed material, it is still a good place to start as far as establishing a presence within your community is concerned.

Commitment to the Cause

This is not something that you can buy off a shelf, but it is definitely a key item to have before you start your business. Commitment can be defined as faithfulness to a cause or activity. It is the sheer dedication that will take you through the tough days before you even break even. Commitment calls for you to be loyal to your vision even when everyone else is doubting it, one year after you have set up shop. There are various ways you can use to check whether you really are committed, and therefore ready, to start your small business. These include determining what you are willing to give up to get started. If you are interested in starting a business but are still excited about the prospect of getting a paycheck from your current employer, you are probably not too committed to entrepreneurship. It does not mean that everyone must quit their job to start a business, but it is a little difficult to give one hundred percent to your new company when your employer expects the very same at work. The math just doesn't look right.

A Good Network

During the first year of business, you will be very grateful for the people you know because they will play a big role in getting you your first customer. Your network of family, friends, and colleagues is vital to marketing your business (and even getting you investors) so make sure you are building the right relationships. Keep in mind that the best time to build a relationship is when you do not need it. Many business owners make the mistake of trying to be friends with a potential investor or mentor when they desperately need them. This approach only makes the person feel used. After all, everyone is human and there needs to be some level of appreciation for the human they are and not the things they can provide. Focus on building strong, genuine relationships with the people you come across that are strong-willed and positive-minded. Take them out for lunch. Meet them for drinks after work. You will be so grateful you surrounded yourself with the right people when you start your business and start to see their input trickling in.

Chapter 2: Creating a Workable and Winning Business Plan

A business plan is one of the most important documents that you can create for your business. A business plan outlines your company's goals and objectives, and the steps you'll take to achieving these objectives. The timeframe within which these business goals must be attained is also documented. Your company's business plan will serve as your roadmap for success, detailing what needs to be done and when. This plan will also come in handy when you need to look back and evaluate whether you are on the right track. If you are in the market for a lender, a business plan will come in hand in convincing your preferred bank that your business idea is worth a business loan.

Many entrepreneurs will set off without a business plan, simply because they find the process of creating one tedious and overwhelming. It can be especially discouraging to create a business plan only for it to become outdated in the face of a dynamic business environment. The good news is that you do not have to spend months working on a business plan, however ideal and thorough this might be. If writing is not your forte, you can hire a consultant to create a business plan for you. For this to work well, you will need to do the research yourself and hand over the information to the writer. Alternatively, you can download a business plan template and customize it to suit your business idea. There are thousands of freely available online templates that are easily accessible through a simple Internet search. Whether you outsource the creation of your business plan or undertake it yourself, it is important to be mindful of the key components of a business plan. These include the executive summary, business description, product or service description, market analysis, organization and management, sales strategies, funding requirements, and financial projections.

Executive Summary

The executive summary of your business plan is your elevator pitch and summarizes all the key points of the other sections of your business plan. The executive summary should clearly communicate your value proposition to your audience. In many cases, potential investors will only look at the executive summary of your business plan before deciding whether you are worth the investment or not. For this reason, the executive summary is commonly considered the most important part of your business plan. It is recommended that you write the executive summary last after the other sections of the business plan so that these other sections can inform the content of the summary. Many executive summaries are only a page long. If your executive summary is longer than this, it is still okay as long as it does not go beyond 10% of the entire business plan. The best executive summary is one that stays below the 5% threshold. For instance, if your entire business plan is 50 pages long, an ideal executive summary would be 5% of 50 pages which comes to two and a half pages.

Business Description

While the executive summary provides a teaser of what your business is all about, the business description goes into details of your business and the business model. The business description should include details about your company's inception and the mission statement. These are vital in communicating the origins of your company, and the noble reasons behind its beginnings. Describing your business allows your audience to connect with your brand and the person behind the brand. It gives a sneak peek into your business and allows your business to tell its story.

There are several other questions that you should answer in the business description. These include:

- What is the name of your business?

- What services or products do you provide?

- Who are your target customers?

- What is your competitive advantage?

- Since when have you been in business?

- Who are the owners and decision makers of your company?

- What is your legal structure-are you a sole proprietorship, a partnership, etc.?

- Where is your business located?

Market Analysis

A market analysis is a quantitative and qualitative review of your target market. A market analysis is intended to show your potential investors that you understand your market and that this market is big enough to allow sustainable business. In order to present an in-depth market analysis, you will be required to look into the demographics, market need, customer segmentation, barriers to entry, regulations and your competition. The demographics of a market refers to the data of a population that relates to their characteristics such as race, income level, age, education, occupation, and even gender. This is important information that you'll need to find out about your target market. If you know that your target market is made up of college-educated white males in their thirties, then you can tailor your product to fit their very specific needs. Customer segmentation is the process of arranging your customer base by their demographic characteristics. This division happens so that you can correctly tailor your marketing message in a way that resonates with customers best.

Often, the investors you approach will usually have an idea of what your intended target market is like. After all, when you are an investor these are the things you are required to know. If you demonstrate that you know even more than the investor, you will stand a better chance of getting investment capital. At the same time, you want to know your market better for your own sake, so that you do not get nasty surprises along the way.

Organizational Structure and Management

In this section of the business plan, you should highlight all the qualities, skills, and expertise of your management team. In many cases, investors will be looking to see who will be on board before investing. The investors need to know that you have assembled a team that can stick it out to the bitter end and give them value for their investment. Make sure to highlight each and every relevant qualification, however unnecessary it might look to you. An investor might be drawn to put their money in a project if your chief accountant shares their passion for charitable work and fundraising. Sometimes, you really cannot tell with these investors. You just need to put your best foot forward.

If your business is going to be a sole proprietorship, use the limelight provided by this section to show why you are worthy of a second look and an investment. Talk about your educational qualifications, industry expertise, publications and anything else that would grab attention. The organizational structure and management section should not be anything other than impressive.

Marketing and Sales Strategies

So far, your business plan has managed to convince its audience of the value of your intended product or service, your understanding of the market you'll be playing in, and the human resources who will implement your vision. There's still one thing that investors will be looking to find out: the how. The sales strategy section of the business plan will delve into detailing how you intend to price your product, and how this will tie in with other company numbers.

In this section, you will be required to explain your pricing strategy and should be able to explain why you chose that particular strategy. As a business owner, there are some tried and tested pricing strategies that you can use to determine the cost of your product or service. One of these strategies is referred to as penetration pricing, which is a strategy that involves pricing your product low to attract customers in a competitive market, and then raising the price later when you've gained traction.

Value-based pricing is another pricing strategy that you can consider. Value-based pricing usually involves pricing your product by estimating how much a customer would be willing to pay for it. In short, the price of your product answers the question: how much value does a customer see in this product? If the answer is high, the price can be set as high as you wish. Value-based pricing works best when you are operating in a niche market, such as high-end fashion or when there is a shortage and customers are willing to pay higher for a product or service. Unless you are truly and positively convinced that your product or service is exclusive and highly sought after, you might want to avoid value-based pricing. At least until you have gained loyal customers.

Cost-plus pricing is a simple pricing strategy that involves adding a markup to the costs of producing one unit and then setting that as the price. Most new businesses will prefer to go for cost-plus pricing as it is simple and straightforward. Competitive pricing, on the other hand, involves looking at what your competitors are offering and setting a price that can compete in the same market. If you are about to launch a business that is offering a product that has been in the market for a long time, and that is offered by multiple outlets, you might want to try out competitive pricing.

Other than the pricing strategies, you'll also want to include information on activities that you are undertaking to promote brand awareness. You should include information on already completed, ongoing, and future activities. You will also be required to provide information on where you intend to sell your product or service, and how these will be distributed. If you are a sole proprietorship, you should include a detailed plan of how you intend to sell your product on your own. If you will be outsourcing the sales work to a marketing company or sales team, make sure to mention this. If your company will have a permanent sales team, you can reiterate this information even though you had highlighted it in the Organizational Structure and Management section.

Funding Requirements

By this point, you've told potential investors almost everything they need to know about you, your vision and passion, your product, excellent team, and sales strategy. Investors will usually know by now if you have thought through your plan and if you are worth investing in. Still, there's one piece of information you have yet to provide, and that is how much money you are asking for.

If you have ever watched the TV Show Shark Tank, you may have noticed how some entrepreneurs ask for ridiculous amounts of capital in exchange for a certain percentage of shares, without a full understanding of what informed this amount. The typical outcome is that the entrepreneur is left with a blank look of cluelessness on his face while the Sharks send him on his merry way. If only they had taken the time to understand how much capital they were asking for, and why...

The amount of money you seek as venture capital can discredit your entire business plan, especially if you are unrealistic about it. The process of correctly determining your funding requirements should be preceded by thorough math and basic accounting.

First, you'll need to have your financial numbers well laid out in a manner that shows your expected costs, the financial resources you have to cover these costs and the expected revenue that you'll be getting once you start up your business. Whatever is left after you cover costs with available investment funds and revenue is the approximate amount of funding that you require. As far as estimating revenue, you can benchmark against industry counterparts, while giving room for fluctuations and bad months.

It can sometimes be difficult to arrive at an exact figure when it comes to estimating funding requirements. In such a case, you are allowed to come up with different amounts supported by different scenarios. For instance, you can estimate that a worst-case scenario where you made zero sales within a six-month period will require $50,000 in investment capital, while a best-case scenario of constant sales will require $20,000. Having these numbers will show investors that you have considered all possibilities, which is a trait that all good business people and entrepreneurs should have. Your funding requirements section will do well to be supported by charts and graphs that can easily walk an investor through your financials across a defined timeline.

At this point, you are probably wondering, how do you determine what percentage of equity correlates to a particular amount of capital? This is where the valuation of your business comes in. You have to determine how much your business is worth. For instance, if you ask investors to give you $25,000 for a 10 percent stake, you are essentially saying your business is worth $250,000. How do you arrive at this?

Revenue is often the simplest way of estimating the worth of a company. Many business owners will value their businesses as a multiple of their revenue, with these multiples being determined by industry. Remember that revenue doesn't automatically translate to profit, so your valuation should also consider your profit margin. A business broker can help you correctly determine how much your business is worth, especially if they have dealt with similar businesses in your industry.

Financial Projections

The financial projections section is where you sell your faith and hope to the investors. At this point, you'll be telling potential investors that your business will grow by this much and that the money they invest today will be worth that much in a year's time, or two. When scrutinizing your financial projections, investors and potential partners will be looking out for revenue growth and market trends. If you have already piloted your product on a small scale, include this information in your financial projections. For instance, you may have started with a food truck and now want to open a restaurant. Talk about how much revenue you earned from the food truck, and how much you expect to earn from a restaurant that provides similar meals to an even larger population.

If you are starting fresh with a completely new business and no entrepreneurial history to draw on, you can still put together an impressive financials section. You can use information from similar-sized industry counterparts to write up your sales forecast, expenses budget, cash-flow statement, and income projections. All these are components that should be included in your financial projections. You should also include a break-even analysis in your financial projections.

A break-even analysis is an estimation of when your business will become viable, that is, able to operate on its own without requiring constant injections of cash. Break-even in business is said to occur when a business becomes profitable or is at least able to cater for its own expenses, and this happens when the revenue earned exceeds costs incurred. A break-even analysis will convince potential investors that the business they are investing in can grow and stand on its own, thus allowing them to plan their exit strategy should they choose to.

Chapter 3: Choosing a Legal Structure

The structure you choose for your business comes with some legal and tax implications. It determines the amount of control you will be able to assert in your business and what decisions you can make on your own. As such, it is important to carefully consider the various legal structures and choose the one that works best for what you wish to achieve. There are four types of business structures that owners should consider when setting up shop. These include sole proprietorship, partnership, limited liability company, and corporation. Before you settle on any one structure, it is imperative that you take into consideration the pros and cons of each. Understanding the various features of different legal structures will help you make a sound decision as far as choosing which of these features is best for your business.

Sole Proprietorship

Take a minute and think of some of the small businesses around your city or town. That restaurant owned by the guy from your high school who got a scholarship to culinary school. Your auntie's friend who sells homemade necklaces on Etsy. The local grocer. Your preferred florist. How many people own and run these businesses? Most often than not each of these businesses is owned by a sole trader.

A sole proprietorship refers to the ownership of a business by one individual. This individual is responsible for all the profits, losses and liabilities of the business, and makes all the business decisions. Sole proprietorships are favorable for small businesses as you'll only require yourself to set up shop. The downside of such a business structure is that your personal assets are not separated from business assets. As such, the liabilities you incur as a business might have a direct impact on your personal assets. You might end up losing your home if the business goes under, especially if you had borrowed money to start up the business. Sole proprietorships also have limited capital to work with, as they cannot approach investors who require a stake in the business before investing.

A sole proprietorship may be sometimes referred to as sole trader business. It is one of the oldest and most popular legal structures across the world. If you have no experience running a business before and want to get started with a simple home business, a sole proprietorship structure is a good bet. Later on, should you wish to, you can convert your sole trader business to a limited liability company or partnership.

Sole proprietorships do not pay taxes to the government as independent entities; rather, the owner pays taxes on the total personal income earned. This is referred to as pass-through taxation.

Corporation

A corporation is a business that operates as a separate entity from its owners. A corporation's operations are usually guided by the board of directors, who are elected by the shareholders. The elections are preceded by nominations, which are guided by the nominating entity. The nominating entity can be the founder of the corporation or whichever entity that controls the company. If investors have a controlling stake in the company, they can nominate members for the positions in the board of directors.

Corporations can take loans, enter into contracts, own assets, sue or get sued, hire and fire employees and even pay taxes. The shareholders in a corporation enjoy the profits and gains of the company but are not liable for any debts or obligations. Many well-known businesses such as Toyota, Coca-Cola, and Microsoft are corporations. However, there are corporations that are not formed with the intention of making a profit. These are known as non-profit corporations. The American Red Cross is an example of a non-profit corporation. The main reason why individuals will opt for a corporation is to limit the members' liability.

S-Corporation

An S-Corporation is a type of corporation which meets certain requirements that allow it to be taxed as a partnership would be. Some of the requirements to become an S corporation include:

- The number of shareholders must be 100 or less, not more

- All shareholders must be individuals, with allowances being given for tax-exempt entities such as estates and trusts

- All shareholders must be US citizens

- The corporation must have only one class of stock

S corporations are beneficial to the shareholders in that they do not pay federal taxes, which is a plus when you have just started a business. You can also easily transfer interests without incurring punitive tax consequences. Corporations which are not S corporations are usually denoted as C corporations. C corporations are the 'normal' type of corporations which are taxed as separate entities from their owners.

Partnership
If a second party is enjoined to a sole proprietorship, the legal structure changes and becomes a partnership. A partnership refers to a legal structure where two or more parties or individuals own a business. In a partnership, the parties have a stake in the responsibilities and liabilities of the business. There are three types of partnerships: general partnership, limited partnership, and limited liability partnership. As in the case of sole proprietorships, partnerships have pass-through taxation.

General Partnership
A general partnership is the most basic form of a partnership. A general partnership is seen to be formed when two or more parties come together and agree to start a business. This agreement may be oral. As good practice, there is a need to have proof of partnership such as a written agreement which may be used for future reference and/or disputes. In general partnerships, all parties involved have agency powers, which means they can legally enter into contracts on behalf of the company. All parties in a general partnership have unlimited liability. This has the implication that personal assets can be used to recover business debts, and other partners can take the fall for mistakes committed by any party that is privy to the partnership.

General partnerships are preferable to a lot of entrepreneurs because they are generally easy to form, and the paperwork required is minimal. The partners are each responsible for their own tax liabilities, and files taxes on income earned through the partnership on their personal income tax returns. General partnerships become null and void when a partner dies (if there were only two partners to begin with), when parties agree to dissolve the partnership or when the partnership achieves its intended business purpose and has to be wound up.

Limited Partnership
Limited partnerships are partnerships where one party has unlimited liability while the other party has limited liability. For a business to qualify as a limited partnership, there should be at least one of each. This means that there is a fall guy should anything go wrong. The partner with limited liability can only suffer liability that is commensurate to the level of their investment. That is, a limited partner's personal assets cannot be used to cover business losses and debts. They can only lose what they invested in the first place. The downside of a limited partnership lies squarely on the shoulders of the general partner, seeing that they could lose their personal assets if the business goes belly up.

Usually, the limited liability partners are only able to invest and do not make decisions or exercise control over the business' operations. If a partner with limited liability takes on an active role in the decisions and operations of the company, there is a likelihood of incurring general partner liability.

Limited Liability Partnership

In a limited liability partnership, all parties privy to the partnership are answerable for their own lack of due diligence and cannot take the fall for business mistakes committed by any other party. That is, all the parties in a limited liability partnership are protected against losing their assets should the business go south. In the case of a lawsuit that results in recovery of assets, only the assets registered under the partnership are affected. Partners' personal assets are protected. The parties in this type of partnership have a stake in controlling the day to day operations of the business and can leave the partnership as they wish. New partners can also be easily added to the partnership.

Professions that involve multiple partners contributing invaluable expertise usually prefer limited liability partnerships. These professions include accounting, law and medical practices.

Choosing a Business Partner
If you decide to go for a partnership structure, you might have to deal with the additional task of worrying about where to find partners. Many people who start their business as partnerships have already figured out two or three people who are ready to partner with them. If you are outside of this lucky group, you can still select an appropriate business partner along the way by understanding what makes a good partner.

The best business partners:
- Have demonstrated skills and experience that adds value to your company

- Understand and share in your vision and commitment to succeed

- Can offer credibility and resources to your brand

- Are financially stable and not doing through financial crises, regardless of whether they are providing financial investment or not

- Are respectful people who practice good business and personal ethics

Limited Liability Company
A limited liability company is a cross between a corporation and a partnership, in that the tax obligations are pass-through as in the case of a partnership, and it has limited liability as corporations do. What this means in simple terms is that if you set up your business to be a limited liability company, you will declare taxes on the company's income on your personal returns. However, in the unfortunate event that the company has debts and liabilities that it cannot honor, you will not be personally liable for them. That is, you cannot lose your personal property because of your business' collapse. The owners of a limited liability company are referred to as members and can be individuals, corporations or even other limited liability companies.

What to Consider When Choosing a Legal Structure
The legal structure you choose for your business will have a direct impact on the control you can exercise over your business, payment of taxes and level of liability you incur as a business owner. There are certain factors that you should take into consideration when selecting a legal structure for your business. It is your prerogative to determine how important each of the factors are to you and then choose a structure accordingly. Often, it will take a careful compromise of two or more factors to arrive at the structure that best fits your circumstances.

Capital
Sometimes, you'll have a brilliant business idea but not enough capital. In such instances, you might require some people to chip in some capital, in exchange for some stake in your new company. Partnerships are ideal when you need trusted partners who can contribute to the required start-up capital. If you have enough

money to start your company without seeking alternative funding, you can comfortably opt for a sole proprietorship.

Control

When starting your business, you'll need to determine how much control you wish to exercise in regard to the business decisions and day-to-day operations. If your business is set up as a sole proprietorship, you can call all the shots. If you are in a partnership, you will be required to consult with other partners before making a decision that affects the outcome of the company. Ultimately, the structure you choose for your business will impact the type and level of ownership and control that you will have over the matters of the company.

Complexity

Another consideration you will have to make is the complexity and cost of setting up shop under your preferred legal structure. In the case of a sole proprietorship, most jurisdictions have a pretty straightforward process that typically involves registering a business name and associated accounts. For other structures, the process might be a little more complicated, involving complex reporting processes and structures. When choosing a structure for your first business, it is best to avoid structures with complex requirements if a simpler structure can serve the same purpose.

Continuity

Some entrepreneurs will start companies that are intended to run for a specific amount of time, after which they will be terminated. In such instances, the entrepreneur might want to start with a simple legal structure such as a sole proprietorship. Such a structure will allow for easy and swift dissolution of a company when it has fulfilled its objectives. If you are looking to start a company that can survive and thrive beyond a certain time period, you might want to opt for a structure that supports continuity, even outside of you as a founder. This way, you can be sure that should you meet some unfortunate fate such as being incapacitated, the company will continue, and you will still benefit from it even in your absence.

Limitation of Liability

Starting a business can be scary, especially when your assets are on the line. It can be frightening to think that one wrong move in your company might cost you your entire life's worth of assets and savings. Different types of business carry with them different levels of risks and liability. If you are venturing into what you would consider risky business, you might want to choose a structure that protects you from personal liability. This way, you can distribute your risk and protect your personal assets should your company incur debts and losses.

Tax Implications

Different business structures have different tax implications. For instance, a sole proprietorship is not considered a taxable entity as the business and the owner is the same. As such, in a sole proprietorship, all income is aggregated, and the appropriate tax charged on you and your business' income as the same entity. This is also the same case with partnerships. In the case of a corporation, you will be required to pay taxes on the income earned by the corporation and pay taxes as an individual citizen as well. This is a consideration to be made before you choose a legal structure.

Chapter 4: Getting Funding for Your Business

As a hopeful business owner, you might have all the brilliant ideas yet find yourself missing one key ingredient: money. Start-up capital is a headache for many entrepreneurs, especially since not many people have loads of cash lying around waiting to be invested. Raising the right amount of seed money for your business can mean the difference between a flop that refuses to take off and a successful venture that stands the test of time. There are different approaches that can be taken when it comes to obtaining funding for your business. Some of these approaches will require collaboration with like-minded individuals who have the money and who believe in your vision. This chapter dives into the various ways you can raise cash to start and grow your small business.

Personal Investment

When starting your business, your first investor should be yourself. It is only after you have committed some of your money and/or assets to your business that you can ask others to do so. Personal investment can be made in the form of cash that you have at hand that you had put away for the specific reason of starting your business. Personal investment can also involve putting up your assets as collateral. In some instances, you might have to use some of your savings to kick start your business. It is vital to be careful when it comes to personal investment as you do not want to use up all your savings or assets, as you still need these to go about your everyday personal obligations.

Love Money

If you are lucky, you are surrounded by loved ones who believe in your vision and ability to thrive as an entrepreneur. If this is the case, you can borrow money from your friends and family to start your business. The start-up capital obtained this way is referred to as love money. The terms of credit for love money usually differ, based on the relationship at hand. In many cases, the loved ones will agree to wait to be repaid if and when the business starts making substantial profits. In other cases, love money is given as a gift with no expectation of repayment. When starting a small business, love money is an ideal source of capital as it carries a low risk.

Crowdfunding

Crowdfunding is a term that refers to the practice of raising money for a project by having a large number of people contribute small amounts of money, usually through online crowdfunding platforms. To get started on crowdfunding for your business, you'll need to sign up on a crowdfunding platform, set up a profile for your business or project, set a goal and then publish your request. When it comes to crowdfunding for a business, you'll need to incentivize your contributors with certain rewards. Unlike in crowdfunding for charitable causes where parties give out of the generosity of their hearts, crowdfunding for business requires you to outline what's in it for your contributors. After all, you are asking for their money to start a profitable business. The least they can expect is some sort of reward or payback. As such, entrepreneurs have embraced two common types of crowdfunding: rewards-based and equity-based crowdfunding.

Rewards-based Crowdfunding

As the name suggests, this type of crowdfunding involves donors giving money with the expectation that they will receive a product or service that is commensurate with the value of their donation. Usually, the hopeful business owner will determine the different rewards tiers based on the donation amounts. A $5 donation, for instance, might attract the reward of a hand-written thank you card, while a $500 might grant the donor early access to the product being developed. Rewards-based crowdfunding is a great way to obtain financing for your business idea without being tied down by credit or commitments, as your obligations to the donors are terminated once you ship and deliver the rewards.

Equity-based Crowdfunding

Equity-based crowdfunding involves receiving contributions from donors in exchange for shares in your company. This type of crowdfunding is ideal for businesses that have a solid growth plan, that can afford to bring on board one or more reputable investors. Equity-based crowdfunding usually attracts larger investors, as it's unlikely you'll get any shares for a $5 donation.

Crowdfunding for your business is the right combination of obtaining funds for your business idea while also generating publicity around your company's launch. Crowdfunding is also a great way to build that initial community around your product or service, which you can tap into for subsequent products or services and the growth of your company. On the downside, crowdfunding can be time-consuming and energy-zapping, especially when you fail to meet your goal. In some cases, you will not have access to the funds donated if you do not reach your goal. Also, posting your business ideas online pre-launch and declaring your financials for the world to see can be uncomfortable and even detrimental for some entrepreneurs.

Credit Facilities/Bank Loans

Bank loans are yet another way of obtaining funding for your business idea. Business loans are a form of debt financing. Debt financing is a term that refers to any type of funding where you owe the lender, in that you have incurred a debt with the lender by accepting their money which you'll repay later with interest accrued. Business loans have existed since time immemorial and works in pretty much the same way that loans for individuals work. Typically, a lender will advance you a certain amount of money, which you'll be required to pay back with interest over an agreed period. The simplest business loan structure takes that form, with you as the business owner being expected to make regular payments, failure to which you will be considered to be in default. Business loans may also take other forms depending on the situation at hand. For instance, you might take an equipment loan to purchase equipment for your business. In such a case, the equipment acts as the collateral for the loan. If you are unable to pay back the money loaned to you, the bank may recover their funds by auctioning your equipment. Invoice financing is yet another form of a business loan. This is something you'll probably deal with once you have set up your business and amassed enough regular customers. Invoice financing involves getting a loan against your outstanding invoice amounts. Invoice financing enables business owners to access the monies held up in unpaid invoices, with the promise to repay the lender once the customers fulfill their payments.

As a budding entrepreneur, you'll probably only need a standard term-loan to boost your start-up capital. Getting your ducks in a row is crucial if you hope to impress your bank enough to give you a loan. One of the main things you'll need to do before applying for a business loan is to accurately, and to the best of your ability, determine the start-up costs of your business. It is unlikely that you'll get a loan to finance all your start-up costs, so you must be certain what specific part of the start-up you'll be using the bank loan for.

Your bank will not just take your word for it, so you must prepare all the necessary documentation to convince your lender that you and your business are worth the risk. The documentation you'll need to put together include registration details, your credit score, your business plan and any other information that may be requested by your specific lender. Make sure you get everything in order before finally submitting your application. Typically, your bank will require you to make a case in person, during which you should put your best foot forward when pitching why you believe you qualify for a loan.

Bank loans are a great way to access substantial amounts of start-up capital without letting go of any equity. When repaid on time, bank loans help build up your credit score, which is advantageous when you need to borrow higher amounts later on to expand your company.

Venture Capital

In the simplest terms, a venture capitalist is a very wealthy individual who has the money to invest in promising start-ups. In actuality, venture capital can be given by these wealthy individuals or investments banks and other financing institutions. Venture capital is a form of private equity and involves giving away some ownership of your company in exchange for funding. Venture capitalists are usually very choosy when it comes to giving away capital, and you'll need to demonstrate that you are worth the investment. Often, venture capitalists will prefer tech startups as this is one area that has constantly demonstrated a sustainable market and room for exponential growth. That being said, you can still get funding from venture capitalists if you speak their language. Speaking their language, in this case, means understanding what they look at, and packaging your value proposition to speak to this.

One of the things that venture capitalists look out for is an excellent and experienced management team that can deliver returns on their investment. This is why it is critical to include your experience and expertise in the business plan, as mentioned in Chapter 2. You need to give the investors the confidence that their money is in good hands.

The other thing that investors who provide venture capital consider before handing over their money is the size of the market. If your product is targeting a large market that can generate sales to the tune of millions, investors will get excited about partnering with you. Investors are drawn by the probability that your product will grow and conquer a huge market share, translating into big returns and a powerful market position. If you are targeting a small niche market with minimal opportunity, you will find it harder to get venture capital.

Lastly, investors also look out for your product's competitive edge. If you want investors to fall over themselves in a bid to provide you with funding, you have to really think outside the box as far as designing your product. Your product must be unique and solve a problem in society. It has to be something customers need and haven't been able to get before, and whose competitive edge is long-lasting such that it will not be overtaken in a few years.

Angel Investors

An angel investor is an individual who provides you with capital for your start-up business, in exchange for some ownership of the company. Angel investors are often among the entrepreneur's network of friends and family and will give the capital because they trust the entrepreneur and not necessarily because they have scrutinized the business plan. The origin of the word angel investors can be traced back to Broadway theater when wealthy individuals supported theatrical productions in the form of cash donations. Sometimes, angel investors are also known as seed investors, business angels or private investors.

It can be confusing for a first-time entrepreneur to distinguish between an angel investor and venture capitalist. As mentioned before, an angel investor will often invest based on the relationship that they have with an entrepreneur while venture capitalists go into the details of the product, the business model and the potential returns.

An angel investor often works alone, while venture capitalists are part of companies referred to as venture capital firms. Venture capital firms have various ways of sourcing for capital including from pension funds, corporations and the individuals themselves. The investors constitute the limited partners of a venture capital firm, while the general partners will usually work closely with entrepreneurs and ensure the funds are being utilized profitably.

Another key difference between angel investors and venture capitalists is the amount of funding they can afford to give. Because investors have pooled their resources in a firm, venture capitalists can provide capital to the tune of $7 million plus. Angel investors, on the other hand, will do a modest $25,000 to $100,000 depending on the company and entrepreneur.

An angel investor will often give you money and then retreat the shadows where they can wait for you to sell your product and give them their returns. Venture capitalists provide funding and then stay on to ensure that your product is successful in the market. Venture capitalists will often take on active roles in establishing your company's strategy, recruiting for senior positions and advising the CEOs of the company (that is, you). Venture capitalists are obligated to provide this all-important handholding, while angel investors will do so only if they want to.

Lastly, angel investors invest in a company that is in its early stages, while venture capitalists will jump in at any stage of the company as long as the company demonstrates a potential for growth.

Grants

When you are struggling to get funding for your small business, free money is music to your ears. That is exactly what grants are: free money. In a perfect world, you would start your business with grant money only, since you will never have to pay it back. Unfortunately, the real world operates a little more differently. You might have to supplement grants with another source of capital.

Grants are often provided by the government and other non-governmental organizations and will often require you to meet certain criteria before you can be deemed eligible. Usually, the process of applying for a grant can be tedious and marred by bureaucracy, which is a factor that discourages entrepreneurs. Another reason why many business owners will not rush for grants is that there are often strict rules regarding what you can use the money for. For instance, a foundation might specify that the money given to you can only be used to fund research on how to develop an environmentally friendly product. This means that you will not be able to buy equipment with this money, however much of a priority that is.

The best way to find out which grants are available for your small business idea is to conduct a simple online search.

Chapter 5: Marketing your Business Effectively

A brilliant business that is not well-marketed is akin to a beautiful woman smiling in the dark - nobody will take notice. Regardless of how well-thought out your product or service is you will not reach your intended market unless you execute a flawless marketing strategy. If you are just starting your first business, you might find the creation of a marketing strategy overwhelming. On top of this, you'll also have to create a marketing plan that is informed by the strategy. If you fall short of the skills or time required to create a marketing strategy and plan, you can outsource this work to a consultant. The consultant will then create for you a marketing strategy that contains your value proposition, target customer information, and ways of turning this target customer into actual clients. The strategy will also outline your company's thematic marketing messages. The marketing plan goes into the details of how the marketing strategy will be executed, including outlining key marketing activities against timelines.

A robust marketing strategy will take your company places as far as increased visibility in an increasingly saturated market. That being said, there are other ways you can involve yourself in marketing your business. These ways are easy to execute on your own and do not require you to have a big marketing budget. As an entrepreneur, you will need to internalize these simple means of marketing your business to the point where they become second nature. Doing so will allow you to naturally plug in your business in everyday situations and conversations.

Create a Powerful Elevator Pitch

In the world of business, there's a phenomenon known as an elevator pitch. You will probably have heard it before in corporate and business environments. As a business owner, it will be one of your most powerful conversation tools. An elevator pitch is a crisp and concise description of a concept in a way that succinctly conveys relevant information to a listener. An elevator pitch is a sales pitch that knows what it wants. It is called this because it should be brief enough to be delivered during an elevator ride, which typically averages just under two minutes. In short, when creating an elevator pitch, you should ensure you keep your talking to under two minutes.

There are three components that combine to make a powerful elevator pitch. The first component is the stimulation of interest. At the very beginning, you have to present yourself in a way that communicates that you are offering something of great value in exchange for a few your audience's resources. There is a trick used by successful salespeople that is sometimes referred to as the 100/20 Rule. The 100/20 Rule is based on the premise that for a customer to be willing to give you their $20, you have to be providing more than that, maybe even $100. As such, your elevator pitch should clearly communicate that you are providing a lot of value and asking only for a small investment from your customer. In order to communicate this effectively, you have to believe it first.

The second component of a powerful elevator pitch is the transition. Now that you have your audience's attention, you have to address a specific need that your audience has, and a problem that the will continue to have if they do not take you up on your offer. The idea is not to shock your potential customers into committing their cash to your product or service. The idea is to push the customers towards an a-ha moment where they actually begin to think of how simpler, easier or better their lives would be should they choose your product or service. At this point in your elevator pitch, you might be tempted to over-promise with the intention of hooking the customer. This is not only unethical but disadvantageous to your brand as well. You should always tell the truth as far as what you can deliver is concerned. If you thought through your value proposition and mission statement well, there will be no need to stretch the truth.

Lastly, the third component of your elevator pitch will be the sharing of a vision. Let potential investors and partners understand what your long-term vision for your company is, what value they will be getting in the present and in future and what you need from them to actualize this value and vision. In sharing your vision, keep the 100/20 rule in mind. You want to ensure that what you are asking of them to make your vision come true is way less than what they stand to gain from your vision coming true.

Do not close your elevator pitch on an ambiguous note. You'll need to ensure that you get feedback on your pitch straight away. Ask your audience whether they have any objections regarding moving forward with you. If the answer is no, then you have another win under your belt. If the answer is yes, ask why they object to a partnership. The answer will help you polish up your pitch for the next opportunity. Whatever the outcome, remember that most people do not excel in their very first sales pitch. Practice makes perfect, and the more you work on your pitch and your product, the easier it will be to get buy-in from investors and customers.

Leverage the Power of Social Media

Social media is a powerful marketing tool that you can use to reach a wide audience across the world. As at the end of 2018, there were over three billion social media users in the world. Facebook alone has one billion active users every day. Social media presents a massive opportunity for anyone who is looking to tell the world about their new company. The best thing about social media is that it is free to use. To get people talking about your new company on social media, create a presence by developing shareable content and availing this on your social media pages. Content can be in the form of the written word or short, informative videos that viewers can easily get through. At the very beginning, you might want to stick to sharing snippets of your new company with your friends and followers. Later on, you might want to implement a full-on social media marketing campaign. A social media marketing campaign could be as simple as setting aside some cash for Facebook ads, or as complicated as getting a fully-fledged social media marketing team on board.

Even if you are not social media savvy, you can run a simple marketing campaign on Facebook by signing up for their paid advertisements. A Facebook ad allows you to define your target audience and the intended outcome of your advertisement. You will also have the freedom to set a budget, which starts from as low as $8 for one thousand impressions. What this means is that you can pay as low as $8 for your brand to be shown to one thousand potential customers. If you refine your target criteria accurately, you can make quite the impression within your region of operation without requiring a big advertising budget. Instagram ads work in pretty much the same way and are another area you should explore in as far as leveraging social media.

You can undertake your social media campaign directly or use established personalities to push your product or service. These personalities who can influence potential customers to choose your brand are known as influencers. Micro-influencers, or influencers with follower numbers of between 2,000 and 50,000, are ideal for smaller businesses. A micro influencer can talk to their followers about your product and convince them to buy from you. Most influencers will prefer to be paid in cash, but many of them will still accept freebies in exchange for some bit of publicity. When picking an influencer, make sure to go for someone who speaks the language of your target audience. This means that the influencer should be relatable and possibly someone who has struggled with the problem that you are looking to solve with your product or solution.

Create a Mailing List

When you start your business, the first contact you make with a customer is highly critical. For starters, your product or service should be top notch and your customer service should be exemplary. This will convince them that there is value for money in your company, and possibly keep them coming back for me. A second thing that must happen when you meet that customer for the first time is to get their contact information. Never let a customer leave without sharing their email information or phone number, especially if they are happy with your product or service. This does not mean that you'll accost your walk-in customers and demand that they leave their personal information. Create a simple customer satisfaction form, and include a section for contact information. Collate this contact information and create a mailing list. This mailing list will come in handy when you need to communicate the release of new products, upgrades, or any relevant information that your customers need to know. A website will make it even easier to get your customer's email addresses. Keep in mind though that sending through email blasts every other minute will annoy your customers. As such, make it short, sweet and regular, without being suffocating.

Give Freebies

Everybody loves freebies; well, most people do. Once you launch your company, you might want to start by giving freebies to potential customers. Freebies allow people to experience a product and determine whether it is worth spending money on. Giving away a product you invested in for free might not sound very appealing to an entrepreneur, but remember you have to spend money to make money. A sample or a free trial will go a long way in building your brand's credibility among potential customers. Once the customer is hooked on the free trial since it has made their life that much easier, they will more likely be interested in a paid version. A person that hasn't interacted with the product at all might be more skeptical when it comes to paying for a product.

When it comes to freebies, you'll want to be moderate about how much you give away as you do not want to deplete your entire stock. You might set a grace period during which customers can get your product or service for free. You could even say that a certain product has a 50% discount if it is purchased within a particular period. Such simple tactics will get people talking about your product, and this is a marketing strategy that anyone can execute on a relatively low budget.

Word of Mouth

The Internet has made it possible to interact with people without leaving your house, but it will never replace a genuine and heartfelt face-to-face conversation. As a business owner, your days of lounging inside your house for hours on end will come to an end. You will have to get out there, network, shake a hand here and there, and get to know some people. The impression you make on people on a personal level can make a big difference in getting your brand known. Find platforms and opportunities that allow you to network with the right people and make use of these. Volunteer, sponsor your local Little League team, attend charity events, sign up for that half marathon and be active in community forums. You meet people when you leave the house, and some of these people will end up becoming your investors and partners. Keep your elevator pitch on standby when you attend these events. Tweak it based on the audience and circumstances and deliver it naturally and convincingly.

Tips for Creating a Winning Marketing Strategy and an Executable Marketing Plan

As mentioned earlier in this chapter, you will need to come up with a marketing strategy that will be supported by one or more marketing plans. Not all strategies are created alike, and this explains why some will fail while others go on to succeed. A brilliant marketing strategy can take your brand from obscurity to national and even international popularity. There are several things that you should keep in mind when coming up with a marketing strategy for your business, and these are discussed below.

Know Your Customer

Understanding your customer is the first step towards ensuring your marketing efforts are focused on the right individuals. The best way to go about knowing your customer is to build a buyer persona. A buyer persona is a representation of what your ideal customer might look like. To create an accurate buyer persona, you will need to rely on market research and data gathered from your customers. Armed with your whiteboard and marker, note down where your ideal customer would live, how old they would be, what level of education they would have and even what their personal interests are. You might also want to take a stab at their job title, annual income, relationship status, and their buying motivation.

When you have a persona that includes all the important characteristics of your customer, verify its accuracy by speaking to your customer. A five-minute interview will help you to verify your persona against real, buying customers. Many people do not like to spend time on websites answering interview questions, so you have to make it worth your customers' while. A simple way of doing this is giving a discount on purchases for every interview completed. Once you know who your customer is and what they like and don't care for you can move on to the next step of building your marketing strategy.

Research your Competition

However unique you think your value proposition is, you should never ignore your competition. There is always something to be learned by looking over the fence. It could be that your competitors have figured out something that you are struggling with. It could also be that they have made some terrible mistakes that you can learn from. Whatever the case may be, always remember that there is a lot to learn from looking around you.

Now, when it comes to researching the competition, you'll need to do a little bit of sleuthing. No competitor will open themselves up for scrutiny, unless inadvertently. As such, you'll have to know where to look if you want more information than a Facebook business page can provide. Some of the tools that will come in handy when researching your competition include Mention, Moz's Open Site Explorer, Alexa, and QuickSprout Website Analyzer. These tools are essentially spy tools that can help you understand what customers are saying online about your competitors, what your competitors are struggling with and the missed opportunities that you can take advantage of.

Choose Your Preferred Channels

The channels you choose to market your message could mean the difference between turning your audience into customers or losing the entire message mid-delivery. Tempting as it might be, you should not try out all channels with the hope that at least one of them works. Marketing should not be a gamble. It should be an informed effort that chooses the best fit. The best way to go about organizing your preferred channels is to understand what channels are out there to choose from.

There are three broad categories of channels which are at your business' disposal. These include owned, earned, and paid media. Owned media refers to the channels that you have full control over. These may be your website or even your branded material. Ideally, you should have at least two owned channels. This way, you have an in-house platform that is fully yours to use as you please.

Earned media refers to the publicity and exposure that you get from your online and offline activities. If people are talking about your brand because of content that you have written and shared online, this is an example of earned media. Guest posting is yet another form of earned media.

Lastly, there is paid media, which refers to any media channel that you pay for. Paid media is a way of letting people know about your owned media, and to boost exposure for your earned media. Examples of paid media include Google AdWords, sponsored ads, and even radio commercials. The best way to approach paid media is by setting a budget and trying out different platforms with an objective of determining what platform works best.

Understand your Sales Funnel

A sales funnel, also known as a sales process, is the journey your customer goes through before they purchase your product or service. A very basic sales funnel has four steps. These are awareness, interest, desire, and action, sometimes abbreviated as AIDA. Creating a sales funnel is important as it allows you to determine what needs to be done under every step, what hasn't been getting done and what could be done better. You will be required to find out ways of making customer aware of your brand, how to generate interest and desire, and lastly how to get them to make a purchase.

Once you have all this information figured out, you will have a marketing strategy that you can flesh out with any further details that you seem fit. Remember also to have SMART (**S**pecific, **M**easurable, **A**ctionable, **R**elevant, **T**ime-bound) marketing goals that will allow you to measure how well your marketing strategy and plan are doing.

Chapter 6: Effective Administration Tips for Small Businesses

Most business owners would rather not deal with the administrative tasks of running their organizations. Entrepreneurs flourish when they are making business decisions, winning customers and growing sales. They would prefer to never deal with the clerical duties of a business. The bad news is that the administration of your business is well within your mandate as a business owner. The good news is that you can always hire someone else to do the seemingly mundane tasks for you, so you can focus on your priorities. When it comes to the administration of a business, there are several dockets that stand out as requiring prioritization. These dockets include bookkeeping, budgeting, cash flow management, and tax preparation.

Bookkeeping

Bookkeeping is an accounting term that refers to the process of creating and maintaining records of the financial transactions of an organization. In accounting, a book is a record of all the financial positions of a trader and is the inspiration behind the term bookkeeping. You should never compromise when it comes to keeping accurate records of your financial transactions. For starters, the law requires that you keep such records. Secondly, you need up-to-date records of your financial affairs so that you can always be appraised on the state of your business' finances. Bookkeeping helps you to know when you are in the red and when you are in the clear. Maintaining proper financial records comes in handy during budgeting and tax preparation. It also informs financial analysis which can give you insights regarding your company's financial performance. With updated records, you can field questions from investors and give a proper view of your current standing. Bookkeeping also informs your financial management; you will know how much you spent and whether you can cut back on spending, and how much you are owed and when to expect it. At a very fundamental level, bookkeeping is essential for your peace of mind as you will have a clear view of your finances all the time.

Many people get confused when it comes to distinguishing between a bookkeeper and an accountant. The key distinction is that a bookkeeper maintains records, while an accountant interprets and analyzes these records. An accountant's work is informed by the information that the bookkeeper has recorded. From this information, an accountant may prepare financial statements, perform audits and even create reports for tax purposes.

As a business owner, having a bookkeeper is ideal as it takes off the work from your mostly full plate. However, you might not be able to afford one immediately. If this is the case, you can enlist the use of tried and tested software to ease your workload. Some of the software you can look into for your small business bookkeeping and other accounting needs include Wave, GoDaddy Bookkeeping, QuickBooks Online, Zoho Books, FreshBooks, and Xero. The monthly cost for these software ranges from $5 a month, an amount that is well within the budget of a small business. What's more, this software is available on mobile as well, which means you have a real-time view of your financial data while on the move. You can make good use of your daily commute to update your numbers on your mobile and make any necessary changes. As invoices get paid and income streams in, you will be able to observe deficits turning into surpluses without ever needing to log onto a laptop, unless you want to.

With all financial data kept up to date, it will be relatively easy to create financial statements on your own. If you do not have confidence in your accounting abilities, there are tools to assist in this area as well. One of these tools is something that you'll probably use many times over in the course of your business' lifetime, and that is Microsoft Excel. Microsoft Excel allows you to create financial statements with minimal hassle. To create a financial statement on Excel, open the application, click on new document and choose from the templates available on there. If you do not see what you are looking for, try using the search bar to access thousands of online templates. This is as simple as it gets.

As your business grows and your numbers become more robust, you might need additional reinforcement. NetSuite ERP and Sage Intacct are two tools that thriving business can invest in to make their accounting tasks easier. In the first year of business, accounting software and the occasional freelance bookkeeper should keep your books in good shape. As your business grows, you might want to hire the services of an accountant regularly. Accountants especially come in handy during tax preparation when you have to file your returns.

Budgeting

Budgeting is yet another administrative task that you'll need to worry about as a business owner. A budget is a useful tool that comes in handy in business and in personal life too. In the simplest terms, a budget is an estimation of income versus expenditure over a period of time. There are several approaches to budgeting that a small business can adopt. When you are getting started out without much historical data to count on, zero-based budgeting will likely be the method you prefer. As the name suggests, a zero-based budget starts with a completely new slate with no figures being carried over from the previous budget period. If you opt for a zero-based approach, you have to be able to justify the expenses that you include in your budget. In the absence of company historical data, you may benchmark with industry counterparts for estimates.

The other approach to budgeting is known as value proposition budgeting. Value proposition budgeting involves the inclusion of budget items that are justifiably supported by demonstrated value. This approach involves mainly having a mindset that enables you to weed out anything that is not value-adding to the business. If you include the purchase of particular equipment in the budget, you must support this choice with quantifiable value in as far as showing how the equipment will be useful to the business.

Incremental budgeting is a budgeting technique that is preferred by businesses and companies that have been in business for a while. This type of approach involves using the previous year's actual figures and adding a percentage to estimate the current year's budget. This form of approach is easily understood and is a popular choice in many organizations. The downside of this budgeting approach is that it can easily perpetuate inefficiencies in that is it automatically expected that certain costs will steadily grow every year even though these can be managed otherwise. In the case of companies that have multiple managers, incremental budgeting may promote laxity in the sense that managers feel entitled to have bigger spending budgets regardless of their previous performance.

Activity-based budgeting is the other approach that you can use to come up with a budget for your small business. In this approach, you'll start by defining the final desired output and the activities you'll need to undertake to achieve this outcome. For instance, you might be looking to have a sales campaign to advertise your product or service. In this case, you'll come up with a marketing budget that contains all the activities that you'll need to undertake to successfully complete a sales campaign. These could include brand activation events, event sponsorships, and placement of ads on television and radio. After coming up with a comprehensive list of activities required, you'll then estimate the costs of each activity. The final output from this budgeting process will be an activity-based budget.

Whichever way you choose to go about your budgeting process, the end goal will be to come up with a reliable estimation of your income and expenses within the budget period. When starting your business, it is best to create your own budget yourself, so that you get acquainted with the numbers that will form the basis of your finances. Later on, as your business grows you can mandate your various department heads, if any, to create their own budgets subject to your approval.

Cash Flow Management

Cash flow is an accounting term that is used to refer to the movement of money in and out of an organization or business. Cash flow management is the process of keeping tabs on this movement. As a small business owner, cash flow management is a crucial part of ensuring your business stays afloat. Managing your cash flow helps you know how much money your business has in the present moment, and how much you can expect to have in future. This will enable you to determine whether you will be in a position to honor your financial obligations. You must ensure that there are no prolonged gaps between cash out and cash in because this might result in cash shortages. When you have cash shortages, you will be unable to pay your bills, staff and even suppliers.

The very first step in cash flow management is having an accurate view of your cash flow. The accounting software mentioned in the bookkeeping section of this chapter will come in handy as far as keeping tabs on your cash flow. You can easily analyze and run reports on your cash position. Armed with these reports and analyses, you can embark on applying strategies that will improve your cash flow. One of these strategies is shortening your cash conversion cycle. Cash conversion cycle is the period of time it takes for the investments in your business to turn into cash from sales. In simple terms, the cash conversion cycle looks at how much time a dollar invested in a business takes to move through the production and sales process before it becomes a dollar plus profit. If you have a lengthy conversion period, it might mean that your operations are not efficient and you are taking too long to deliver value, and thus taking too long to get paid. It could also mean that you have a credit period that is not reasonable for your type of business.

A strategic approach to solving your cash flow problems if your best bet if you are looking for a long-term solution. In some cases, however, you might find yourself facing cash flow problems that require immediate solutions. When this happens, many businesses will resort to short-term credit. Credit gives business owners some bit of reprieve in that they have cash to meet their immediate financial needs, while they wait for what is owed to them to be paid up.

As a business owner, you should not delegate cash flow management to third parties. While an accountant can be hired to prepare reports and financial statements for you, it is best to tackle cash flow problems head on. You are the best person to make the financial decisions for your business.

Tax Preparation

Most people are not fond of taxes, and for good reason. For starters, taxes are mostly expensive. You'd have a lot more on your paycheck if you did not pay taxes. Secondly, on top of paying tax, you are expected to later on file returns to reinforce the fact that you have been paying taxes. It is almost like adding salt to injury. As if that is not enough, every once in a while, a new tax bill is introduced that throws the spanner into the works. As a new business owner who is used to handling only their personal tax matters, it is easy to become overwhelmed by your business' tax requirements.

Understanding your business' tax obligations is the very first step towards getting some clarity on tax preparation. First things first, there are different types of taxes depending on the industry you are in, the jurisdiction (federal, state and local taxes) and the type of legal structure you operate under. It is critical to be clear on what taxes you are required to pay before you even start your business, and you should also be aware of how your tax obligations change as your business evolves.

For starters, all businesses must pay income tax, regardless of their size. Income tax is tax that is levied on the profit your business makes. If you have a sole proprietorship, you'll pay your income tax through your personal returns. This type of arrangement is referred to as pass-through tax and also applies in the case of partnerships.

Sales tax is the other type of tax that you'll be required to pay to the government if you are in business. Sales tax is quite simply, tax on money made from the sale of products and services. Sales tax is usually charged to the end user. In the case of your business, this will be your customer. Many products move through several stages and players of the supply chain before making it to the end user. In such instances, players in this supply chain are required to obtain documentation showing that they are not end-users, but resellers. The final reseller ultimately passes this to the customer, who will pay a price for the product or service that is inclusive of the sales tax. You will usually be required to pay the sales tax collected quarterly or monthly, depending on the state you are located in. Payment of sales tax must be supported by a report on all sales made, including the sales that were taxable and exempt.

If you are lucky enough to own property on top of owning a small business, you must pay property tax to your local authority. This is usually the city or town council that has jurisdiction over your property's location. Other taxes that your small business might be expected to pay include excise tax, sometimes referred to as excise duty, which is levied on items such as fuel and transportation. If you have employees, you will be required to pay employment or payroll taxes as well.

When it comes to tax preparation, you cannot afford to gamble with your business's future. It is best to consult a tax professional for a thorough breakdown of your tax obligation and for assistance in the filing of returns. Once you get the hang of it, you can file your business' taxes on your own. Before then, it is best to err on the side of caution. The last thing you require when running a small business is run-ins with the law, and the penalties imposed by the Internal Revenue Service are not exactly friendly; especially not when you are operating on tight budgets in the first place.

Chapter 7: Why Small Businesses Fail in the First Year

There is no running away from the fact that not all small business started thriving and become successful ventures that their owners can be proud of. Early on while researching the feasibility of your business idea, you might come across statistics on business failure. This is not exactly what you want to think about while starting a business, but it is something that requires acknowledgment. Bloomberg reports that 8 out of 10 businesses fail within the first eighteen months, a discouraging statistic that might have you second-guessing yourself even before you start. While failure is a very real possibility when starting a business (or anything for that matter) it should not be your ultimate eventuality. Understanding the threats that your business faces and the pitfalls business owner fall prey to is key to ensuring you insulate your business against failure. Many businesses that have failed have faced similar red flags that eventually led to their demise. Recognizing these red flags will go a long way in avoiding a similar fate.

Insufficient Due Diligence/Research

You've had this burning desire in you to start a beauty business. You have the capital, the passion, and even the location. You know a few resources who would come in handy as salespersons and even beauty stylists. You know there's a market for beauty products and services in your area because you've seen how much walk-in traffic your local beauty parlor has. You're ready to get started. Or so you think.

Unfortunately, entrepreneurs that start businesses without properly investigating the market are setting themselves up for failure. When launching a brand-new business, hearsay and gut instinct are not sufficient. You have to arm yourself with data and all relevant information regarding the market you are about to enter. Is there a quantifiable need? What are the barriers to entry? Who is your competition? What strategies has your competition applied to win customers? Can you measure up? If you have to take six months to do proper research on your market, do so. You might think it is a lot of time to hold off starting your business, but the due diligence will pay off in the end when your startup survives the first year and a half.

Poor Planning and/or Lack of a Business Plan

Writing a business plan is tiring and definitely not many people's hobby. Unfortunately, in business, you cannot wing it without a plan. You are sinking your hard-earned capital into a business, and the least you can do is have a solid plan to back it up. In the absence of a business plan, you will lose sight of your objectives and road map to success. Even though you are a seasoned business owner, you'll still need a business plan for your subsequent businesses. Not having a business plan may also come across as lack of commitment, from an investor's point of view. This might cost you funding, leading to the collapse of your company. A business plan will also come in handy in your absence when you require your employees to run the business without you for one reason or another. Lack of continuity planning will cost your business by ensuring that your business can only survive if you are present. As an entrepreneur, you will need to take breaks here and there to replenish your mental and physical energy. Proper planning ensures that you can take such breaks because everyone else that is left behind understands what their role in the company is.

Bad Location

You've done sufficient research on your market and come up with a stellar business plan. You're now ready to open shop and serve your customers. Two months post-launch, you are still struggling to get walk-in clients. What might be the problem? Location, that's what. Many businesses that have a solid plan and business model still fail because they chose the wrong location for their premises. If your location is not easily accessible or is hidden away in obscurity, not many customers will walk in. It might be because the customers feel the journey is not worth the effort, or they simply do not know where to find you. When choosing a location for your business, consider whether the community living nearby makes up your target market. You should also consider the affordability of the premises so that you do not incur too many costs leasing or buying the place, as this could negatively impact your business. If the location is well-known for the products or services you are providing, this is a plus. Consider too the growth prospects of the area. Is it likely to become a thriving business hub in the near future? If the answer is yes, it is probably a good location, all other factors considered.

Lack of Experience and Poor Management

You do not need to have ten years of experience in entrepreneurship to run a business, but you need to know a few basics. You also need to be open to learn how to properly run a business. If it means reading books, attending short courses and being actively mentored by people who have run companies before, go for it. Many individuals make the mistake of thinking that since they have worked in a certain sector before as employees, they have all the information to run a company. The truth of the matter is that being the top employee in a company is not the same as being the owner. As an employee, many decisions are made for you; as the owner, you will find yourself making all the decisions and being responsible for the company's survival. If you make the wrong decisions regarding products, human resources, and especially finances, you will most likely end up in the 80% of startup failure. While you might be book smart in understanding which numbers go where, work on filling the gaps created by your lack of experience with ongoing learning. When it comes to management, make sound decisions that are supported by facts, and do not delegate decision-making and running of everyday operations to third parties.

Starting a Business for Wrong Reasons

Most people want to be rich. There are very few people who would complain if they won the lottery, if there are any at all. Aspiring for wealth is fine, but it is not a good reason to start a business. Yes, many entrepreneurs start businesses with the aspiration that someday the business will be profitable, and they'll be able to pay themselves and reinvest in the company and expand and so forth. However, for many successful ventures, this is usually not the main goal. To thrive in business, you have to have a reason or reasons that surpass monetary gains. You need to be passionate about solving a particular customer need. You need to have particular knowledge or skill that can positively impact the market. You have to bring your best value to the market, or else you'll be failing in less than eighteen months. It is not wrong to want to succeed in business and become a millionaire, but if you are getting into business for a get rich quick scheme, you will more likely than not fail terribly.

Premature Expansion

You've started your business in one location and it's doing so well in the first six months that you are considering expanding into another location. A lot of entrepreneurs equate expansion to success, when in fact this might not be the case. Many successful businesses have continued to serve customers in the very same location that started out in. It does not make them any less successful. Expansion is not solely based on location either. It could also be in the product or service catalog. You might have noticed that your initial product is doing very well in the market and now want to introduce a few more products.

There are key questions you need to ask yourself before venturing into the expansion, and top on the list is whether you are financially ready for it. Expansion requires capital, and if the market response is not commensurate to the investment you just might sink yourself and your enterprise. At the same time, you should not be afraid of expanding especially if all signs point to a need for expansion. Once you have established a solid customer base and a decent and predictable cash flow, look out for the green light that your business is ripe for an enterprise. If you are unable to fulfill customer needs in a timely manner, you might want to think about expansion. Another key indicator that you might want to expand is if your employees are overstretched. In either scenario, you can come up with a plan to grow your business in terms of production capacity, location, product catalog and so on.

Too Little Financing

If you want to succeed in your business in the first year and beyond, you have to be realistic in your demands as far as finances are concerned. Before you get the hang of entrepreneurship, you might think that asking for too much startup capital will put off interested investors. You might also think that approaching your local lender with a modest loan requirement will work to your advantage. Unfortunately, underestimating your financial needs will only work to your detriment. Six months later when you have exhausted your finances, you'll go out looking for more funds and no lender will be interested since you have existing loans needing to be repaid. When estimating your capital requirements, consider what you'll need to start your business and the funds you'll require to stay in business as well. Be realistic about how long you'll need before you can break even. After doing the math, ask for the money you require. Second guessing yourself and undercutting figures so that you do not scare investors away will only ruin your prospects of survival and success.

Lack of Web Presence

There are approximately four billion Internet users worldwide. According to statistics released by research giant Statista, 1.8 billion of these users purchased items online. The modern-day consumer wants to get their goods fast and conveniently. While the thrill of window-shopping in brick and mortar stores is still very real, many customers would rather forego it if it means getting their item delivered to their doorstep. If you are starting a business in 2019, you cannot afford to not have web presence. This is the very first place a customer will go to look you up. Even if you do not offer deliveries for your product, at least have a website that will allow customers to interact with your brand. Lack of web presence is a red flag that many customers are not willing to overlook. In this era where there is software that allows you to create your own website, you cannot afford to run a business without a website. At the very least, set up active social media pages where potential customers can find you and ask you any pertinent questions that they might have.

Getting Stuck in the Comfort Zone

As an entrepreneur, you have to be dynamic and change with the times if you are hoping to be successful. The modern-day consumer is fickle and easily excitable. They know that they have many options to choose from and are eager to keep up with trends. It is your job to keep up with these trends, and your customers' constantly changing needs and meet them somewhere in the middle. That product that caused a buzz last year might not get a second look this year. Your business model from two years back might need some refreshing. If you do not evolve, your business will not survive. Every once in a while, you will need to step out of your comfort zone and introduce some new angles to your products, services and overall, your business. This is the only way you will remain relevant in the very dynamic environment of entrepreneurship.

Lack of a Unique Value Proposition

Businesses that have no unique value to offer their customers eventually collapse after being in business for a short while. As an entrepreneur, you have to be very clear on what your unique value proposition is and this is what differentiates you from your competitors. This unique value proposition is what entitles you to remain standing in the face of competition and a dynamic business environment. If you are offering something that your customers cannot find anywhere else, you will stay in business with relative ease. However, if you are providing a product or service that is generic and can be gotten anywhere else, and probably at cheaper prices, you will have a very hard time staying in business. Your value proposition is something that you should consider very early on when starting your business. The value proposition that you decide on sets the tone for your business, and informs the investors you'll go after, your pricing, target market, location and a whole lot of operational decisions in your company. Any time there is ambiguity regarding a decision to be made, you have to go back to your value proposition. Why are you doing this (running the business)? What are you offering your customers? Are they willing to pay for it? Will they be willing to pay for it in the coming year? In short, your value proposition is your guiding light, which should be constantly readjusted to meet the evolving needs of your customers.

Poor Leadership Skills

As a business owner and company founder, you are the top leader who will be looked upon to direct the business towards success. This leadership role is critical and requires you to bring your A-game if you're hoping to succeed. Unfortunately, not all entrepreneurs have inborn leadership skills. You might have the best experience and financial management skills, and still be a poor leader. Good leaders are distinguished by their glowing attributes which include courage, integrity, humility and razor-sharp focus. You have to be the kind of leader that inspires your employees to work better and harder towards the achievement of the business objectives. When the business hits rocky times, you have to be the pillar of strength that inspires your workers to hold on and work towards getting out of the trenches. Your commitment and passion as a leader will take you places others might think unreachable. Whether you are running a partnership or a sole proprietorship, you have to put your best leadership foot forward. If you are unclear about how to be a good leader, you can take leadership courses, read books on leadership or get mentored by a leader you admire. If you can do all three, even better. While not everyone is born a leader, you have it within you to be made into one through learning and observation.

Chapter 8: Surviving Your First Year in Business

The first year of your business is a crucial period that can make or break your enterprise. It has often been said that the first year is the year that a lot of start-ups struggle with, as they try to find their footing in a world riddled with competition. Statistics show that eight out of 10 businesses fail within the first eighteen months, news that is not comforting to an entrepreneur. With the right tactics, however, you can go on to become one of the two entrepreneurs who succeed. The decisions you make within your business' first year will lay a foundation for success or failure. As such, you will have to be extremely deliberate about the choices you make, if survival and success are what you are aiming for. You can ensure you are still standing by the end of your first year by taking steps to cultivate the right habits around your business and personal life.

Keep your Support System Close

When you first start your business, you'll need to ensure that the people closest to you are part of the journey. Dealing with the stresses of running a new business can lead to lots of stress, and cause you to want to push people away. Sometimes you'll think you are the only one who truly understands the struggles and stresses that you are going through. While this might be so, it is necessary that you keep your loved ones in the loop because they'll come in handy on days when everything seems to be going downhill. Your partner may not have the best ideas on how to obtain funding, but they'll be there when you are nearing burnout. When your would-be investors turn you down and bring your hopes crashing down, your spouse will be waiting with open arms and a home-made meal. This is important. It might sound like a hipster thing to say, but your soul needs nourishing when you are in the thick of running a new business. This nourishing will come from the people who care deeply about you as a friend, son, brother, or partner.

Expect Some Self-Doubt

There will be moments when self-doubt will creep in and take over all the confidence you had previously felt about starting a business. Anybody that tells you that the first year of starting a business is all great and full of heaps of confidence is lying. Your first year will be punctuated by moments where you truly doubt your decision to quit your job to start a business. There will be times when you will start to fill a job application because you cannot see yourself surviving for another month. Anticipating this kind of self-doubt is important in being prepared to deal with it. When the self-doubt checks in, remind yourself of why you started this journey in the first place. Remember the vision that motivated you in the first and the goals that you have set for yourself and your business. Keep your eye on the prize and push harder. Success exists for people like yourself; it is within reach and highly attainable, even though you might have to cross some valleys to get there.

Set Aside Enough Money

During your business' first year, you'll be lucky if you make enough profit to pay yourself. If you make any money, most if not all of it will be reinvested into your business. As such, you should be prepared to go for months without a paycheck. Foregoing a salary can be challenging, especially if you were used to drawing one every month. It is necessary to ensure that you have set aside enough money to cover your personal expenses for the period that you will not be making any profits from the business, which is usually a year to eighteen months. Setting aside enough savings will ensure that you do not compromise your quality of living. You will also not have to worry about your household bills while trying to run a business. In the same breath, you should also have enough money to cover the expenses of the business for at least a year. You will be required to sink in a lot of money to establish a foundation for your business. Think of the services you might have to pay for; the equipment purchases, legal fees, and installation of certain fixtures should you choose to have a physical office...these will cost you a pretty penny. Be prepared for this.

Keep your expenses low

It is said, you must spend money to make money. Every entrepreneur is conscious of this. That being said, you must be very conscious of where you spend your money when you're just getting started in business. Spending frivolously will run a hole in your finances, and your business to the ground. A practical way of keeping your expenses low is hiring permanent employees only when necessary and outsourcing the rest of the work to freelancers. Also, consider working from home if having a physical office is not crucial. Cut back on your advertising expenses by making the most of free advertising platforms such as your social media pages. Reconsider where you have your business lunches; your clients will understand if you do not take them to the most expensive restaurant in the city. Keeping your expenses low doesn't mean you'll have to be stingy towards your business; it means you'll only spend money where it is the only option, without which you'd be doing your business injustice.

Stay Conscious of Being Busy versus Being Productive

You've just launched your very first business. You're excited about your new adventure and cannot wait to see yourself on Forbes 400. While you dream of a future full of good fortune and infinite success, you're taking steps to ensure this comes true. So, you're going to meetings with potential clients and investors, holding briefs with consultants, preparing proposals, pitching and being everywhere all at once, it seems. At the end of the day, you're dog-tired from all the busyness of the day. This busyness should not fool you into thinking you're making progress. There's a big difference between busyness and productivity, and the difference lies in what is achieved at the end of the day. If you are neck-deep in meetings with potential clients and have no clients at the end of the month, you're busy but not productive. Beware of the allure of wanting to feel wanted and needed, at the expense of your business. In your first year, there might be many calls made and many meetings scheduled; determine the value of each and respond appropriately. A day that ends at noon with two sales made is more fruitful than a never-ending day of chasing potential clients who are unwilling to sign on the dotted line.

Focus on the Customer

You've come up with this amazing innovation that is going to blow everyone's mind. Twelve months later, no one seems to be mind-blown. You invested a tidy sum into your business, and you have yet to break even. Sales are tricking in at a discouraging rate. You're just about to close shop. What happened to your amazing innovation? You probably did not pay attention to the customer, that's what. The feedback you'll get from your customers during your first year in business is crucial. Pay keen attention to this feedback and then align your product or service to fit in with the customer requirements. A lot of entrepreneurs focus too much on the product and not enough on the customer. The end result is that the customer feels ignored and takes their business elsewhere. If your customer service is topnotch, customers will be willing to cut you some slack even if you're fumbling with your first product, because they know version two of that product will meet all their needs.

Build a Wide Network

However much of an indoors person you are, your first year of business will call for you to get out of your comfort zone and network with as many people as you can. As a business person, the people you know will come in handy when it comes to getting funding, opening doors, sounding off ideas and even getting clients. If there are industry networking events in your area, attend them and introduce yourself to a few people. Call your mentor and invite them out for lunch. Make some phone calls and grab some drinks with that former boss that you always liked. People are assets; use them to grow your business.

Track your Progress

As a business person, you'll very quickly learn that it is not enough to assume that you are doing well. You must have the numbers to back up every statement that you make about your business. If you say that sales increased, you must have numbers showing last month's sales compared to the current month's sales. If you are projecting a certain amount of revenue, you must produce the numbers behind these projections. In business, numbers don't lie. Numbers track progress, and they tell you if you are headed in the right direction. Numbers are what you'll take to potential investors when you need to raise capital for your business. Investors want to know how much your business is worth now and in future, and you can only determine this if you know how much revenue you've been making and can project to make in future. If you're not good with numbers, hire someone who is.

Stretch Your First Year

A calendar year might be twelve months, but the truth of the matter is that a year in business takes longer than that. Most business persons give themselves timelines regarding when they should have started making profits. For instance, an entrepreneur might say I'll give myself a year and if I am not making a profit by then I'll call it quits. Limiting yourself to one year is impractical. Many businesses require at least 18 months before they can start making profits. Allowing yourself these additional six months might be the difference between a flop and a successful venture. Give yourself some more wiggle room as far as timelines and watch what can happen when you are a little more patient.

Make Technology Your Friend

As an entrepreneur, there are a lot of tasks that require your attention. Some of these tasks are strategic while others are operational. Wherever possible, make use of technology to make your load easier on the operational side. For instance, automate recurring payments so that you do not have to go through the struggle of paying each and every payment every month. There are several softwares that you can use to automate payments. These include PaySimple, Ariba, Invoicera and even Slickpie, which is free to use. Automating your payment process will take off some work off your hands and also make it easier to track your expenses as you can easily run reports on this software. At the very beginning of your business, you might want to keep your expenses low by opting for free or affordable software. Later on, as your business grows, you can look into other software solutions that are targeted at bigger businesses. Examples include Procurify and SAP Business ByDesign.

Take a Break

Entrepreneurial burnout is a real thing. Your business' first year will most likely be fraught with emotional, physical, financial and mental exhaustion. Whether you are starting your very first business or are launching another business, your first year will most likely be draining. As a business owner, it is crucial that you stay conscious of what your limits are and take a break when you see yourself approaching these limits. You cannot run a business when you are burned out unless you mean running it to the ground. In formal employment, you could take a break and go on leave for a few days without worrying that the company will close down. In your business, you're worried to death that a few days of absence will take you back a couple of hundred steps. Regardless, prioritize your well-being and take a break when you need to. Take time away to center yourself; only after doing so will you be in the right frame of mind and body to run a successful business. You do not have to book a trip to Bali (remember you're keeping your expenses low) but if you can afford a Friday afternoon massage and a weekend getaway it will be much better than cracking under pressure.

Start Afresh

It is one thing to demonstrate unwavering commitment and yet another to continue flogging a dead horse. Sometimes, even the best-laid plans do not work out. Many entrepreneurs have stories of businesses that started out well and promisingly, only to fail spectacularly later on. Sometimes, the difference between failure and success is an unexpected natural event. You may have started your small carwash business and found the first few months to be highly encouraging, only for a raging storm to pass through your town and destroy everything you had started. Or it could be that the bubble burst and left your real estate business in shambles. Whatever the case may be, you are allowed to start afresh if things are not looking up. It is not quitting; it is more like rebooting. Many entrepreneurs are scared of looking like they gave up. It is a warranted fear considering there are people who gave them money who are scrutinizing their every move. A wise person once said, you should not hold onto a mistake just because you spent a lot of time making it. If your business is destroyed beyond repair, hold your head up and start over.

Chapter 9: Scaling your Business

One of the best moments in your life as an entrepreneur is when your business finally becomes profitable. This is a defining moment for many businesses and marks a major milestone and is a testament to the viability of the brand in the market. A business that is profitable can pay for its own expenses, with a surplus being left over to serve as income for the owner and for re-investment as well. On average small businesses will typically require two to three years of operations before they become profitable. If your business is consistently profitable over a period of time, you can start thinking about scaling and expansion.

It is relatively easy to tell when you have become profitable. You'll find yourself with some change left over after paying for your business' expenses. However, as has been the theme of this book, it is best to support your gut instinct with numbers. Using metrics to measure profitability is the best way to go about it. When you have numbers, you can track how your business is growing, how far you're off your preferred mark and what changes you need to make to achieve this. Entrepreneurs usually use several financial metrics to calculate their profitability. These metrics include gross profit margin, net profit margin, and return on capital employed.

Gross Profit Margin

Your gross profit is the amount of money left over when you deduct your cost of goods from net sales revenue. The net sales revenue is all the money you get from your sales minus any returns, discounts, and allowances that you give out. To calculate your gross profit margin, you'll need to divide your gross profit by the net sales. The gross profit margin measures how feasible a certain product or service is. If the percentage is high, it shows that you are retaining more money from sales than you are spending on production. The reverse is true if the gross profit margin is low.

Net Profit Margin

Your net profit is the amount of money left over after you have deducted all your expenses from your net sales or revenue. Your net profit margin is this amount expressed as a percentage of your revenue or net sales. There is no set figure that has been universally agreed on as a good net profit margin. However, there exists statistics on industry benchmarks that you can use to measure how well you are doing as a business. A simple Google search filtered by country or region should yield useful results on various benchmarks that are often group by industry.

Return on Capital Employed (ROCE)

Return on Capital Employed, abbreviated as ROCE, is yet another profitability ratio that you can apply to determine how well your business is ready and whether you are ripe for expansion. This ratio is obtained by expressing your earnings before interest and tax as a percentage of your total assets less current liabilities. Total assets less current liabilities constitute capital employed.

This profitability ratio is preferred by investors as it clearly shows which company would be a better investment. Simply comparing the earnings of a company may be deceiving, as a company X might make more than company Y when in fact company X employed a great deal of capital to make those numbers. Ideally, investors will choose a company that is able to extract a great deal of value from a little capital.

After working out your profitability ratios and coming up with impressive numbers, it is usually time to start thinking about proactive growth. Proactively growing your business means consciously seeking ways of growing your sales and revenue, so that you can boost your income and serve a larger clientele. Unfortunately for my business owners, there is a lot of confusion in this area, especially in regard to differentiating between scaling and growth.

In a business context, growth refers to the increase in revenue brought on by an increase in resources. For instance, if a professional services firm wins more clients, it might need to hire additional consultants to serve the client. In this case, the firm will grow its revenue thanks to the additional income stream from the new clients and spend more money paying salaries to its additional employees. Scaling, on the other hand, involves growing your revenue exponentially, while only adding resources at a phased pace. Scaling increases your profit margin at a rapid rate, while growth might make a decent but not necessarily mind-blowing difference to your margins. As a business owner, you should pay attention to growth and scaling as they are both important. However, for long-term success, you should be more concerned with scaling.

Besides sustained profitability, there are other signs that indicate that your business is ready for scaling up. One of these is having a reliable team and infrastructure in place. In order for a business to expand strategically, you require to have the right people, technology and process in place to support expansion. You also require to have a plan. Scaling your business is similar to starting a new business in that you are introducing aspects that were previously not existing. You're introducing a new customer service unit, a new or upgraded product line, a new component of the supply chain and numerous other firsts. Just as you would with a new business, you will have to be systematic and strategic about your scaling.

Scaling Your Business in Five Simple Steps

Step #1: Commit to Scaling

Many entrepreneurs are excited to see their businesses grow. They want to see their customer base growing and their revenues increasing. However, not very many entrepreneurs want to scale their businesses. The thought itself is scary as there are many unknowns and usually multiple detractors pointing out why it is not the right time yet. If you are looking to step out of the shadows and expand your business to formidable levels, it is important to strongly desire the journey and commit to the process. Once you make scaling your business a priority, come up with a plan outlining the activities that you'll undertake and commit to the plan.

Step #2: Automate your business processes

If all your processes are carried out manually, you will always be in need of additional resources to cater to your growing customer base. Automating your processes takes care of this need by reducing your human capital requirements. As a small business, there are some processes you can easily automate so that your human resources can focus their skills and abilities on other more important operational areas. Examples of these processes are data capturing, invoicing and payments, purchase order and sales order processes. It is often expensive to automate everything at once, and for this reason, it is recommended that small business owners phase their automation projects. Your low-hanging fruits as far as automation goes are those processes that are repetitive and require fairly priced tools to automate.

Step #3: Identify your core strength and competitive edge

In order to scale your business, you will need to be clear on what sets you apart from the competition. Your competitive edge is the factor that entitles you to seek higher prices and gain more customers. It is the factor that motivates customers to remain loyal to you. Your competitive advantage is what you should be focused on investing in when it comes to strategically expanding, or scaling, your business. When you put the right resources in the right areas, your business will grow exponentially.

Step #4: Focus on what matters

There are likely to be hundreds of activities that are undertaken in your business' everyday operations. However much you want to switch up everything for the sake of optimization, you will not really be able to focus your energy on all tasks and activities without losing something in between. After determining what your competitive edge is, it will be relatively easy to decide what is a priority in moving your business forward and what is not. If an activity or operational item is not a priority, do not give it too much of your energy and attention. A mistake many business owners make is trying to micromanage everything in their business operations. Some things really aren't that consequential. For instance, if part of your scaling involves reducing production costs, you should not do an entire sweep of the costs in your business to the extent that you are even looking at stationery. It only wastes your time and the $60 dollars saved on a ream of printer paper will not make much difference to your bottom-line. Focusing on what matters also means that at some point you will be required to outsource the non-core activities of your operations so that you can focus on what defines your brand. Outsourcing is a term used to refer to the practice of using an external service provider to carry out activities that could otherwise be carried out internally. Administrative tasks, accounting, and marketing are a few examples of activities that can be outsourced by small businesses.

Step #5: Build a formidable network

The relationships you foster around you are critical in the development and success of your business. Many a time it has been said that in entrepreneurship, it is more of who you know and less of what you know. While this may be debatable depending on your school of thought, it is easy to see that having business mentors and potential investors within your network gives you a leg up on someone who does not. Your network is going to play an important role in getting the word out about your products and services. When you begin to grow and scale, you need the formidable force of a strong, solid network that is interested and invested in seeing you succeed.

Signs that Your Business is Not Ready for Scaling

Sometimes, the signs that you are not ready for scaling are more pronounced and easier to spot. As a business owner, you need to know the signs of distress to look out for, especially if you are considering growth and scaling as a near future goal. If your business experiences any of the following signs, you'll need to hold off the scaling until further notice:

Lack of confidence in your revenue model

A revenue model is a component of the business model, and specifically outlines your revenue sources, value to offer and even how to price your value. A revenue model that is predictive in nature allows you to anticipate revenue and plan accordingly. For instance, if you know that out of every 50 sales calls, you get one client paying $100 for a service, you'll easily determine how many calls you need to make to earn $1000. If you are able to isolate such metrics in your revenue streams, it is likely that you are ready for growth. If you are not sure about certain details of your revenue model, you might want to hold off until you are one hundred percent certain.

A fledgling accounting system and inability to forecast your cash flow

So, you have been serving 500 customers since inception and you want to grow your business to serve 300 more. Logically, this means that you will incur more variable costs in a bid to produce the additional 300 or more units. Can you forecast how higher your costs will be if you grow to 800 customers? If your answer is no, you are not ready for scaling. A company that is ready for growth will have a strong accounting system that has their actual and forecasted numbers in place. This kind of clarity will enable you to plan accordingly for your growth and expansion.

Uncertainty about your brand and vision

You've started your business and have been performing decently over the course of three years. You feel like you are ready to scale, except for the niggling feeling at the back of your head. You no longer feel excited about your brand or your vision. You have found yourself constantly questioning your business' ethos. What to do? Scaling should never be undertaken against a backdrop of fear and doubt. You have to be certain of your brand, your vision and mission, and your ethos, before you can replicate this on a larger scale. If you need some time out to reaffirm what you knew and believed about your brand when you started it, do so. If the end result is still uncertainty, there's nothing wrong about getting back to the drawing board. Many entrepreneurs have had to start over when they realized they were on the wrong path.

Too Much on Your In-tray

Scaling is almost like starting a new business all over again. You have to commit to the process and put it many hours of your time. If you are dealing with numerous commitments (even personal ones), you are probably not ready to start scaling. Hold off until you can give your full and undivided attention to this most-important period.

Chapter 10: Best Practices for Small Businesses

Sometimes as a business owner, you'll need a quick feel of how well you are performing as a small business. This chapter outlines several practices that are considered the most effective when it comes to running a small business. Over time, you can check to see how you are performing against industry standards and re-adjust accordingly. The practices are grouped alphabetically for ease of reference.

Accounting

Accounting is one of the most crucial aspects of your small business. This docket helps you track your money at all times. It shows what is coming in, what is going out, what you owe and what is owed to you. Flaws in the accounting docket can have a detrimental impact on your business as a whole. There are several best practices that you should adopt in accounting:

- Whatever your professional background is, ensure you familiarize yourself with the different financial statements to the extent of being able to interpret them in the context of your business

- Separate your business' finances from your personal finances

- Automate repetitive tasks such as payments and invoicing

- Make only essential purchases, even after you start making a profit

- Implement necessary controls to curb wastage, fraud, and errors

- Pay your bills on time

- Define a schedule for closing your books and stick to it

- Pay your taxes on time

- Monitor your cash flow and especially the accounts receivables

- Hire a reputable accountant or accounting firm to help with the heavy lifting

Automation

Automation is one of those exciting buzzwords that many entrepreneurs love to talk about. In a bid to keep up with the Joneses, many entrepreneurs have found themselves approaching automation the wrong way. Just because your competition has automated certain processes doesn't mean you should rush to replicate that automation in your operations. These are the best practices you should have in mind when you start to think of automating your small business processes:

- Start slowly by automating the non-critical processes and then build up to the customer-centric processes

- Choose the right automation tools that are in line with your business goals as far as capabilities and scalability are concerned

- Set goals that will help you determine the success and return on investment of the automation

- Manage your various stakeholders and their stakeholder behaviors by defining process owners and involving your staff in the automation process

- Train your users on the automated process

- Make automation a continuous improvement process rather than a one-off project

- Have a back-up plan to ensure your process continue uninterrupted in the event of technology glitches

Branding

When it comes to branding, the message you want to send out there is one of coherence and uniformity. Whatever message you send through your social media pages should be replicated on your website. Identify your marketing themes and messages and share them appropriately on your various channels. The message should remain similar across all channels. The only changes to be made should be those that tailor the marketing message in a way that allows the message to be easily consumed on a particular channel.

Benchmarking

Seeing as you will not be operating in a vacuum, it is always important to pause and see what other industry players are doing. If you are struggling in some areas, you can borrow the practices applied by counterparts who seem to have figured out how to solve the problem. As a small business owner, these are the best practices you should keep in mind when benchmarking:

- Start as early as possible so that you can come up with a road map soonest possible

- Phase your benchmarking activities and have timelines defining when you should implement your findings

- Choose competitors who are most similar to your company in terms of size, industry, business model, etc.

- At the same time, challenge yourself by looking outside your industry for companies who have figured out processes that you are struggling with

- Define your benchmarking metrics so that you can be in a position to compare apples to apples

- Keep in mind that the only way you'll change your company's metrics to measure up with the competitors is by improving your operations and not mulling over the statistics and feeling bad about your performance

Contract Management

The contracts you prepare for your business transactions can make or break you. If you are coming from an environment where word of mouth was considered a sufficient form of agreement, you might find the process of preparing contracts nerve-wracking. Whatever you do, never engage in a business relationship that is not supported by a contract. This might be the very relationship that takes you to the cleaners. To ensure that you are legally protected at all times:

- Determine which contract templates to use by checking what standard forms are available and passing these through a legal specialist or lawyer

- Avail these standard templates across your organization

- Standardize the negotiation process so all staff know what is expected

- Make use of contract management software to reduce workload and repetitive tasks

- Have a central repository for all your contract documents

Customer Service

You could have the best product in the market but if your customer service is lacking your potential clients will run the opposite direction. Key to getting your customer service right is treating your employees as your first customer. It has been said before that once you treat your employees well, they are able to treat your customers even better. Prioritizing your employees as customers means creating and supporting a culture that prioritizes employee welfare. Another best practice in customer service is drafting customer service standards that your employees are supposed to abide by when serving customers. Having a clear document that acts as a guideline and sets expectations means that there is no room left for ambiguity.

Many businesses are focused on impressing the customer during the sale and forget the very important after-sale period which can make or break a customer's loyalty. A best practice in customer service is to follow up with your customer after they have already made a purchase. It could be simply to thank them for the purchase or get their feedback on the same. Whatever the reason may be, it shows your customer that you care about them even after they have already spent their money on your product.

Data and Decisions

As much as possible, small business owners should always rely on data to back up their decisions. Data-driven decision making is beneficial in many ways, including enabling entrepreneurs and management teams to approach decisions rationally instead of relying merely on past experience or gut instinct. The data you gather along the various steps of your business operations is an asset that should be used for the good of your company.

Efficiency vs. Effectiveness

It is often easy to confuse efficiency with effectiveness. This is a confusion that many businesses owners face, especially in application. To illustrate this difference in the simplest way possible, efficiency is doing things right while effectiveness is doing the right things. As a business owner, you want to ensure that you have struck a balance between efficiency and effectiveness. This is the best way to ensure that you get high returns on your investment and reduce your costs, for instance.

There are several ways you can make your business more efficient. The very first thing you need to do is identify what is inefficient, that is, what is not working right. To identify inefficiencies in your business, you can start by taking baseline measurements across factors such as customer satisfaction scores, hours spent in meetings, delivery times and even administrative expenses. These measurements will give you an indication of where you should be looking for inefficiencies. After determining that a process is indeed inefficient, you should then start looking for its root cause.

Giving your customers power in their hands is another way of making your business more efficient. If you run a travel agent business, allowing customers to create their own itinerary where possible is a form of giving them power. It ensures that part of the process is handed over to the customer to do it just right, as they want to, and frees you up to focus on other aspects of the customer experience. On the other hand, you can improve effectiveness in your business by listening to your customer and providing the right quality of products and services.

Feedback

As your business grows, you might not always be available to take charge of all the daily operations. At the same time, you want to keep your finger on the pulse of things so that you do not lose touch with an entity you created in the first place. In such circumstances, it is necessary to solicit feedback from your team so that you know which areas are inefficient and could use improvement. Feedback from your customers is also highly valuable, as it helps you know whether you are meeting the customers' needs from the horse's mouth.

Growth Hacking

Growth hacking is a term that refers to the strategies that a start-up employs to ensure massive growth within a short time and on a limited budget. The expected outcome of growth hacking is to gain as many customers as possible without breaking the bank. Often times, growth hacking takes the form of content and product marketing and advertising. It utilizes readily available and often free-to-use channels such as blogs, podcasts, social media, search engine optimization, affiliate marketing, and even referrals. A growth hacker differs from the traditional marketer in that the growth hacker is inspired by a singular goal, and that is to grow a business rapidly to the best of their human ability.

Meetings and Conferences

The truth is that while millions of meetings are held across the world every month, at least half of those could be emails. You might probably have experienced it at your workplace: your boss gets agitated about something and calls for a meeting. Or your colleague who's excited about something they have achieved calls for a meeting to gloat. So there you are, seated in the meeting room and wondering why this information you're hearing now could not be shared in an email. This is the kind of inefficiency that you do not want to replicate in your new company. As far as meetings go, keep the following in mind:

- Adopt collaboration tools such as Slack, Microsoft Teams and Asana that reduce the need for meetings

- Meet only if it creates value

- Plan for the meeting in advance and circulate an agenda

- Do not deviate from the meeting's agenda

- Ensure everyone understands that they are required to show up on time

Outsourcing

Business process outsourcing can be focused on either back-end operations or customer-facing functions such as marketing. Whichever function you choose to hand over to a third-party, it is necessary to ensure that you do it correctly. For starters, it is important to determine what function is safe to outsource and what should be performed in-house. As an initial cut off, all core activities of a business are performed in-house. If you are a manufacturing company, you cannot afford to outsource the production process. Anything else that is non-core is up for grabs. Make sure you select a trustworthy third-party and train them well on how you like certain things to be done. Just because you have outsourced does not mean you have given up all say in the matter. It is important that the vendor is attuned to your brand's vision and mission.

Processes

Always document your processes, showing clearly all the steps involve from beginning to end, and the roles played by the process owners. When processes are documented, it makes it easier for new employees to be on-boarded, and for existing employees to refer to the documents in the event of ambiguity. Undocumented processes contribute to significant time wastage in many small businesses.

Payroll

In the beginning, your company will have very few people on its payroll, if at all. As you grow and onboard more employees, you'll need to make sure that you are handling the payroll process correctly. One of the things you'll need to do is ensure that your employees clearly understand what their salaries are. During onboarding, provide your new staff with information on how their net pay is arrived at, when it is paid and how vacation days are calculated.

Automate your payroll process so that you do not have to invest your energy in repetitive manual tasks. If you are lacking the budget to automate your payroll process, you can make use of free payroll software. Many providers will allow you a free version of their payroll software as long as you have a limited number of employees. Examples of free payroll software include TimeTrex, HR.my, and Payroll4Free.com.

Record-Keeping

Keep your records well-organized and up to date to ensure that you can always access information whenever you need it. Documents are an essential part of your business, whether they are printed or electronic. It is also important to come up with a document management policy so that you can communicate your company's preferred organization, storage, and disposal practices.

Regulatory Awareness

It's probably the last thing you want to think about as an entrepreneur, but you should be up to date with any legal changes affecting your business. If you are not keen on getting embroiled in the legalese, always consult an attorney to break down the laws for you.

Social Media

Whether you run an online business or operate a physical store social media will eventually become a part of your business. Seeing as this is your predicament, the best you can do is ensure that you know how to deal with social media as a component of your commercial activities. Here are some key things to remember:

- Hire a social media manager--you'll probably not have the time to engage everyone across all social media platforms on top of ensuring your social media marketing activities are on time

- Be careful of what your brand endorses or appears to endorse; the Internet requires careful navigation and one wrong move could bring your brand crashing down

Software

As your business grows, you'll probably want to invest in software that is robust and that which supports your scaling aspirations. With so many software solutions available in the market, it can be tempting to delegate the selection process to a more knowledgeable party instead of dealing with it yourself. Unfortunately, you'll learn early on that delegating the important tasks in your small business will often times leave you in a mess, especially when you are just getting started. You need to get things right in the early days otherwise you'll spend your teething months fixing problems that you could have avoided.

When selecting software, have a clear picture of what your needs are and how each of the software options you have provide a solution for these. Software salesmen can be very convincing, and your confusion will be magnified when you are not clear on what you need.

Buy software that is suited for your industry, so that you can get all the components you need. If you are in the manufacturing industry, do not try to integrate tools that are best suited for the service industry. Another best practice to keep in mind is to integrate software in your operations over-time instead of adopting a big bang approach. Big bang implementation is whereby you replace your existing enterprise resource planning system with a completely new one all at the same time. It is a direct contrast to the phased approach where you stagger your rollouts.

Chapter 11: Essential Soft Skills for Successful Entrepreneurs

As a business owner, you will need more than your technical skills to succeed. Yes, it's crucial to understand how the important parts of your business work, but you are more likely to exert more influence if you have the right soft skills. Building up your soft skills is how you are going to win investors, clients, and employees. So, what exactly should you have under your belt as far as soft skills are concerned?

Leadership Skills

The phrase leadership skills have been used so many times when talking to entrepreneurs that it somehow lost its impact. And truth be told, many entrepreneurs believe they are leaders already. After all, they came up with an idea and saw it to action. Unfortunately, this is not what leadership is about. You might be a market leader and still lack the essential leadership skills required to motivate your staff. A good leader is one who understands the human side of the people they interact with. They are able to cut through the boardroom talk and appeal to the emotional side of people. A strong leader inspires and leads from the front. They are not afraid to lead and serve at the same time. Excellent leaders take time to listen before they offer their opinion. They disagree respectfully and with reason, not for the sake of asserting their authority.

Some people seem to have a knack for leadership. Others require a little more motivation. If you are struggling with building up your confidence as a leader, you should take steps to ensure this doesn't cause the downfall of your business. You can train yourself to become a better leader by motivating yourself to acknowledge your achievements and abilities, and the opportunity you have been presented with to become a role model. If this fails, you can enlist the help of a leadership coach who will help you decide what your leadership style is and how you can improve upon it.

Time Management

You've gone from being employed and probably having someone (your boss) plan your time to being your own boss and accounting for your time to no one else but you. Sounds a little overwhelming, right? Right. It the beginning, you'll probably be excited about being your own boss and getting to choose what you'll do and when. It will be an exciting concept until you realize that you have achieved very little at the end of the day. You will probably have spent hours in meetings, hours chasing after clients and even more hours figuring out the administrative details. Sooner rather than later, you'll realize that time management is a skill that you need to have if you wish to succeed in business.

Some simple tips you can use to manage your time better is ensuring that you do not get bogged down by calls and emails. Constantly refreshing your email is surprisingly one of the top time wasters. Answering all phone calls will leave you with very little time to manage your business. Take stock of all your daily activities and notice where you spent a lot of time yet didn't create any value. Cut out all non-value adding activities and learn to say no a little bit more.

Communication

The way you communicate can cost you friends and win you enemies. As an entrepreneur, your communication style is the very first impression you make, and you know what they say—you do not get a second chance to make a first impression. Communication is not just the way you speak to a group of investors gathered in a boardroom. It is also the way you listen, write and present. If you are a good communicator, you will have a very easy time passing your brand message to the audience.

- Here are some tips on how to become a better communicator:

- Always figure out the message you want to pass across beforehand

- Speak clearly and concisely

- Stay respectful of different cultural environments

- Observe email etiquette

- Listen before answering—never interrupt unless the building is on fire

- Mind your body language

- Embrace differences in opinion without being argumentative—it is okay to not agree on some things

Flexibility

Most successful entrepreneurs are strong-willed persons with strong convictions about certain matters. However, they are also quick to adapt to changing circumstances because they understand that it is what they need to do to survive. As an entrepreneur, you have to be willing to be agile in your thought process and decisions, otherwise, you will be left behind. If something does not go as planned, change direction and see what happens. If the market doesn't respond as you had hoped, understand the reasons and strategize. Change is as good as rest, and if you're not willing to change you'll be one very tired entrepreneur.

Being flexible as a person means that you will be in a better position to be flexible in business. Flexible businesses are able to keep up in dynamic market environments. They can respond to the changing needs of customers better and more easily.

A simple way to improve your flexibility is by engaging in creative activities that challenge you to think outside the box. You might also want to look into emotional intelligence and how to tap into it. Emotional intelligence is your ability to recognize your emotions and those of others and respond appropriately.

Problem-solving

Entrepreneurship is anything but smooth sailing. Even with a foolproof business plan and the backing of seasoned investors, you will still encounter problems that you did not anticipate. Problem-solving is a skill that you will need to have when this happens. Problem-solving does not just refer to solving huge business problems. It could be as simple as finding a solution for when your flight is delayed or canceled. These decisions will impact you and your business in one way or another. You have to be prepared to have a solution to every challenge that you encounter.

Teamwork

Teamwork is a term that is used to refer to the collaborative energy and effort of a team, that is aimed at achieving a common goal. Even as the boss, you will still need to be part of a team. Entrepreneurship calls for a lot of collaboration, even in a sole proprietorship. Even as a sole trader, you will still need to collaborate with your vendors and freelancers at particular points in time. To be an excellent team player, entrepreneurs must:

- Demonstrate genuine interest in a cause, business-related or otherwise

- Be reliable

- Listen to others

- Contribute actively

- Show up

- Always offer their help whenever possible

- Show support and respect for others

Whether you are meeting with your in-house team to discuss your marketing strategy or planning a local charity event, you will be required to demonstrate teamwork as a leader.

Negotiation Skills

In a way, negotiation skills are related to communication in that you will be speaking with the intention of getting what you want. That being said, negotiation is a very specific niche that has more dire consequences than communication. If you are a bad negotiator, you might cost your business essential leverage. As you try to win investors and clients, you will run into seasoned negotiators who have no qualms about taking you for everything that you are worth. It is important to know how to throw back a punch in the negotiation room, as you do not want a situation where everyone is walking all over you.

There are some tips that you can apply to become a better negotiator, including:

- Understand yourself, and your needs and wants. Figure out the areas you cannot compromise on, and the areas where you are willing to leave a little room open for compromise

- Understand the other party just as well as you understand yourself, so you know what they want, and which buttons can be pushed for appropriate responses

- Give yourself time to become a good negotiator—good negotiators are made, and it takes a whole lot of time and practice

- Attend training on negotiation - classroom training on negotiation skills are a good place to simulate real-life scenarios for a better understanding

Networking

Networking can be a nerve-wracking affair for many entrepreneurs. What do you say to a seasoned, self-made and successful entrepreneur that you've always admired when you finally meet at that networking affair? Many an entrepreneur has found themselves tongue-tied when faced with such a scenario. It is a natural reaction to be at a loss for words. It happens to the best of us. In the beginning, networking is likely to be a dreadful affair, especially if you lean towards the introverted side. However, you can still make it bearable by using some tried and tested tips that other entrepreneurs have used.

For starters, you should be authentic. Do not put on an act for the sake of impressing your audience. Speak what is true and dear to your heart, and your authenticity will shine through. Secondly, never second guess yourself. Leave the second guessing to those private moments when you are in the comfort and safety of your home. Once you are in the throes of networking, believe in yourself and what you have to offer. Be bold and composed, and let the world know about you and your brand.

The other thing you should do when it comes to networking is to be memorable. If nobody remembers you after you left the room, you have failed in networking. To ensure that your presence lingers long after you have left, introduce yourself properly and adequately. You are not just Rob. You are Rob from Company X that did Y and Z. Rob is forgettable. Rob with the drone photography company that did that one viral article with the sheep that photobombed some wedding pictures is somewhat memorable. Do not be afraid to be on the spotlight as far as introducing yourself goes. You have earned your place in the spotlight.

Being memorable also calls for effort in remembering other people's names. You do not just want to keep repeating the Rob story without remembering people's names. This comes off as aloof and will not win you very many fans or friends. When speaking, make eye contact and repeat the other person's name. People remember people who remember their names.

Personal Branding

Closely related to being memorable, your personal brand is key to standing out. Your personal brand is who you are as a person outside of your business, what you stand for, what interests you have and the overall aura surrounding your career and business interests. Personal branding is the reason why the world knows about Apple and Steve Jobs as well. Personal branding is the reason why Richard Branson and Virgin Atlantic are synonymous. Personal branding is also the reason why you cannot discuss Microsoft without mentioning Bill Gates. These great men and entrepreneurs managed to show the world the great value they have as individuals, outside of being successful business owners.

A simple way to build your personal brand is by using your social media accounts to establish yourself as a trustworthy source of information and expertise. People gravitate towards the experts that they can trust. If you build a large community around you that believes in your credibility, you are one step ahead as far as building your personal brand is concerned.

Stress Management

Running a business is a high-stress activity. There will be days when you will be running on fumes. Stress management will come in to help you figure out how to properly run on those fumes. Most business owners understand that entrepreneurship is not all fun and games. Unfortunately, stress usually creeps on most people gradually and without many indications until it is too late. Stress management is a soft skill that you can learn so you can be in a better position to identify your stressors and wind down after a hectic day. Managing your stress will help you stay in good health, which is crucial for the effective management of a business.

Being Personable

To succeed in entrepreneurship, you need to be personable. Being personable means being pleasant in manner and appearance. Simply put, you have to be a nice person if you want to succeed as a business owner. Being personable does not mean being a pushover. It only means that you have to tame the inner voice that always has a comeback for every inconvenience be it a person or an event. Even if you do not get along with some people, you'll need to be patient enough to allow for respectful interaction. Once you get into business, you'll quickly realize that many of the people you need will not exactly be nice, but you have to be better than them. Better to bite your tongue, especially if speaking does nothing besides waste your time.

Empathy

At a fundamental level, you have to appreciate that the people you work with are human and going through a life which is somewhat unpredictable a lot of the time. Your account is not just a number-cruncher but a father as well. Your administrative assistant arranges your travel and rushes home to her baby. Understanding the human aspect of your employees and colleagues will help you to show more empathy for their respective circumstances. When your bookkeeper misses a day because they have to take a sick child to hospital, show empathy by allowing them the day without being begrudging. Say thank you as much as possible. Hand out gifts when your employee is celebrating a special occasion. These little things that show that you are human and that your employees are human, will go a long way in solidifying a caring culture at your business.

Work-Life Balance

Your business is important, but so is your life outside of it. Many entrepreneurs have no qualms about burning the midnight oil at the expense of their social lives. The excuse they give is that they have to make sacrifices so that they can enjoy the fruits later. The truth of the matter is that, if you were unable to accomplish something during the day when the sun was shining and your productivity was top-notch, you will not do so at eleven o'clock at night while half-asleep. Work-life balance ties in with time management. You have to draw boundaries about when to work and when to go home to your loved ones, be they friends, family or loyal pets. This balance is key to touching base with your overall purpose in the Universe. As a leader or boss, your employees might have a hard time coping with your work-life balance especially during those moments when they need to consult on something. To navigate this, make sure you communicate your schedule. For instance, let your staff know that you are available for meetings on critical matters for an hour every afternoon. Also let them know that you do not pick up calls beyond a certain time unless it is an emergency. If you allow yourself to carry your work home, it will be a matter of time before you have exhausted yourself beyond your limits.

Conclusion

As you can tell by now, starting a small business is well within the reach of a dreamer who commits to their dream. However, it calls for a lot of conscious effort in different aspects impacting you as an entrepreneur and as a person. Entrepreneurship is not the place for auto-pilot. Everything you do as an entrepreneur will have a corresponding impact that will either move you towards or away from success. An encouraging thing to remember is that many entrepreneurs have started with only a vision and learned everything else along the way. When you are committed to achieving success, even the stumbling blocks you'll face on the journey will be learning moments.

If you have nothing else, start with a vision and work your way from there. Look for inspiration from friends, family, successful entrepreneurs, struggling business owners, businesses that took over the world, and businesses that collapsed soon after launch. There is something to be learned from every scenario.

Keep an open mind and be open to correction. You might be the smartest software developer there ever was but there will still be someone who knows something that you do not. Be patient with yourself and be patient with the process. Nobody has ever figured it out on the first day. Rome itself took longer to build.

Lastly, take care of yourself as a human being and individual. Your business exists because of you. You do not exist because of the business. Unlike the chicken and the egg, it is very clear that you preceded the business, and your wellbeing should always take precedence over the business. Going to work while sick and overworking yourself to the extent of missing your loved one's important days is reckless. Do not be reckless. Reckless entrepreneurs do not survive very long.

References

I. Agarwal, N. (2019). 8 Best Automated Invoice Processing Software | FormGet. Retrieved from https://www.formget.com/best-automated-invoice-processing-systems/

II. Best Accounts Payable Software | 2019 Reviews of the Most Popular Systems. (2019). Retrieved from https://www.capterra.com/accounts-payable-software/

III. Helpful Tips for Surviving Your First Year in Business. (2019). Retrieved from https://www.thebalancecareers.com/tips-for-surviving-your-first-year-in-business-3515786

IV. Issa, E., & Zimmermann, J. (2019). Crowdfunding for Business: What You Need to Know. Retrieved from https://www.nerdwallet.com/blog/small-business/crowdfunding

V. Marquit, M., & Marquit, M. (2019). Essential Soft Skills for Entrepreneurs. Retrieved from https://due.com/blog/soft-skills-need-develop/

VI. Number of internet users worldwide 2005-2018 | Statista. (2019). Retrieved from https://www.statista.com/statistics/273018/number-of-internet-users-worldwide/

VII. Review, H. (2019). Use Your 118 Seconds Wisely | TIME.com. Retrieved from http://business.time.com/2012/04/04/use-your-118-seconds-wisely/

VIII. Surviving Your First Year As A Small Business Owner. (2019). Retrieved from https://www.forbes.com/sites/allbusiness/2015/05/11/surviving-first-year-as-small-business-owner/#184edc8d8e55

IX. The Pros and Cons of Crowdfunding Your Business. (2019). Retrieved from https://www.thebalancesmb.com/raising-money-for-your-business-with-crowdfunding-985178

Lightning Source UK Ltd.
Milton Keynes UK
UKHW051247070223
416538UK00026B/879